# HEALTHY EATING

What the press said about parts of this book:

'It must be the most useful down-to-earth guide I have
ever read'
**Today**

'A very useful little guide.'
**Cosmopolitan**

'Anyone who wants to make the most of their new
healthy eating habits would do well to invest in a book
by Isabel Skypala.'
**Daily Telegraph**

'A handy guide.'
**Daily Express**

'Sensible Ms Skypala, who is chief dietician at
London's Brompton Hospital, realises that not all
health-conscious people wish to be vegetarians.'
**Sunday Express**

'Want to know exactly what's in the food you eat? Two
new books, Your Guide to A Healthy Diet
(incorporated in Healthy Eating), will tell you
everything from the calories in a kidney to the calcium
in a courgette.'
**The Star**

# HEALTHY EATING

Isabel Skypala

Editor: Susan Lewis

**WISEBUY PUBLICATIONS**

*First published 1988*

*Copyright © 1987, 1988 Isabel Skypala*

**Further copies of HEALTHY EATING
can be obtained from Wisebuy Publications,
25 West Cottages, London NW6 1RJ, price £3.95
plus 50p p+p (UK) or £6 airmail including p+p.**

Parts of this book were published in 1987
in Your Guide to a Healthy Diet: Meat, Fish and
Dairy Foods and Fruit, Vegetables and Nuts.

**British Library Cataloguing in Publication Data**
Skypala, Isabel
   Healthy eating.
   1. Nutrition—Handbooks, manuals, etc.
   I. Title
   613.2     TX353

ISBN 0-9509751-8-4

*Typesetting by MC Typeset Ltd., Chatham, Kent
Reproduced, printed and bound in Great Britain by
Hazell Watson & Viney Limited
Member of BPCC plc
Aylesbury Bucks*

# Contents

1 **Food Facts**                                                     7
Calories. What you should weigh. Weight for height charts.
Protein. Fat. Saturated fat. Polyunsaturated fat. Mono-
unsaturated fat. Carbohydrates. Sugar. Starch. Fibre.

2 **Minerals**                                                       17
Calcium. Iron. Zinc. Copper. Sodium and salt.
Potassium. Magnesium. Phosphorus.

3 **Vitamins**                                                       24
Vitamin A. Vitamin C. Vitamin D. Vitamin E. B Vitamin
Complex. Vitamin B1 or Thiamin. Vitamin B2 or Ribo-
flavin. Niacin or Vitamin B3. Vitamin B6 or Pyridoxine.
Vitamin B12. Folic acid. Pantothenic acid. Biotin.

4 **What the experts suggest**                                      34
Recommended daily intakes. Children aged: one to six;
seven to 12. Teenagers aged 13 to 18. Women: aged 19 to
54; pregnant or breast feeding; over age 55. Men: aged 19
to 64; over age 65.

5 **What's in your food**                                           44
How to read the food tables in the following three
chapters.

6 **Meat, fish and dairy foods** 46
Over 100 foods analysed highlighting how much fat,
protein and calories exist alongside valuable vitamins,
calcium, iron and other minerals.

7 **Fruit, vegetables and nuts** 108
Compare the nutritional content of fresh and tinned foods
sold by most greengrocers and supermarkets.

8 **Everyday foods** 166
Bread, cereals, biscuits, cakes, drinks, sweets, spreads
and all those other foods you and your family eat everyday.

*Index* 231

# About the author

Isabel Skypala is Chief Dietitian at the Brompton Hospital, one of three London hospitals which form the National Heart and Chest Hospitals Group.

Over the last eight years at the Brompton, she has been involved in all dietary aspects of heart disease and the management of food allergies. She has also carried out research work with young people suffering from cystic fibrosis.

Isabel Skypala has a degree in nutrition and dietetics from Leeds Polytechnic where she qualified in 1979.

Isabel would like to thank her dietetic colleagues and her sister, Pauline, for all their advice and help.

# 1

# Food facts

Eating a healthy diet has never been easier. The variety of foods available today is huge compared with even ten years ago. But the increase in choice has brought great confusion about which foods to choose and how much to eat. This book will help you find out what you are getting from your daily diet so that you can make a healthier food choice.

Fortunately many doctors, dietitians and others involved in health education are now in agreement about what constitutes a healthy diet. Reports have been produced giving facts and figures and some of the myths about food are beginning to disappear. However it is hard for most people to translate some of these health messages into practical hints for every day eating.

To help you help yourself and your family, Chapters 1 to 3 describe what you need to know about the different nutrients in food such as protein, fat, sugar, fibre, minerals and vitamins and tell you which foods contain the most. Chapter 4 tells you how much of each nutrient the experts in the UK and the USA suggest you should eat each day depending on your age and sex. And Chapters 5 to 8 contain information on over 300 foods showing the nutritional contents of the foods you are likely to eat regularly.

## Calories

A calorie is a measure of energy and the calorie value of a food indicates how much energy that food provides after you have eaten it. Most foods contain calories in the form of protein, fat, carbohydrate, and sometimes alcohol, but not in equal proportions. Compared to protein and carbohydrate, fat provides twice the number of calories. Vitamins and minerals do not have a calorie value.

For a healthy diet, it is important that your calorie intake comes from a variety of foods. Although protein can be used to provide calories, its main function is the promotion of tissue growth and repair. So it is important not only to eat enough calories, but also make sure a sufficient number of those calories comes from carbohydrate and fat.

Everyone needs a different number of calories, depending on their age, sex, and occupation. Even if you are just lying down and doing nothing, your body still uses up about half of your daily calorie intake. Women usually use less calories than men while resting and you also need less the older you get.

The rest of your calorie requirement depends on the amount of energy you use up during the day. Everyone has very different energy needs and they may not match the recommended intakes. If you are fit and well and not overweight there is no need to worry if you are eating a lot more than the recommended intake. However, remember that your requirements will change as you grow older.

Currently 35% to 39% of the population are overweight and so much more likely to develop heart disease and diabetes. If you are overweight, the sensible way to try and lose it is to eat small regular meals and avoid a lot of fried and sugary foods, and alcohol. It is also important to take some exercise such as swimming, cycling or brisk walking. Taking moderate exercise three to four times a week is better than very vigorous exercise once a week. Even just walking to the next bus stop, or climbing the stairs instead of taking the lift or escalator helps to use up calories.

## What you should weigh

Your weight depends not only on the amount of fat you are carrying, but also on your frame or build. Large bones or bulky muscles can mean you weigh more than the average person of your height. If you are not sure of your frame size, you can get a rough idea by looking at the size of your hands and feet, or the breadth of your shoulders. If they are smaller than other people's of the same size, then you probably have a small frame for your height.

Muscle weighs heavier than fat, and if you are trying to lose weight, but are also taking regular strenuous exercise, you may increase your muscle mass as well as losing fat. This may result in a slight weight gain for a short period although you will probably look thinner.

The charts on p. 10 show what is an acceptable weight for your height. These weights were recommended by the Royal College of Physicians in 1983.

## Protein

The amount of food eaten in the UK has decreased this century but the proportion of protein has remained the same. A lot of protein comes from animal sources such as meat, fish, eggs, cheese, and milk. However a good deal also comes from vegetables sources such as peas, beans, lentils, cereals and nuts.

People usually eat more protein than the recommended intake but this is not thought to be harmful. Recent guidelines suggest a healthy diet should contain more protein from fish, vegetables and cereals, and less from red meat and milk products. So although protein intakes would stay the same, the diet would contain less fat and more starchy carbohydrate.

Vegans, who eat no animal protein at all, need to make sure that they are having a good mixture of vegetable and cereal protein. Well balanced vegetarian and vegan diets can be very nourishing and healthy, since they are usually quite low in fat and high in fibre.

Protein is needed for growth and development. A new baby needs five times more protein per kilogram of body weight than an adult. This requirement becomes less as the child develops and the growth rate slows down. A deficiency of protein is rare in children in this country but affects many children in third world countries, who have low calorie intakes and use protein for energy and not for growth and development.

However, one group of people in the UK who might develop protein deficiency are the elderly, especially those who live alone. Although they have the lowest requirement, they often eat very

## Women's weight for height chart

| Height (without shoes) | | Weight (without clothes) | |
|---|---|---|---|
| ft | in | st lb to st lb | kg   kg |
| 5 | 0 | 6 12 to  8 13 | 44 to 57 |
| 5 | 1 | 7  1 to  9  1 | 45 to 58 |
| 5 | 2 | 7  3 to  9  3 | 46 to 59 |
| 5 | 3 | 7  7 to  9  8 | 48 to 61 |
| 5 | 4 | 7  9 to  9 10 | 49 to 62 |
| 5 | 5 | 7 12 to 10  0 | 50 to 64 |
| 5 | 6 | 8  2 to 10  5 | 52 to 66 |
| 5 | 7 | 8  4 to 10  7 | 53 to 67 |
| 5 | 8 | 8  9 to 10 11 | 55 to 69 |
| 5 | 9 | 8 13 to 11  2 | 57 to 71 |
| 5 | 10 | 9  3 to 11  8 | 59 to 74 |

## Men's weight for height chart

| Height (without shoes) | | Weight (without clothes) | |
|---|---|---|---|
| ft | in | st lb to st lb | kg   kg |
| 5 | 3 | 8  2 to 10  3 | 52 to 65 |
| 5 | 4 | 8  4 to 10  5 | 53 to 66 |
| 5 | 5 | 8  6 to 10  7 | 54 to 67 |
| 5 | 6 | 8 11 to 11  2 | 56 to 71 |
| 5 | 7 | 9  1 to 11  6 | 58 to 73 |
| 5 | 8 | 9  3 to 11  8 | 59 to 74 |
| 5 | 9 | 9  8 to 11 13 | 61 to 76 |
| 5 | 10 | 10  0 to 12  5 | 64 to 79 |
| 5 | 11 | 10  3 to 12  8 | 65 to 80 |
| 6 | 0 | 10  7 to 13  2 | 67 to 84 |
| 6 | 1 | 10 11 to 13  7 | 69 to 86 |
| 6 | 2 | 11  2 to 13 11 | 71 to 88 |
| 6 | 3 | 11  8 to 14  6 | 74 to 92 |

little protein because of low incomes, poor cooking facilities and infirmity.

These days more people are involved in fitness training where emphasis is often placed on diet particularly protein. People in training often eat up to 5,000 calories a day, a lot of which comes from large amounts of protein. Although your calorie requirement goes up during training, your need for protein does not and eating large amounts of protein has no effect on athletic performance.

## Fat

Although in many cases we eat less calories now than 100 years ago, the percentage of calories coming from fat has increased. On average nearly half of our calories (42%) comes from fat. That means we are eating less starchy carbohydrate and therefore less fibre. This change in eating habits is thought to be one of the causes of heart disease and bowel cancer.

When food was rationed during the 1939–1945 world war, only 33% of calorie intake came from fat. This is now thought to be the amount a healthy diet should provide and to achieve this most people need to cut down substantially on their fat intake.

Most foods contain a mixture of three types of fat: saturated, polyunsaturated and mono-unsaturated, but some contain much more than others. All three types of fat contain the same number of calories.

**Saturated fat** is found in large quantities in animal fats which tend to be solid at room temperature. Milk fats like butter, cheese, cream and milk; meat fat like lard; and many margarines; all contain a lot of saturated fat.

**Polyunsaturated fat** usually comes from vegetable oils which are often liquid at room temperature. They include sunflower, safflower and corn oils; polyunsaturated margarines; and fish oils.

**Mono-unsaturated fat** is predominant in olive oil, peanut oil and rape seed oil.

Studies have shown that a diet high in fat, especially saturated fat, raises the level of cholesterol in the blood. Cholesterol is a product of fat digestion. A high blood cholesterol level is one of the risk factors for heart disease. Polyunsaturated fat can lower blood cholesterol levels but its effect is only half as strong as the cholesterol-raising ability of saturated fat. The effect of mono-unsaturated fat is less certain although it may also have a similar cholesterol-lowering effect.

Currently half of people's fat intake comes from saturated fat and only one eighth from polyunsaturated fat. So as well as reducing your total fat intake, you should also consider the type of fat you eat.

If you wish to control your fat intake, think about both visible and hidden fats. Visible fats include butter, cream, margarine and cooking oils. Fat is also hidden in cakes, biscuits, pastry and many other foods, as you will see when you check through the food descriptions. Changing from ordinary milk to semi-skimmed or skimmed milk, and using a low-fat spread will reduce your fat intake. Eating less cheese and red meat, and more chicken without the skin, fish and vegetable dishes, as well as low fat cheese, will also help.

Although children should be encouraged to eat less fat, those under five should not be given skimmed milk. This is because they get a large percentage of their calories from milk, and skimmed milk contains half the calories of whole milk. Children over three can be given semi-skimmed milk if they are eating a good and plentiful variety of food.

## Carbohydrates

Sugar, starch and fibre are the three main types of carbohydrates. Throughout the world they provide most of the energy in the diet. In poor countries 90% of the calories may come from carbo-hydrates whilst in affluent countries it might only be 40%.

## Sugar

The most simple of all the carbohydrates are the sugars which include glucose, fructose (fruit sugar), sucrose (cane and beet sugar) and lactose (milk sugar). Sugar (sucrose) intake in the UK

**Most fat in a portion**

| | |
|---|---|
| Cornish pastie | 48.6 g. |
| Pork pie | 39.1 g. |
| Sausages pork fried | 37.0 g. |
| Meat pie | 36.9 g. |
| Chocolate bar, milk | 30.3 g. |
| Lamb shoulder roast | 31.0 g. |
| Chocolate bar, plain | 29.2 g. |
| Cheesecake | 28.6 g. |
| Whitebait fried | 28.5 g. |
| Goose | 26.9 g. |
| Lasagne | 25.8 g. |
| Salami | 25.3 g. |
| Mackerel fried | 24.9 g. |
| Plaice fried in breadcrumbs | 24.7 g. |

*Recommended daily amount for adults in the UK 57 g. to 88 g.; in the USA 54 g. to 83 g. (see Chapter 4 for different age and sex). See individual foods for saturated and polyunsaturated amounts.*

**Most sugar, both natural and added, in a portion**

| | |
|---|---|
| Chocolate bar, plain | 59.5 g. |
| Chocolate bar, milk | 56.5 g. |
| Toffee apple | 37.9 g. |
| Coco Cola | 34.6 g. |
| Tinned fruit salad | 32.5 g. |
| Fruit crumble | 30.9 g. |
| Marzipan | 29.5 g. |
| Trifle | 28.0 g. |
| Gateau | 24.7 g. |
| Mango | 24.5 g. |
| Fruit cake | 24.1 g. |
| Peaches, tinned | 24.0 g. |
| Fruit pie | 21.6 g. |
| Iced bun | 20.8 g. |

*Recommended daily amount of added sugar for adults in the UK 50 g.; in the USA 45 g. to 69 g. (see Chapter 4 for different age and sex).*

reached a maximum in 1974 when the average intake was 2lbs a week. Although this has gone down over the last decade, it is still causing concern and some reports suggest people should halve their current intake. Sugar has been linked to dental decay.

The reason why so much sugar is eaten is partly that it is a good preservative and used in many different foods. A high sugar content helps to extend the shelf-life of food by stopping the growth of moulds. People develop a sweet tooth if they become accustomed to sweet foods early on in life.

Pure sugar only gives you calories although honey and some of the very dark brown sugars contain very small amounts of minerals. Cutting down on sugar will help you lose weight without missing out on any essential nutrients. Many people believe sugars such as honey to have restorative properties. There is no evidence that honey or brown sugar are good for you or any better than white sugar. A well balanced diet provides all the calories most people, including children, need.

The best way to start eating less sugar is by gradually reducing the amount you add so that your taste buds will get used to a less sweet taste. Using a sugar substitute will not help you lose your sweet tooth. Cut down on sweets and chocolates especially in between meals. Avoid soft drinks and squashes sweetened with sugar. Even unsweetened natural fruit juice contains sugar in the form of fructose from the fruit so dilute it if you normally drink a lot. Check food labels to see how high sugar comes on the list of ingredients. If it is near the top, or listed in several different ways (sucrose, glucose, honey), you can be sure that the product contains a lot of sugar.

## Starch

The second main type of carbohydrate is starch which is broken down into glucose in the body and found in cereals such as wheat and rice and some vegetables. In the past many 'slimming' diets have recommended that starchy foods should be eaten in small amounts or even cut out completely. Now reducing diets encourage people to eat normal or only slightly smaller amounts of starchy foods and to avoid fatty and sugary foods.

Bread, potatoes and other starchy foods can provide significant amounts of protein, iron, calcium and vitamin C. Today's guidelines to cut down on fat will mean eating more of these starchy foods.

## Fibre

Fibre or roughage is found in the indigestible fibrous parts of fruit and vegetables such as the stalk, skin, leaves, and core, and the husk of cereal grains. Over the last century our fibre intake has fallen by two thirds and most of us only eat 20 g. a day compared to people living in rural Africa who eat between 50 g. to 120 g. of fibre a day.

This falling intake has been linked with an increase in such problems as constipation, bowel cancer and heart disease. So most recent medical reports say fibre intakes should be increased to 30 g. a day. You should not do this by just taking large amounts of wheat bran and not changing your diet, as this can create more problems than it solves.

You can easily increase your fibre intake by changing to wholemeal bread and by eating plenty of fresh fruit and vegetables, raw and well washed with the skins on where possible. Try porridge or a wholegrain breakfast cereal but remember to check the label for sugar content. Beans and lentils contain a lot of fibre. Dried beans should be soaked and boiled for ten minutes

**Most fibre in a portion**

| | |
|---|---|
| Baked beans | 16.4 g. |
| Kidney beans | 14.0 g. |
| Chickpeas | 12.0 g. |
| All-Bran | 11.5 g. |
| Peas | 9.6 g. |
| Bran | 9.2 g. |
| Plantain | 9.0 g. |
| Blackberries, 18 | 6.6 g. |
| Chilli con carne | 6.4 g. |
| Spinach | 6.3 g. |
| Leeks | 6.2 g. |
| Sweetcorn | 5.7 g. |

*Recommended daily amount for adults in the UK 30 g.*

before slow cooking. If you eat a lot of pasta or rice you should try the wholegrain varieties as they are much tastier and higher in fibre.

Remember to drink plenty of fluids when you increase your intake of fibre since it is very absorbent.

# 2

# Minerals

## Calcium

You need calcium for bones and teeth, so a good intake is important, especially for children, expectant and nursing mothers, and the elderly. A young child's skeleton is replaced completely within one to two years. In adults, this replacement continues but much more slowly until the age of 40 when the bones gradually begin to break down. Before birth, and during breast feeding, the calcium needs of the baby are met by a supply from the mother. So if the mother is not eating enough calcium she will become deficient.

**Most calcium in a portion**

| | |
|---|---|
| Tofu (soya bean curd) | 709 mg. |
| Spinach | 600 mg. |
| Sardines | 550 mg. |
| Pilchards | 540 mg. |
| Ravioli | 516 mg. |
| Whitebait | 516 mg. |
| Macaroni cheese | 387 mg. |
| Goat's milk | 364 mg. |
| Milk, skimmed | 364 mg. |
| Cheese sauce | 364 mg. |
| Scone | 341 mg. |
| Milk, semi-skimmed | 350 mg. |
| Milk, fresh whole | 336 mg. |
| Milk, skimmed powder | 333 mg. |

*Recommended daily amount for adults in the UK 500 mg. to 1,200 mg.; in the USA 800 mg. to 1,200 mg. (see Chapter 4 for different age and sex).*

Most calcium in the diet comes from milk, skimmed milk having the same amount as full cream milk. Other sources are cheese, water in hard water areas, and tinned fish containing bones, such as pilchards and sardines. Calcium is often added to flour, so bread can be an important source for some people. Soya milk may also be fortified with calcium.

In the UK calcium intakes are often much higher than the recommended intake because of all the milk and cheese eaten. High calcium intakes are not harmful, but there is probably nothing to be gained from eating more than 1,000 mg. a day unless you are pregnant or breast feeding.

## Iron

Iron is found in animal and vegetable foods. Foods rich in iron in a form that is easily absorbed include liver, red meat, and blood products such as black pudding and haggis. Reasonable amounts of iron are also found in eggs, oats, wholemeal bread, chocolate and some cereals, pulses, and green vegetables. Because the body only uses up 10% of its iron intake, eat the recommended daily amounts given in Chapter 4 to ensure you get enough.

The iron found in eggs and vegetables is not as easily used as that found in meat and offal, but vitamin C helps the body to absorb both sources of iron. Recent reports suggest that the best way to increase iron intake and prevent deficiency, is by eating more fruit and vegetables to aid iron absorption, rather than by eating more meat which is high in fat.

A lack of iron in the diet causes a blood disorder called iron-deficiency anaemia, which is still relatively common in the UK. People most likely to be affected are women of child bearing age, particularly those who do not eat meat, fish or eggs.

## Zinc

Much is still to be learned about this mineral but we know it is part of several substances known as enzymes, without which necessary reactions cannot take place in the body. Zinc is found in many foods but meat is a particularly good source.

It is quite rare for anyone in Britain to develop zinc deficiency,

**Most iron in a portion**

| | |
|---|---|
| Liver, pig's | 17.8 mg. |
| Liver, lamb's | 10.5 mg. |
| Kidney, lamb's | 8.9 mg. |
| Venison | 7.5 mg. |
| Cockles | 6.5 mg. |
| Heart | 6.5 mg. |
| Chickpeas | 6.2 mg. |
| Chilli con carne | 6.2 mg. |
| Black pudding | 6.0 mg. |
| Goose | 5.5 mg. |
| Pilchards | 4.9 mg. |
| All-Bran | 4.8 mg. |
| Steak, grilled | 4.5 mg. |
| Spinach | 4.0 mg. |
| Kidney beans | 3.8 mg. |

*Recommended daily amount for adults in the UK 10 mg. to 15 mg.; in the USA 10 mg. to 60 mg. (see Chapter 4 for different age and sex).*

**Most zinc in a portion**

| | |
|---|---|
| Oysters | 18.00 mg. |
| Liver, pig's | 8.60 mg. |
| Steak | 6.80 mg. |
| Beef roast | 5.88 mg. |
| Lamb leg roasted | 5.52 mg. |
| Lamb shoulder roasted | 5.16 mg. |
| Gammon rasher | 4.80 mg. |
| Pork chop | 4.72 mg. |
| Chilli con carne | 4.60 mg. |
| Liver, lamb's | 4.60 mg. |
| Veal fillet | 4.50 mg. |
| Corned beef | 4.48 mg. |
| Crab | 4.25 mg. |

*Recommended daily amount for adults in the USA: 15 mg. to 25 mg. (see Chapter 4 for different age and sex). No UK recommendation.*

although diets which are very high in cereal fibre may cause deficiency due to the binding of zinc by a substance called phytate which is present in wheat bran and which prevents the absorption of zinc in the body. The average British diet provides about 10 mg. of zinc a day. There is no UK recommended daily intake but the USA has a recommended daily intake of 15 mg. a day, which is 50% higher than the average UK intake.

Some people might benefit from zinc supplements. Small-for-date babies may have mothers who have low blood zinc levels, so supplementation during pregnancy may be important especially for vegetarians. Extra zinc might also help leg ulcers to heal more quickly in people who have low blood levels. People who have a poor food intake such as the elderly, or those who have cancer, are often unable to taste and smell food normally which might be due to a lack of dietary zinc. It could also be important to supplement the diets of people who cannot absorb food properly.

## Copper

If you eat a variety of foods grown in different areas, you are unlikely to become deficient in copper. The daily diet contains about 2.5 mg. of copper, most of which comes from green vegetables, fish and liver. Copper plays a part in the formation of blood. Copper deficiency usually only occurs in a genetically inherited condition where the sufferer cannot absorb copper. Premature babies may develop copper deficiency unless they are fed on a proper modified baby milk, since cows milk is a very poor source of copper.

## Sodium and salt

Sodium is probably one of the most widespread nutrients in food, but the amount naturally present is small. Foods which contain a lot have usually had it added in the form of sodium bicarbonate or salt (sodium chloride). One gram of salt contains 388 mg. of sodium. Sodium is an essential part of all body cells, but the average daily intake of salt is 12 times higher than the one gram of salt needed each day to meet requirements. Luckily, the body has the ability to lose most of this excess sodium in the urine.

**Most salt found in a portion**

| | |
|---|---|
| Gammon rasher | 8.3 g. |
| Smoked haddock | 4.7 g. |
| Chickpeas | 4.4 g. |
| Porridge | 3.9 g. |
| Vegetable soup, tin | 3.9 g. |
| Cornish pastie | 3.6 g. |
| Sausages, beef | 3.6 g. |
| Tomato soup, tin | 3.6 g. |
| Egg omelette with salt | 3.5 g. |
| Chicken soup, tin | 3.4 g. |
| Oxtail soup | 3.4 g. |
| Minestrone soup, packet | 3.3 g. |
| Sausages, pork | 3.2 g. |
| Kipper | 2.9 g. |

*Recommended daily amount for adults in the UK 9 g.; in the USA 5 g.*

Because most people eat more sodium than they need, the effect of sodium on blood pressure has been closely studied. It is still not clear whether cutting salt intakes will lower blood pressure in everyone, but there is an effect in people who already have high blood pressure. In Britain, one person in five is likely to develop high blood pressure.

If you want to eat less salt, look for foods which contain only small amounts naturally. All fresh foods are suitable. It will help to avoid meat products such as sausages, bacon and ham and cured fish such as kippers and smoked haddock. Look for vegetables which are not tinned in brine, and try low salt baked beans. Tinned soups and bottled sauces are also high in salt.

A third of your salt intake is added during cooking and at the table. If you want to add less salt to food, it is easier to stop adding it at the table and still add a small amount during cooking. It will take time to get used to food without added salt so persevere and leave the salt cellar in the cupboard.

## Potassium

Potassium is an essential part of muscle tissue in the body. It is very rare for most people to either need extra potassium or to reduce the amount they eat, except when they have specific medical conditions, or are on particular drugs which rid the body of too much potassium.

Potassium is lost from the body in much the same way as sodium and the amount you lose is small and corresponds to the amount you eat. Potassium is closely associated with protein so if body muscle is being broken down and lost more potassium will be needed.

Potassium is found in a wide variety of foods, fruit, vegetables and meat being the best sources.

## Magnesium

Together with calcium, magnesium is another important part of bone. Half the amount contained in the body is found in the skeleton. It also plays a part in many reactions which happen in the body and all human tissue contains small amounts of magnesium.

Most foods contain some magnesium, including green vegetables since magnesium is an essential part of the green colour chlorophyll. Cereals and vegetables between them can contribute up to two thirds of the daily magnesium intake. Meat, fish and nuts are also good sources.

**Most magnesium in a portion**

| | |
|---|---|
| All-Bran | 148.0 mg. |
| Chickpeas | 134.0 mg. |
| Potato chips | 111.0 mg. |
| Bran | 148.0 mg. |
| Cashew nuts | 106.0 mg. |
| Chocolate bar, plain | 100.0 mg. |
| Kidney beans | 100.0 mg. |
| Mackerel | 77.0 mg. |
| Chilli con carne | 76.0 mg. |
| Marzipan | 72.0 mg. |
| Pilchards | 70.2 mg. |

*Recommended daily amount for adults in the USA 300 mg. to 450 mg. (see Chapter 4 for different age and sex). No UK recommendation.*

# Phosphorus

Phosphorus is present in all natural foods as it is a major part of all plant and animal cells. Generally foods which are high in calcium and protein are also rich in phosphorus. It is also used as a food additive and 10% of the phosphorus eaten has been added artificially. Deficiency is unknown in man. Phosphorus is mainly found in your bones with the kidneys controlling the level in the blood. In the past, the only concern with phosphorus has been with very young babies being fed on cows milk, which contains more phosphorus than breast milk. However there is now a wide range of modified baby milks.

# 3

# Vitamins

## Vitamin A

Vitamin A is found in both animal and vegetable foods. The animal source is a substance called retinol, which is present in full cream milk, butter, cheese, egg yolk, liver and some fatty fish. The richest natural sources of retinol are fish liver oils such as cod liver oil.

The vegetable source is called beta carotene which is converted to retinol inside the body. The amount of retinol yielded from beta carotene is only one sixth of its original weight. Green vegetables such as cabbage and lettuce contain a lot of carotene but only in the dark outer leaves. Yellow and red fruits and vegetables,

**Most vitamin A in a portion**

| | |
|---|---|
| Liver, lamb's, fried | 21,640 µg. |
| Liver, pig's, braised | 12,180 µg. |
| Vegetable curry | 1,426 µg. |
| Pate | 1,318 µg. |
| Carrot | 1,200 µg. |
| Spinach | 1,000 µg. |
| Sweet potato | 866 µg. |
| Eel | 760 µg. |
| Melon, canteloupe | 599 µg. |
| Nectarine | 550 µg. |
| Mixed vegetables | 533 µg. |

*Recommended daily amount for adults in the UK 750 µg. to 1,200 µg.; in the USA 800 µg. to 1,200 µg. (see Chapter 4 for different age and sex).*

especially carrots, also contain good amounts of carotene. Vegetable oils contain no beta carotene except for red palm oil. In the UK vitamin A is added to margarine.

Vitamin A is essential for vision in dim light but it is very unusual for anyone in the Western World to suffer from a deficiency. One of the reasons why deficiency is so rare is that this vitamin can be stored in the liver. Most people store 90 mg. to 150 mg. which is enough to meet normal requirements for months or even years, without eating any more. Occasionally these stores can get low, particularly in old age when people may not eat as well. Because vitamin A is stored, taking extra amounts can cause side effects and very large amounts are dangerous.

## Vitamin C

Vitamin C is mainly found in fruit and vegetables. Good sources include citrus fruits, blackcurrants, strawberries and kiwi fruit. For many people, potatoes provide most of their vitamin C intake because although they only contain moderate amounts of the vitamin, they are usually eaten in larger quantities than most other vegetables and fruit.

**Most vitamin C in a portion**

| | |
|---|---|
| Blackcurrants | 112 mg. |
| Lemon | 80 mg. |
| Pepper, green | 80 mg. |
| Strawberries | 72 mg. |
| Orange | 70 mg. |
| Kiwi fruit | 60 mg. |
| Cabbage, red raw | 49 mg. |
| Brussell sprouts | 48 mg. |
| Tomatoes, tinned | 36 mg. |
| Gooseberries | 34 mg. |
| Grapefruit | 32 mg. |
| Potato chips | 26 mg. |
| Spinach | 25 mg. |

*Recommended daily amount for adults in the UK 30 mg. to 80 mg.; in the USA 60 mg. to 100 mg. (see Chapter 4 for different age and sex).*

Vitamin C prevents scurvy, increases the absorption of iron, and helps wounds to heal. It might also have a role to play in the prevention of gastric cancer and strokes, and in the lowering of blood cholesterol levels. The recommended intake in the UK is 30 mg. a day. However, the recommended intake in other countries is much higher, particularly the USA where it is 60 mg.

Most people eat more than 30 mg. a day although 10% of households in the UK have been estimated to consume less. Recently, some people have been taking many times the UK recommended intake of vitamin C in order to prevent a variety of illnesses including the common cold. Since at this high dosage most of the vitamin does not appear to be absorbed, it is not clear whether this type of therapy is effective or whether it might even be harmful in the long term.

## Vitamin D

The amount of vitamin D occurring naturally in food is small and restricted to very few foods such as oily fish, eggs and liver. Some foods like margarine are fortified with the manufactured form of the vitamin. However, most vitamin D does not come from food but is produced when your skin is exposed to sunlight by the action of ultra-violet light on a substance found in the oily secretions of human skin.

Vitamin D, like vitamin A, is stored in the liver and kidneys, which is useful since less is produced in the winter because there is less sunlight. Vitamin D is necessary for the formation of normal bones and is involved in controlling the amount of calcium in the blood. It takes calcium from the bones if there is not enough in the blood and acts in response to the body's changing need for calcium.

Too little vitamin D will cause joint problems and bone deformities, particularly in the young and old, even if the diet contains enough calcium, since it cannot be used without the action of vitamin D. Expectant mothers should have good intakes of the vitamin even before they conceive as babies lay down a reserve of vitamin D from the mother before they are born. Elderly housebound people often have low levels of vitamin D because of a poor food intake and lack of sunshine.

Vitamin D can have toxic effects at high doses but this only applies to oral vitamin D as the body regulates against overproduction of vitamin D from sunshine. An intake of only 50 μg. a day over a period of time is known to be toxic. The recommended intake for most people is 10 μg. a day.

**Most vitamin D in a portion**

| | |
|---|---|
| Mackerel | 46.40 μg. |
| Herring, grilled | 29.70 μg. |
| Kipper | 28.00 μg. |
| Herring, pickled | 20.25 μg. |
| Pilchards | 14.40 μg. |
| Salmon | 13.13 μg. |
| Sardines | 7.50 μg. |
| Tuna fish | 5.30 μg. |
| Egg omelette | 2.00 μg. |
| Danish pastry | 1.77 μg. |
| Liver, pig's | 1.19 μg. |

*Recommended daily amount for adults in the UK 10 μg.; in the USA 5 μg. to 11.25 μg. (see Chapter 4 for different age and sex).*

## Vitamin E

Good sources of vitamin E are vegetable oils, nuts, oily fish like tuna, egg, wholewheat cereals, avocado pear and spinach.

Vitamin E has a protective effect on polyunsaturated fats both in food and in the body. It is found in all your cell membranes and may have a role in preventing a large number of degenerative disorders. Your requirement depends on the amount of polyunsaturated fat you eat. Western diets provide 5 mg. to 10 mg. a day and some people appear to maintain good health on a quarter of this amount. For this reason there is no recommended daily intake in the UK for this vitamin although the USA has one of 8 mg. to 11 mg. a day for most adults.

People who might need extra vitamin E are those with liver problems or who cannot digest fats. It has also been recommended in the treatment of many conditions including sterility and skin disorders, as well as to delay aging and improve sexual function. There is still no real evidence that it can improve any of these.

**Most vitamin E in a portion**

| | |
|---|---|
| Tuna fish in oil | 5.80 mg. |
| Marzipan | 5.46 mg. |
| Sweet potato | 5.20 mg. |
| Twix | 3.50 mg. |
| Cornish pastie | 3.09 mg. |
| Asparagus | 3.12 mg. |
| Sunflower seed oil | 2.43 mg. |
| Tomatoes, tinned | 2.40 mg. |
| Avocado pear | 2.40 mg. |
| Hazel nuts | 2.10 mg. |

*Recommended daily amount for adults in the USA 8 mg. to 11 mg. (see Chapter 4 for different age and sex). No UK recommendation.*

# B Vitamin Complex

# Vitamin B1 or Thiamin

Good amounts of vitamin B1 are found in meat, particularly pork, wholewheat products, potatoes and some nuts. Beef extract, some fish, beans and pulses are also good sources. If sugar cane and cereals are refined, the vitamin is lost and so many manufactured foods such as breakfast cereals have the vitamin added. Because

**Most vitamin B1 in a portion**

| | |
|---|---|
| Gammon rasher | 1.32 mg. |
| Pork chop | 1.19 mg. |
| Pork leg | 0.78 mg. |
| Kidney | 0.42 mg. |
| Plaice | 0.41 mg. |
| All-Bran | 0.40 mg. |
| Heart | 0.36 mg. |
| Duck | 0.31 mg. |
| Kidney beans | 0.30 mg. |
| Rice, brown | 0.30 mg. |
| Kellogg's Corn Flakes | 0.30 mg. |

*Recommended daily amount for adults in the UK 0.9 mg. to 1.1 mg.; in the USA 1.05 mg. to 1.55 mg. (see Chapter 4 for different age and sex).*

vitamin B1 is soluble in water much can be lost during cooking especially if sodium bicarbonate is added to the water. So only use a small amount of water or better still steam vegetables or cook them in a microwave oven.

Vitamin B1 is concerned with the breakdown of carbohydrate in the body. A small amount is stored but most is lost in the urine. Since it cannot be accumulated, it is almost impossible to take too much. Although the UK recommended figure is one of the lowest in Europe, it is believed to be adequate.

## Vitamin B2 or Riboflavin

Liver, kidney, milk, meat, fish and yeast extracts are good sources of vitamin B2. Some foods, like breakfast cereals, are fortified with it. Vitamin B2 is soluble in water and although ordinary cooking methods will not completely destroy it by heat, it is often thrown away with the water the food is cooked in. It is also destroyed by ultra-violet light and most vitamin B2 contained in milk will be lost if it is left on the doorstep all day.

In the UK, vitamin B2 deficiency is not common except amongst people who have a very poor food intake or follow a very restricted diet.

**Most vitamin B2 in a portion**

| | |
|---|---|
| Liver, lamb's | 4.62 mg. |
| Liver, pig's | 3.25 mg. |
| Kidney | 1.72 mg. |
| Heart, lamb's | 1.20 mg. |
| Mackerel | 0.84 mg. |
| Beef extract | 0.81 mg. |
| All-Bran | 0.60 mg. |
| Duck | 0.56 mg. |
| Milk, skimmed | 0.56 mg. |
| Milk, fresh whole | 0.53 mg. |
| Pilchards | 0.52 mg. |
| Steak | 0.47 mg. |

*Recommended daily amount for adults in the UK 1.3 mg. to 1.8 mg.; in the USA 1.25 mg. to 1.75 mg. (see Chapter 4 for different age and sex).*

## Niacin or Vitamin B3

Niacin, also known as nicotinic acid and vitamin B3, is found in many foods but only in small amounts. Meat, liver, offal, fish, wholemeal cereals and beans are the best sources. Some processed foods have it added. Unlike other B vitamins, the body can make niacin from certain high protein foods such as milk and eggs. Heat does not destroy this vitamin but large amounts can be lost in the cooking water since it is water soluble.

Many cereals contain good amounts of niacin but it is useless because it is present in a bound form and only treatment with an alkaline substance can release it. Niacin can easily be produced synthetically and also occurs naturally in the body in the form of nicotinamide. It is related chemically to nicotine but behaves very differently and is not harmful even in large amounts. Pellagra, the condition caused by a lack of niacin, is very rare in this country.

**Most niacin in a portion**

| | |
|---|---|
| Mackerel | 27.94 mg. |
| Pilchards | 19.98 mg. |
| Chicken breast, roast | 19.89 mg. |
| Pork chop | 18.36 mg. |
| Liver, pig's | 17.80 mg. |
| Gammon rasher | 17.70 mg. |
| Turkey, roast | 16.68 mg. |
| Steak | 16.20 mg. |
| Liver, lamb's | 15.90 mg. |
| Tuna | 15.80 mg. |

*Recommended daily amount for adults in the UK 15 mg. to 21 mg.; in the USA 13.5 mg. to 18.5 mg. (see Chapter 4 for different age and sex).*

## Vitamin B6 or Pyridoxine

Fish, liver and meat contain the most. Potatoes have reasonable amounts. The average British diet provides about 2 mg. of vitamin B6 a day. The UK does not give a recommended daily amount for this vitamin. However the USA recommends 2 mg. to 2.5 mg. a day for adults.

It is very rare for anyone to develop a deficiency of vitamin B6 except in association with another disorder such as severe malnutrition. But some women taking oral contraceptives may get relief from headaches and sickness by taking extra vitamin B6. Also some women find that premenstrual tension is helped by taking quite large amounts of this vitamin, sometimes up to 200 mg. a day. This beneficial effect has yet to be proved by scientific research.

**Most vitamin B6 in a portion**

| | |
|---|---|
| Salmon, fresh | 0.91 mg. |
| Cod in batter | 0.85 mg. |
| All-Bran | 0.72 mg. |
| Cod, grilled | 0.72 mg. |
| Herring, grilled | 0.68 mg. |
| Liver, pig's | 0.67 mg. |
| Plaice | 0.65 mg. |
| Kipper | 0.64 mg. |
| Banana | 0.61 mg. |
| Pork chop | 0.55 mg. |
| Rabbit | 0.55 mg. |
| Chilli con carne | 0.50 mg. |

*Recommended daily amount for adults in the USA 2 mg. to 2.6 mg. (see Chapter 4 for different age and sex). No UK recommendation.*

## Vitamin B12

Vitamin B12 is unique because it is not found in any plants. Sources include liver, kidney, oily fish and meat. Estimated intakes of vitamin B12 range from 3 µg. to 32 µg. a day in the UK. So people who eat a mixed diet will take in more than the normal requirement of 2 µg. to 4 µg. a day, as will vegetarians who eat milk and dairy products. Vegans who eat no animal foods often need to take vitamin B12 supplements. Vitamin B12 is the only B vitamin that can be stored in large amounts in the liver, most adults having a five year supply.

**Most vitamin B12 in a portion**

| | |
|---|---|
| Liver, lamb's | 85.0 μg. |
| Kidney | 59.0 μg. |
| Sardines | 28.0 μg. |
| Liver, pig's | 27.3 μg. |
| Mackerel | 26.4 μg. |
| Pilchards | 21.6 μg. |
| Rabbit | 13.2 μg. |
| Herring, grilled | 13.0 μg. |
| Kipper | 12.3 μg. |
| Heart | 11.2 μg. |
| Salmon, fresh | 6.6 μg. |

*Recommended daily amount for adults in the USA 3 μg. to 4 μg. (see Chapter 4 for different age and sex). No UK recommendation.*

# Folic acid

There are very few rich natural sources of this vitamin, green vegetables and liver being the two main ones. Folic acid is lost from food if it is stored for a long time, exposed to light or cooked. So store vegetables in a dim light and eat as soon as possible.

A normal diet contains about 100 μg. to 300 μg. a day and although only a quarter of this is completely absorbed, it is thought to cover most people's requirements in the UK. No daily amounts are officially given in the UK but in the USA 400 μg. a day is recommended and this rises to 800 μg. during pregnancy.

A lack of folic acid can cause a type of anaemia. This is unlikely to happen in most people but some need extra folic acid such as pregnant women, the elderly and certain groups of Asians. If women have folic acid deficiency before they conceive, it is possible they are more likely to have babies with malformations of the central nervous system, such as spina bifida. Therefore, since folic acid requirements increase during pregnancy, it is important that the diet is already rich in folic acid before conception. Blood levels of folic acid are lower in old people than in younger ages. This means some elderly people may become deficient if they do not eat enough food containing this vitamin.

**Most folic acid in a portion**

| | |
|---|---|
| Liver, lamb's | 252.0 µg. |
| Spinach | 140.0 µg. |
| Liver, pig's | 115.0 µg. |
| Brussel sprouts | 104.0 µg. |
| All-Bran | 100.0 µg. |
| Cabbage, red, raw | 81.0 µg. |
| Kellogg's Corn Flakes | 75.0 µg. |
| Chickpeas | 74.0 µg. |
| Kidney beans | 72.0 µg. |
| Peas, frozen | 62.4 µg. |

*Recommended daily amount for adults in the USA 400 µg. to 800 µg. (see Chapter 4 for different age and sex). No UK recommendation.*

## Pantothenic acid

This vitamin is present in all living things and is so widely distributed in natural foods that a deficiency is unlikely. The only people who might develop one are those who eat mostly processed foods. Most pantothenic acid is found in liver, kidney, yeast, egg yolk, and fresh vegetables. Cooking will destroy pantothenic acid but only if the temperature goes above boiling point. Frozen foods especially meat will lose a lot during thawing. There is no good reason for taking extra. Although a lack of the vitamin causes the greying of hair in rats, supplements will not prevent the development of grey hair in man.

## Biotin

Biotin can be found in a variety of foods, liver, kidney, eggs and fish being the best sources. The human body uses only a few micrograms of biotin daily and can usually get all it needs from the many micro-organisms that are present in food or living in the intestines. A deficiency of biotin cannot occur naturally in man. All recorded instances of a deficiency have been associated with the consumption of raw eggs because they contain a protein which combines with biotin to make it unusable. Cooking eggs releases the vitamin.

# 4

# What the experts suggest

There are two main sets of dietary guidelines and these are summarised in this chapter. The first are the official recommended daily amounts (RDAs) of certain nutrients for different age groups and sex. Every country has its own figures and the UK recommendations by the Department of Health and Social Security (DHSS), last revised in 1979, are given together with those recommended in the USA in 1980 by the Food and Nutrition Board, National Academy of Sciences – National Research Council.

The second set of dietary guidelines come from various reports produced by groups of experts. These reports do not cover all nutrients but give recommendations on specific aspects and often describe how dietary changes can be achieved.

The most important report of the 1980s was the NACNE report and its recommendations are also summarised on the following pages. This report was a discussion paper on proposals for nutritional guidelines for health education in Britain produced by the Health Education Council in 1983. Another significant report was one on diet and cardiovascular disease, known as the COMA report, which was produced by the DHSS in 1984. The most recent report on diet, nutrition and health was produced by the British Medical Association in 1986.

The recommendation for sugar intake applies only to added sugar which is added to drinks or found in cakes, biscuits and sweets for example. It does not include those foods which contain sugar naturally such as in fruit and vegetables.

Only use the following recommendations as a guide. Different people may need different amounts. A dash (–) means no recommendations have been made.

# Children aged one to six years

**UK** Official recommended daily amounts unless otherwise stated.

**Food Facts**
Energy 1,100 to 1,740 kcal.
Protein 27 to 43 g.
Total fat –
Saturated fat –
Polyunsaturated fat –
Carbohydrate –
Sugars –
Fibre –

**Minerals**
Calcium 600 mg.
Iron 8 mg.
Zinc –
Copper –
Sodium –
Potassium –
Magnesium –
Phosphorus –

**Vitamins**
Vitamin A 300 µg.
Vitamin C 20 mg.
Vitamin D 10 µg.
Vitamin E –
Vitamin B1 0.5 mg.
Vitamin B2 0.75 mg.
Niacin 8.5 mg.
Vitamin B6 –
Vitamin B12 –
Folic acid –
Pantothenic acid –
Biotin –

Children's requirements are very varied so only use these figures as a guide.

**USA** Official recommended daily amounts unless otherwise stated.

**Food Facts**
Energy 1,300 to 1,700 kcal.
Protein 23 to 30 g.
Total fat –
Saturated fat –
Polyunsaturated fat –
Carbohydrate –
Sugars –
Fibre –

**Minerals**
Calcium 800 mg.
Iron 12.5 mg.
Zinc 10 mg.
Copper –
Sodium –
Potassium –
Magnesium 175 mg.
Phosphorus 800 mg.

**Vitamins**
Vitamin A 450 µg.
Vitamin C 45 mg.
Vitamin D 10 µg.
Vitamin E 5.5 mg.
Vitamin B1 0.8 mg.
Vitamin B2 0.9 mg.
Niacin 10 mg.
Vitamin B6 1.1 mg.
Vitamin B12 2.25 µg.
Folic acid 150 µg.
Pantothenic acid –
Biotin –

Young children need varied healthy meals, not a very low fat, high fibre diet. Give them full cream milk and butter, not low fat substitutes.

# Children aged seven to 12 years

**UK** Official recommended
daily amounts unless
otherwise stated.

**USA** Official recommended
daily amounts unless
otherwise stated.

**Food Facts**
**Energy** 1,900 to 2,280 kcal.
**Protein** 47 to 57 g.
**Total fat** –
**Saturated fat** –
**Polyunsaturated fat** –
**Carbohydrate** –
**Sugars** –
**Fibre** –

**Food Facts**
**Energy** 2,400 to 2,700 kcal.
**Protein** 34 to 45 g.
**Total fat** –
**Saturated fat** –
**Polyunsaturated fat** –
**Carbohydrate** –
**Sugars** –
**Fibre** –

**Minerals**
**Calcium** 650 mg.
**Iron** 11 mg.
**Zinc** –
**Copper** –
**Sodium** –
**Potassium** –
**Magnesium** –
**Phosphorus** –

**Minerals**
**Calcium** 1,000 mg.
**Iron** 10 to 18 mg.
**Zinc** 12.5 mg.
**Copper** –
**Sodium** –
**Potassium** –
**Magnesium** 300 mg.
**Phosphorus** 1,000 mg.

**Vitamins**
**Vitamin A** 487 µg.
**Vitamin C** 22.5 mg.
**Vitamin D** 10 µg.
**Vitamin E** –
**Vitamin B1** 0.85 mg.
**Vitamin B2** 1.1 mg.
**Niacin** 12.5 mg.
**Vitamin B6** –
**Vitamin B12** –
**Folic acid** –
**Pantothenic acid** –
**Biotin** –

**Vitamins**
**Vitamin A** 850 µg.
**Vitamin C** 47.5 mg.
**Vitamin D** 10 µg.
**Vitamin E** 7.5 mg.
**Vitamin B1** 1.3 mg.
**Vitamin B2** 1.5 mg.
**Niacin** 17 mg.
**Vitamin B6** 1.7 mg.
**Vitamin B12** 3 µg.
**Folic acid** 350 µg.
**Pantothenic acid** –
**Biotin** –

**Children's requirements are very
varied so only use these figures as
a guide.**

**Adults develop a taste for sweet
and salty foods in childhood so
don't add extra salt or sugar to
children's food.**

# Teenagers aged 13 to 18 years

**UK** Official recommended daily amounts unless otherwise stated.

**USA** Official recommended daily amounts unless otherwise stated.

**Food Facts**
Energy 2,150 to 2,880 kcal.
Protein 53 to 72 g.
Total fat –
Saturated fat –
Polyunsaturated fat –
Carbohydrate –
Sugars –
Fibre –

**Food Facts**
Energy 2,750 kcal.
Protein 45 to 56 g.
Total fat –
Saturated fat –
Polyunsaturated fat –
Carbohydrate –
Sugars –
Fibre –

**Minerals**
Calcium 650 mg.
Iron 12 mg.
Zinc –
Copper –
Sodium –
Potassium –
Magnesium –
Phosphorus –

**Minerals**
Calcium 1,200 mg.
Iron 18 mg.
Zinc 15 mg.
Copper –
Sodium –
Potassium –
Magnesium 337 mg.
Phosphorus 1,200 mg.

**Vitamins**
Vitamin A 737 µg.
Vitamin C 27 mg.
Vitamin D 10 µg.
Vitamin E –
Vitamin B1 1.02 mg.
Vitamin B2 1.55 mg.
Niacin 17.5 mg.
Vitamin B6 –
Vitamin B12 –
Folic acid –
Pantothenic acid –
Biotin –

**Vitamins**
Vitamin A 900 µg.
Vitamin C 55 mg.
Vitamin D 10 µg.
Vitamin E 8.5 mg.
Vitamin B1 1.25 mg.
Vitamin B2 1.3 to 1.7 mg.
Niacin 16.2 mg.
Vitamin B6 1.9 mg.
Vitamin B12 3 µg.
Folic acid 400 µg.
Pantothenic acid –
Biotin –

**Young people's requirements are very varied so only use these figures as a guide.**

**If teenagers will not eat proper meals, wholemeal toasted sandwiches or jacket potatoes with various fillings are good substitutes.**

# Women aged 19 to 54 years

**UK** Official recommended daily amounts unless otherwise stated.

## Food Facts
Energy 2,150 kcal.
Protein 54 g.
Total fat 69 g.[1]
Saturated fat 23 g.[1]
Polyunsaturated fat 11.5 g.[1]
Carbohydrate 286 g.[1]
Added sugar 50 g.[1]
Fibre 30 g.[1]

## Minerals
Calcium 500 mg.
Iron 12 mg.
Zinc –
Copper –
Sodium 3,496 mg. (9 g. salt)[1]
Potassium –
Magnesium –
Phosphorus –

## Vitamins
Vitamin A 750 µg.
Vitamin C 30 mg.
Vitamin D 10 µg.
Vitamin E –
Vitamin B1 0.9 mg.
Vitamin B2 1.3 mg.
Niacin 15 mg.
Vitamin B6 –
Vitamin B12 –
Folic acid –
Pantothenic acid –
Biotin –

[1]Recommended in the NACNE report produced by the Health Education Council in 1983.

**USA** Official recommended daily amounts unless otherwise stated.

## Food Facts
Energy 2,050 kcal.
Protein 44 g.
Total fat 66 g.[2]
Saturated fat 22 g.[2]
Polyunsaturated fat 22 g.[2]
Carbohydrate 262 g.[2]
Added sugar 54 g.[2]
Fibre –

## Minerals
Calcium 800 mg.
Iron 18 mg.
Zinc 15 mg.
Copper –
Sodium 1,942 mg. (5 g. salt)[2]
Potassium –
Magnesium 300 mg.
Phosphorus 800 mg.

## Vitamins
Vitamin A 800 µg.
Vitamin C 60 mg.
Vitamin D 6.25 µg.
Vitamin E 8 mg.
Vitamin B1 1.05 mg.
Vitamin B2 1.25 mg.
Niacin 13.5 mg.
Vitamin B6 2 mg.
Vitamin B12 3 µg.
Folic acid 400 µg.
Pantothenic acid –
Biotin –

[2]Recommended in a report called Dietary Goals for the United States, produced by the U.S. Senate Committee on nutrition in 1977.

# Pregnant women

**UK** Official recommended daily amounts unless otherwise stated.

**USA** Official recommended daily amounts unless otherwise stated.

**Food Facts**
Energy 2,400 kcal.
Protein 60 g.
Total fat 77 g.[1]
Saturated fat 25 g.[1]
Polyunsaturated fat 12 g.[1]
Carbohydrate 320 g.[1]
Added sugar 50 g.[1]
Fibre 30 g.[1]

**Minerals**
Calcium 1,200 mg.
Iron 13 mg.
Zinc –
Copper –
Sodium 3,496 mg. (9 g. salt)[1]
Potassium –
Magnesium –
Phosphorus –

**Vitamins**
Vitamin A 750 µg.
Vitamin C 60 mg.
Vitamin D 10 µg.
Vitamin E –
Vitamin B1 1 mg.
Vitamin B2 1.6 mg.
Niacin 18 mg.
Vitamin B6 –
Vitamin B12 –
Folic acid –
Pantothenic acid –
Biotin –

[1]Recommended in the NACNE report produced by the Health Education Council in 1983.

**Food Facts**
Energy 2,350 kcal.
Protein 74 g.
Total fat 75 g.[2]
Saturated fat 25 g.[2]
Polyunsaturated fat 25 g.[2]
Carbohydrate 300 g.[2]
Added sugar 62 g.[2]
Fibre –

**Minerals**
Calcium 1,200 mg.
Iron 30 to 60 mg.
Zinc 20 mg.
Copper –
Sodium 1,942 mg. (5 g. salt)[2]
Potassium –
Magnesium 450 mg.
Phosphorus 1,200 mg.

**Vitamins**
Vitamin A 1,000 µg.
Vitamin C 80 mg.
Vitamin D 11.25 µg.
Vitamin E 10 mg.
Vitamin B1 1.45 mg.
Vitamin B2 1.55 mg.
Niacin 15.5 mg.
Vitamin B6 2.6 mg.
Vitamin B12 4 µg.
Folic acid 800 µg.
Pantothenic acid –
Biotin –

[2]Recommended in a report called Dietary Goals for the United States, produced by the U.S. Senate Committee on nutrition in 1977.

# Breastfeeding women

**UK** Official recommended daily amounts unless otherwise stated.

**Food Facts**
Energy 2,750 kcal.
Protein 69 g.
Total fat 88 g.[1]
Saturated fat 29 g.[1]
Polyunsaturated fat 14 g.[1]
Carbohydrate 366 g.[1]
Added sugar 50 g.[1]
Fibre 30 g.[1]

**Minerals**
Calcium 1,200 mg.
Iron 15 mg.
Zinc –
Copper –
Sodium 3,496 mg. (9 g. salt)[1]
Potassium –
Magnesium –
Phosphorus –

**Vitamins**
Vitamin A 1,200 µg.
Vitamin C 60 mg.
Vitamin D 10 µg.
Vitamin E –
Vitamin B1 1.1 mg.
Vitamin B2 1.8 mg.
Niacin 21 mg.
Vitamin B6 –
Vitamin B12 –
Folic acid –
Pantothenic acid –
Biotin –

[1]Recommended in the NACNE report produced by the Health Education Council in 1983.

**USA** Official recommended daily amounts unless otherwise stated.

**Food Facts**
Energy 2,550 kcal.
Protein 64 g.
Total fat 82 g.[2]
Saturated fat 27 g.[2]
Polyunsaturated fat 27 g.[2]
Carbohydrate 326 g.[2]
Added sugar 68 g.[2]
Fibre –

**Minerals**
Calcium 1,200 mg.
Iron 30 to 60 mg.
Zinc 25 mg.
Copper –
Sodium 1,942 mg. (5 g. salt)[2]
Potassium –
Magnesium 450 mg.
Phosphorus 1,200 mg.

**Vitamins**
Vitamin A 1,200 µg.
Vitamin C 100 mg.
Vitamin D 11.25 µg.
Vitamin E 11 mg.
Vitamin B1 1.55 mg.
Vitamin B2 1.75 mg.
Niacin 18.5 mg.
Vitamin B6 2.5 mg.
Vitamin B12 4 µg.
Folic acid 500 µg.
Pantothenic acid –
Biotin –

[2]Recommended in a report called Dietary Goals for the United States, produced by the U.S. Senate Committee on nutrition in 1977.

# Women aged over 55 years

**UK** Official recommended daily amounts unless otherwise stated.

**Food Facts**
Energy 1,790 kcal.
Protein 44.5 g.
Total fat 57 g.[1]
Saturated fat 19.2 g.[1]
Polyunsaturated fat 9.6 g.[1]
Carbohydrate 238 g.[1]
Added sugar 50 g.[1]
Fibre 30 g.[1]

**Minerals**
Calcium 500 mg.
Iron 10 mg.
Zinc –
Copper –
Sodium 3,496 mg. (9 g. salt)[1]
Potassium –
Magnesium –
Phosphorus –

**Vitamins**
Vitamin A 750 µg.
Vitamin C 30 mg.
Vitamin D 10 µg.
Vitamin E –
Vitamin B1 0.85 mg.
Vitamin B2 1.45 mg.
Niacin 15 mg.
Vitamin B6 –
Vitamin B12 –
Folic acid –
Pantothenic acid –
Biotin –

[1]Recommended in the NACNE report produced by the Health Education Council in 1983.

**USA** Official recommended daily amounts unless otherwise stated.

**Food Facts**
Energy 1,700 kcal.
Protein 44 g.
Total fat 54 g.[2]
Saturated fat 18.2 g.[2]
Polyunsaturated fat 18.2 g.[2]
Carbohydrate 217 g.[2]
Added sugar 45 g.[2]
Fibre –

**Minerals**
Calcium 800 mg.
Iron 10 mg.
Zinc 15 mg.
Copper –
Sodium 1,942 mg. (5 g. salt)[2]
Potassium –
Magnesium 300 mg.
Phosphorus 800 mg.

**Vitamins**
Vitamin A 800 µg.
Vitamin C 60 mg.
Vitamin D 5 µg.
Vitamin E 8 mg.
Vitamin B1 1 mg.
Vitamin B2 1.2 mg.
Niacin 13 mg.
Vitamin B6 2 mg.
Vitamin B12 3 µg.
Folic acid 400 µg.
Pantothenic acid –
Biotin –

[2]Recommended in a report called Dietary Goals for the United States, produced by the U.S. Senate Committee on nutrition in 1977.

# Men aged 19 to 64 years

**UK** Official recommended daily amounts unless otherwise stated.

**Food Facts**
Energy 2,400 to 2,900 kcal.
Protein 66 g.
Total fat 85 g.[1]
Saturated fat 28 g.[1]
Polyunsaturated fat 14 g.[1]
Carbohydrate 352 g.[1]
Added sugar 50 g.[1]
Fibre 30 g.[1]

**Minerals**
Calcium 500 mg.
Iron 10 mg.
Zinc –
Copper –
Sodium 3,496 mg. (9 g. salt)[1]
Potassium –
Magnesium –
Phosphorus –

**Vitamins**
Vitamin A 750 µg.
Vitamin C 30 mg.
Vitamin D 10 µg.
Vitamin E –
Vitamin B1 1 mg.
Vitamin B2 1.6 mg.
Niacin 18 mg.
Vitamin B6 –
Vitamin B12 –
Folic acid –
Pantothenic acid –
Biotin –

[1]Recommended in the NACNE report produced by the Health Education Council in 1983.

**USA** Official recommended daily amounts unless otherwise stated.

**Food Facts**
Energy 2,400 to 2,900 kcal.
Protein 56 g.
Total fat 83 g.[2]
Saturated fat 27 g.[2]
Polyunsaturated fat 27 g.[2]
Carbohydrate 332 g.[2]
Added sugar 69 g.[2]
Fibre –

**Minerals**
Calcium 800 mg.
Iron 10 mg.
Zinc 15 mg.
Copper –
Sodium 1,942 mg. (5 g. salt)[2]
Potassium –
Magnesium 350 mg.
Phosphorus 800 mg.

**Vitamins**
Vitamin A 1,000 µg.
Vitamin C 60 mg.
Vitamin D 6.25 µg.
Vitamin E 10 mg.
Vitamin B1 1.45 mg.
Vitamin B2 1.65 mg.
Niacin 18.5 mg.
Vitamin B6 2.2 mg.
Vitamin B12 3 µg.
Folic acid 400 µg.
Pantothenic acid –
Biotin –

[2]Recommended in a report called Dietary Goals for the United States, produced by the U.S. Senate Committee on nutrition in 1977.

# Men aged over 65 years

**UK** Official recommended daily amounts unless otherwise stated.

**Food Facts**
**Energy** 2,150 to 2,400 kcal.
**Protein** 57 g.
**Total fat** 73 g.[1]
**Saturated fat** 24 g.[1]
**Polyunsaturated fat** 12 g.[1]
**Carbohydrate** 303 g.[1]
**Added sugar** 50 g.[1]
**Fibre** 30 g.[1]

**Minerals**
**Calcium** 500 mg.
**Iron** 10 mg.
**Zinc** –
**Copper** –
**Sodium** 3,496 mg. (9 g. salt)[1]
**Potassium** –
**Magnesium** –
**Phosphorus** –

**Vitamins**
**Vitamin A** 750 µg.
**Vitamin C** 30 mg.
**Vitamin D** 10 µg.
**Vitamin E** –
**Vitamin B1** 0.99 mg.
**Vitamin B2** 1.6 mg.
**Niacin** 18 mg.
**Vitamin B6** –
**Vitamin B12** –
**Folic acid** –
**Pantothenic acid** –
**Biotin** –

[1]Recommended in the NACNE report produced by the Health Education Council in 1983.

**USA** Official recommended daily amounts unless otherwise stated.

**Food Facts**
**Energy** 2,050 to 2,400 kcal.
**Protein** 56 g.
**Total fat** 71 g.[2]
**Saturated fat** 23 g.[2]
**Polyunsaturated fat** 23 g.[2]
**Carbohydrate** 284 g.[2]
**Added sugar** 59 g.[2]
**Fibre** –

**Minerals**
**Calcium** 800 mg.
**Iron** 10 mg.
**Zinc** 15 mg.
**Copper** –
**Sodium** 1,942 mg. (5 g. salt)[2]
**Potassium** –
**Magnesium** 350 mg.
**Phosphorus** 800 mg.

**Vitamins**
**Vitamin A** 1,000 µg.
**Vitamin C** 60 mg.
**Vitamin D** 5 µg.
**Vitamin E** 10 mg.
**Vitamin B1** 1.2 mg.
**Vitamin B2** 1.4 mg.
**Niacin** 16 mg.
**Vitamin B6** 2.2 mg.
**Vitamin B12** 3 µg.
**Folic acid** 400 µg.
**Pantothenic acid** –
**Biotin** –

[2]Recommended in a report called Dietary Goals for the United States, produced by the U.S. Senate Committee on nutrition in 1977.

# 5

# What's in your food

All the foods in the following three chapters are given in portions which you normally eat so that you can calculate what is in the food on your plate. The portions are approximate as the size of foods vary as well as the amount people consider to be a normal serving. For instance potatoes and cuts of meat and fish rarely come in exactly the same size each time you eat them and a plateful of spaghetti can differ quite significantly from what your neighbour serves up. In these cases the weights given under each portion will help you assess the true amounts.

The foods on the following pages have been divided up into three chapters: meat, fish and dairy foods coming together, then fruit, vegetables and nuts followed in the last chapter by bread, cereals, drinks, sweets, spreads and all those other foods you eat everyday. They have been assembled in this way to make for easy comparison when planning and analysing your meals.

The weight of the foods are given in grams (g.) and ounces (oz.). There are 28 g. to one ounce. The amount of energy a food gives you is described in kilocalories (kcalories) usually known as calories. If you want to convert them into kilojoules (the metric measure of calories), multiply the kilocalories by 4.184.

There are three figures given for fat: total fat, saturated fat and polyunsaturated fat. Where the latter two figures do not equal the total fat figure, the difference is mono-unsaturated fat (see p 11).

The carbohydrate figure includes both sugars and starch, with sugars given separately below it. Sugars include both natural and added sugar. Fibre is not included in the carbohydrate total and is given separately. Fibre is not absorbed into the body (see p 15).

The amount of minerals in a food is given in milligrams (mg.). There are 1,000 mg. to a gram. Remember that 388 mg. of sodium is equivalent to one gram of salt. Some vitamins are given in micrograms (μg.). There are 1,000 μg. to a milligram.

The figures in this Guide have been calculated from the following sources: *McCance and Widdowson's The Composition of Foods* by Paul and Southgate (HMSO) and Supplements; *The Handbook of Clinical Dietetics* by the American Dietetic Association (Yale University Press); *Food Tables* by Bender and Bender (Oxford University Press); Nutrition Branch, Ministry of Agriculture, Fisheries and Food; and the manufacturers of brand named foods.

# 6

# Meat, fish and dairy foods

Over 100 portions of meat, fish and dairy foods are analysed highlighting how much fat, protein and calories exist alongside valuable vitamins, calcium, iron and other minerals. The hints at the bottom of each food will help you decide what to pick for you and your family. The weight given for meat and fish is their weight after they have been cooked.

# Anchovies

**Portion** Four anchovies.

**Weight** 20 g., about ⅔ oz.

**Food Facts**
**Energy** 56 kcal.
**Protein** 5 g.
**Total fat** 3.98 g.
**Saturated fat** Not known.
**Polyunsaturated fat** Not known.
**Carbohydrate** Not known.
**Sugars** None.
**Fibre** None.

**Minerals**
**Calcium** 59 mg.
**Iron** 0.8 mg.
**Zinc** 0.6 mg.
**Copper** 0.03 mg.
**Sodium** 786 mg.
**Potassium** 45 mg.
**Magnesium** 11.2 mg.
**Phosphorus** Not known.

**Vitamins**
**Vitamin A** 12.4 µg.
**Vitamin C** Not known.
**Vitamin D** Not known.
**Vitamin E** Not known.
**Vitamin B1** None.
**Vitamin B2** 0.02 mg.
**Niacin** 0.76 mg.
**Vitamin B6** Not known.
**Vitamin B12** 2.2 µg.
**Folic acid** 3.6 µg.
**Pantothenic acid** Not known.
**Biotin** Not known.

Anchovies add a strong and distinctive flavour to salads, pizzas and pasta dishes without increasing the calorie value too much.

# Bacon, back grilled

**Portion** Two rashers grilled without rind.

**Weight** 40 g., about 1½ oz.

**Food Facts**
**Energy** 162 kcal.
**Protein** 10.1 g.
**Total fat** 13.5 g.
**Saturated fat** 5.4 g.
**Polyunsaturated fat** 0.98 g.
**Carbohydrate** None.
**Sugars** None.
**Fibre** None.

**Minerals**
**Calcium** 4.8 mg.
**Iron** 0.6 mg.
**Zinc** 1.2 mg.
**Copper** 0.06 mg.
**Sodium** 808 mg.
**Potassium** 116 mg.
**Magnesium** 6.4 mg.
**Phosphorus** 64 mg.

**Vitamins**
**Vitamin A** None.
**Vitamin C** None.
**Vitamin D** None.
**Vitamin E** 0.04 mg.
**Vitamin B1** 0.17 mg.
**Vitamin B2** 0.07 mg.
**Niacin** 3.68 mg.
**Vitamin B6** 0.11 mg.
**Vitamin B12** None.
**Folic acid** 0.4 µg.
**Pantothenic acid** 0.2 mg.
**Biotin** 0.8 µg.

Try to cut the fat off your bacon before you grill it. Bacon contains a lot of salt.

# Bacon, back fried

**Portion** Two rashers fried without rind.
**Weight** 40 g., about 1½ oz.

## Food Facts
**Energy** 186 kcal.
**Protein** 10 g.
**Total fat** 16.2 g.
**Saturated fat** 6.5 g.
**Polyunsaturated fat** 1.18 g.
**Carbohydrate** None.
**Sugars** None.
**Fibre** None.

## Minerals
**Calcium** 5.2 mg.
**Iron** 0.52 mg.
**Zinc** 1.04 mg.
**Copper** 0.05 mg.
**Sodium** 764 mg.
**Potassium** 120 mg.
**Magnesium** 8 mg.
**Phosphorus** 68 mg.

## Vitamins
**Vitamin A** None.
**Vitamin C** None.
**Vitamin D** None.
**Vitamin E** 0.07 mg.
**Vitamin B1** 0.16 mg.
**Vitamin B2** 0.08 mg.
**Niacin** 3.96 mg.
**Vitamin B6** 0.12 mg.
**Vitamin B12** None.
**Folic acid** 0.4 µg.
**Pantothenic acid** 0.1 mg.
**Biotin** 1.2 µg.

If you want to fry bacon, try to use a non-stick pan that needs little or no added fat.

# Bacon, streaky

**Portion** Three rashers grilled without rind.
**Weight** 30 g., about 1 oz.

## Food Facts
**Energy** 126 kcal.
**Protein** 7.3 g.
**Total fat** 10.8 g.
**Saturated fat** 4.3 g.
**Polyunsaturated fat** 0.7 g.
**Carbohydrate** None.
**Sugars** None.
**Fibre** None.

## Minerals
**Calcium** 3.6 mg.
**Iron** 0.45 mg.
**Zinc** 0.87 mg.
**Copper** 0.04 mg.
**Sodium** 597 mg.
**Potassium** 87 mg.
**Magnesium** 4.8 mg.
**Phosphorus** 48 mg.

## Vitamins
**Vitamin A** None.
**Vitamin C** None.
**Vitamin D** None.
**Vitamin E** 0.4 mg.
**Vitamin B1** 0.12 mg.
**Vitamin B2** 0.05 mg.
**Niacin** 2.64 mg.
**Vitamin B6** 0.07 mg.
**Vitamin B12** None.
**Folic acid** 0.3 µg.
**Pantothenic acid** 0.1 mg.
**Biotin** 0.6 µg.

Make a bacon sandwich with wholemeal bread, lettuce and tomato using only a little bacon.

# Beefburger

**Portion** One fried beefburger.

**Weight** 50 g., about 1¾ oz.

**Food Facts**
Energy 132 kcal.
Protein 10.2 g.
Total fat 8.6 g.
Saturated fat 3.6 g.
Polyunsaturated fat 0.34 g.
Carbohydrate 3.5 g.
Sugars None.
Fibre None.

**Minerals**
Calcium 16.5 mg.
Iron 1.55 mg.
Zinc 2.1 mg.
Copper 0.14 mg.
Sodium 440 mg.
Potassium 170 mg.
Magnesium 11.5 mg.
Phosphorus 125 mg.

**Vitamins**
Vitamin A None.
Vitamin C None.
Vitamin D None.
Vitamin E 0.29 mg.
Vitamin B1 0.01 mg.
Vitamin B2 0.11 mg.
Niacin 4 mg.
Vitamin B6 0.1 mg.
Vitamin B12 1 µg.
Folic acid 7.5 µg.
Pantothenic acid 0.2 mg.
Biotin 1 µg.

**Grill beefburgers, don't fry. Buy ones which are 100% meat. They cost more but will not shrink so much.**

# Beefburger in a bun

**Portion** One McDonald's hamburger.

**Weight** 103 g., about 3¾ oz.

**Food Facts**
Energy 252 kcal.
Protein 13.6 g.
Total fat 9.9 g.
Saturated fat 4.8 g.
Polyunsaturated fat 0.4 g.
Carbohydrate 29 g.
Sugars 1.4 g.
Fibre 0.8 g.

**Minerals**
Calcium 69 mg.
Iron 1 mg.
Zinc Not known.
Copper Not known.
Sodium 396 mg.
Potassium 143 mg.
Magnesium Not known.
Phosphorus Not known.

**Vitamins**
Vitamin A 2.4 µg.
Vitamin C Not known.
Vitamin D Not known.
Vitamin E Not known.
Vitamin B1 0.2 mg.
Vitamin B2 0.06 mg.
Niacin 3 mg.
Vitamin B6 0.04 mg.
Vitamin B12 0.5 µg.
Folic acid Not known.
Pantothenic acid Not known.
Biotin Not known.

**A beefburger makes a change from a lunch-time sandwich and contains less fat than most people realise.**

# Beef cheeseburger

**Portion** One McDonald's cheeseburger.
**Weight** 117 g., about 4 oz.

**Food Facts**
**Energy** 300 kcal.
**Protein** 15.8 g.
**Total fat** 14.2 g.
**Saturated fat** 7.3 g.
**Polyunsaturated fat** 0.7 g.
**Carbohydrate** 29.1 g.
**Sugars** 1.3 g.
**Fibre** 0.8 g.

**Minerals**
**Calcium** 153 mg.
**Iron** 1.1 mg.
**Zinc** Not known.
**Copper** Not known.
**Sodium** 579 mg.
**Potassium** 153 mg.
**Magnesium** Not known.
**Phosphorus** Not known.

**Vitamins**
**Vitamin A** 47.4 µg.
**Vitamin C** Not known.
**Vitamin D** Not known.
**Vitamin E** Not known.
**Vitamin B1** 0.21 mg.
**Vitamin B2** 0.05 mg.
**Niacin** 2.9 mg.
**Vitamin B6** 0.04 mg.
**Vitamin B12** 0.8 µg.
**Folic acid** Not known.
**Pantothenic acid** Not known.
**Biotin** Not known.

If you are weight watching, do not have fries or chips with your burger.

# Beef, minced

**Portion** A ¼lb of raw minced beef, cooked with some onion.
**Weight** 70 g., about 2½ oz.

**Food Facts**
**Energy** 91 kcal.
**Protein** 9.2 g.
**Total fat** 4.5 g.
**Saturated fat** 1.8 g.
**Polyunsaturated fat** 0.16 g.
**Carbohydrate** 3.9 g.
**Sugars** 0.9 g.
**Fibre** 0.3 g.

**Minerals**
**Calcium** 15.4 mg.
**Iron** 0.84 mg.
**Zinc** 1.4 mg.
**Copper** 0.07 mg.
**Sodium** 219 mg.
**Potassium** 139 mg.
**Magnesium** 9.8 mg.
**Phosphorus** 62 mg.

**Vitamins**
**Vitamin A** None.
**Vitamin C** None.
**Vitamin D** None.
**Vitamin E** 0.07 mg.
**Vitamin B1** 0.03 mg.
**Vitamin B2** 0.08 mg.
**Niacin** 3.29 mg.
**Vitamin B6** 0.09 mg.
**Vitamin B12** 0.7 µg.
**Folic acid** 2.8 µg.
**Pantothenic acid** 0.2 mg.
**Biotin** None.

Up to a third of the raw weight of minced beef can be fat. So try to buy good quality mince which contains less fat.

# Beef, roast

**Portion** Four slices of topside including fat.
**Weight** 120 g., about 4¼ oz.

## Food Facts
**Energy** 256 kcal.
**Protein** 31.9 g.
**Total fat** 14.4 g.
**Saturated fat** 6 g.
**Polyunsaturated fat** 0.5 g.
**Carbohydrate** None.
**Sugars** None.
**Fibre** None.

## Minerals
**Calcium** 7.2 mg.
**Iron** 3.12 mg.
**Zinc** 5.88 mg.
**Copper** 0.16 mg.
**Sodium** 57.6 mg.
**Potassium** 420 mg.
**Magnesium** 27.6 mg.
**Phosphorus** 240 mg.

## Vitamins
**Vitamin A** None.
**Vitamin C** None.
**Vitamin D** None.
**Vitamin E** 0.38 mg.
**Vitamin B1** 0.08 mg.
**Vitamin B2** 0.37 mg.
**Niacin** 13.6 mg.
**Vitamin B6** 0.35 mg.
**Vitamin B12** 2.4 µg.
**Folic acid** 18 µg.
**Pantothenic acid** 1 mg.
**Biotin** None.

**Roast beef is the leanest and lowest in calories out of all red meats.**

# Beef stew

**Portion** One ladleful.

**Weight** 170 g., about 6 oz.

## Food Facts
**Energy** 202 kcal.
**Protein** 16.3 g.
**Total fat** 12.7 g.
**Saturated fat** 5.4 g.
**Polyunsaturated fat** 0.6 g.
**Carbohydrate** 6.1 g.
**Sugars** None.
**Fibre** None.

## Minerals
**Calcium** 32.3 mg.
**Iron** 2.04 mg.
**Zinc** 3.06 mg.
**Copper** 0.17 mg.
**Sodium** 680 mg.
**Potassium** 340 mg.
**Magnesium** 23.8 mg.
**Phosphorus** 124 mg.

## Vitamins
**Vitamin A** 453 µg.
**Vitamin C** None.
**Vitamin D** None.
**Vitamin E** 0.25 mg.
**Vitamin B1** 0.07 mg.
**Vitamin B2** 0.17 mg.
**Niacin** 6.46 mg.
**Vitamin B6** 0.22 mg.
**Vitamin B12** 1.7 µg.
**Folic acid** 8.5 µg.
**Pantothenic acid** 0.5 mg.
**Biotin** None.

**A stew will be just as tasty if you add more vegetables and use less meat. The carrots make it high in vitamin A.**

# Black pudding

**Portion** 4 slices fried.

**Weight** 30 g., about 1 oz.

**Food Facts**
**Energy** 91 kcal.
**Protein** 3.9 g.
**Total fat** 6.6 g.
**Saturated fat** Not known.
**Polyunsaturated fat** Not known.
**Carbohydrate** 4.5 g.
**Sugars** None.
**Fibre** None.

**Minerals**
**Calcium** 10.5 mg.
**Iron** 6 mg.
**Zinc** 0.39 mg.
**Copper** 0.11 mg.
**Sodium** 363 mg.
**Potassium** 42 mg.
**Magnesium** 4.8 mg.
**Phosphorus** 33 mg.

**Vitamins**
**Vitamin A** None.
**Vitamin C** None.
**Vitamin D** None.
**Vitamin E** 0.07 mg.
**Vitamin B1** 0.03 mg.
**Vitamin B2** 0.02 mg.
**Niacin** 1.14 mg.
**Vitamin B6** 0.01 mg.
**Vitamin B12** 0.3 μg.
**Folic acid** 1.5 μg.
**Pantothenic acid** 0.2 mg.
**Biotin** 0.6 μg.

Although quite a high calorie
addition to a cooked breakfast,
black pudding is very high in iron.
However it is an acquired taste.

# Butter

**Portion** Enough for one slice
of bread.

**Weight** 7 g., about ¼ oz.

**Food Facts**
**Energy** 51 kcal.
**Protein** None.
**Total fat** 5.7 g.
**Saturated fat** 3.4 g.
**Polyunsaturated fat** 0.15 g.
**Carbohydrate** None.
**Sugars** None.
**Fibre** None.

**Minerals**
**Calcium** 1 mg.
**Iron** 0.01 mg.
**Zinc** 0.01 mg.
**Copper** None.
**Sodium** 60 mg.
**Potassium** 1 mg.
**Magnesium** 0.1 mg.
**Phosphorus** 1.7 mg.

**Vitamins**
**Vitamin A** 58 μg.
**Vitamin C** None.
**Vitamin D** 0.05 μg.
**Vitamin E** 0.14 mg.
**Vitamin B1** None.
**Vitamin B2** None.
**Niacin** 0.01 mg.
**Vitamin B6** None.
**Vitamin B12** None.
**Folic acid** None.
**Pantothenic acid** None.
**Biotin** None.

Butter contains exactly the same
amount of calories as margarine,
but is often hard to spread as thinly
as soft margarine.

# Camembert-type cheese

**Portion** One matchbox sized cube.
**Weight** 30 g., about 1 oz.

**Food Facts**
Energy 90 kcal.
Protein 6.8 g.
Total fat 7 g.
Saturated fat 4.1 g.
Polyunsaturated fat 0.19 g.
Carbohydrate None.
Sugars None.
Fibre None.

**Minerals**
Calcium 114 mg.
Iron 0.23 mg.
Zinc 0.9 mg.
Copper 0.02 mg.
Sodium 423 mg.
Potassium 33 mg.
Magnesium 5.1 mg.
Phosphorus 87 mg.

**Vitamins**
Vitamin A 71 µg.
Vitamin C None.
Vitamin D 0.05 µg.
Vitamin E 0.18 mg.
Vitamin B1 0.01 mg.
Vitamin B2 0.18 mg.
Niacin 1.85 mg.
Vitamin B6 0.06 mg.
Vitamin B12 0.36 µg.
Folic acid 18 µg.
Pantothenic acid 0.4 mg.
Biotin 1.8 µg.

This type of cheese contains less fat and calories than cheddar. Brie cheese is lower in fat than camembert.

# Cheddar cheese

**Portion** One matchbox sized cube.
**Weight** 30 g., about 1 oz.

**Food Facts**
Energy 121 kcal.
Protein 7.8 g.
Total fat 10 g.
Saturated fat 6 g.
Polyunsaturated fat 0.27 g.
Carbohydrate None.
Sugars None.
Fibre None.

**Minerals**
Calcium 240 mg.
Iron 0.12 mg.
Zinc 1.2 mg.
Copper 0.01 mg.
Sodium 183 mg.
Potassium 36 mg.
Magnesium 7.5 mg.
Phosphorus 156 mg.

**Vitamins**
Vitamin A 103 µg.
Vitamin C None.
Vitamin D 0.08 µg.
Vitamin E 0.24 mg.
Vitamin B1 0.01 mg.
Vitamin B2 0.15 mg.
Niacin 1.87 mg.
Vitamin B6 0.02 mg.
Vitamin B12 0.45 µg.
Folic acid 6 µg.
Pantothenic acid 0.1 mg.
Biotin 0.5 µg.

Avoid eating cheese and biscuits after your meals if you want to cut down on calories.

# Cheese and tomato pizza

**Portion** A quarter of a large pizza.
**Weight** 97 g., about 3½ oz.

**Food Facts**
Energy 227 kcal.
Protein 9.1 g.
Total fat 11.2 g.
Saturated fat 4.9 g.
Polyunsaturated fat 0.7 g.
Carbohydrate 24.1 g.
Sugars None.
Fibre None.

**Minerals**
Calcium 232 mg.
Iron 1.07 mg.
Zinc 1.16 mg.
Copper 0.13 mg.
Sodium 329 mg.
Potassium 174 mg.
Magnesium 18.4 mg.
Phosphorus 164 mg.

**Vitamins**
Vitamin A 105 µg.
Vitamin C 2.9 g.
Vitamin D 0.06 µg.
Vitamin E 0.68 mg.
Vitamin B1 0.11 mg.
Vitamin B2 0.14 mg.
Niacin 2.98 mg.
Vitamin B6 0.08 mg.
Vitamin B12 0.29 µg.
Folic acid 23.3 µg.
Pantothenic acid 0.3 mg.
Biotin 2.9 µg.

**Try making pizzas at home using wholemeal floor for the base and a small amount of cheese on top.**

# Cheese spread

**Portion** One triangle.
**Weight** 10 g., about ⅓ oz.

**Food Facts**
Energy 28 kcal.
Protein 1.8 g.
Total fat 2.3 g.
Saturated fat 1.36 g.
Polyunsaturated fat 0.06 g.
Carbohydrate 0.1 g.
Sugars None.
Fibre None.

**Minerals**
Calcium 51 mg.
Iron 0.07 mg.
Zinc 0.3 mg.
Copper 0.01 mg.
Sodium 117 mg.
Potassium 15 mg.
Magnesium 2.5 mg.
Phosphorus 44 mg.

**Vitamins**
Vitamin A 19.7 µg.
Vitamin C None.
Vitamin D 0.01 µg.
Vitamin E Not known.
Vitamin B1 None.
Vitamin B2 0.02 mg.
Niacin 0.44 mg.
Vitamin B6 Not known.
Vitamin B12 Not known.
Folic acid 0.7 µg.
Pantothenic acid Not known.
Biotin Not known.

**It is better to give children a mild cheese rather than cheese spread in their sandwiches as its protein content is low.**

# Chicken, roast

**Portion** Breast and leg with some skin.
**Weight** 130 g., about 4½ oz.

## Food Facts
**Energy** 280 kcal.
**Protein** 29.4 g.
**Total fat** 18.2 g.
**Saturated fat** 6 g.
**Polyunsaturated fat** 2.73 g.
**Carbohydrate** None.
**Sugars** None.
**Fibre** None.

## Minerals
**Calcium** 11.7 mg.
**Iron** 1.04 mg.
**Zinc** 1.82 mg.
**Copper** 0.16 mg.
**Sodium** 93.6 mg.
**Potassium** 351 mg.
**Magnesium** 27.3 mg.
**Phosphorus** 221 mg.

## Vitamins
**Vitamin A** None.
**Vitamin C** None.
**Vitamin D** None.
**Vitamin E** Not known.
**Vitamin B1** 0.08 mg.
**Vitamin B2** 0.22 mg.
**Niacin** 13.65 mg.
**Vitamin B6** Not known.
**Vitamin B12** None.
**Folic acid** Not known.
**Pantothenic acid** Not known.
**Biotin** Not known.

The skin accounts for the increase in calories as compared to values for chicken breast or leg. Remember this if weight-watching.

# Chicken breast, roasted

**Portion** One whole chicken breast without skin.
**Weight** 130 g., about 4½ oz.

## Food Facts
**Energy** 184 kcal.
**Protein** 34 g.
**Total fat** 5.2 g.
**Saturated fat** 1.7 g.
**Polyunsaturated fat** 0.79 g.
**Carbohydrate** None.
**Sugars** None.
**Fibre** None.

## Minerals
**Calcium** 11.7 mg.
**Iron** 0.65 mg.
**Zinc** 1.3 mg.
**Copper** 0.14 mg.
**Sodium** 92 mg.
**Potassium** 429 mg.
**Magnesium** 33 mg.
**Phosphorus** 286 mg.

## Vitamins
**Vitamin A** None.
**Vitamin C** None.
**Vitamin D** None.
**Vitamin E** 0.1 mg.
**Vitamin B1** 0.1 mg.
**Vitamin B2** 0.18 mg.
**Niacin** 19.89 mg.
**Vitamin B6** 0.45 mg.
**Vitamin B12** None.
**Folic acid** 9.1 µg.
**Pantothenic acid** 1.4 mg.
**Biotin** 2.6 µg.

Chicken breast is quick to cook and ideal for stir-fried dishes. The meat will stretch further if vegetables are added. Also try grilling.

# Chicken leg, roasted

**Portion** One leg, meat without skin and bone.
**Weight** 130 g., about 4½ oz.

**Food Facts**
Energy 201 kcal.
Protein 30 g.
Total fat 9 g.
Saturated fat 2.9 g.
Polyunsaturated fat 1.36 g.
Carbohydrate None.
Sugars None.
Fibre None.

**Minerals**
Calcium 11.7 mg.
Iron 1.3 mg.
Zinc 2.73 mg.
Copper 0.17 mg.
Sodium 118 mg.
Potassium 377 mg.
Magnesium 28 mg.
Phosphorus 247 mg.

**Vitamins**
Vitamin A None.
Vitamin C None.
Vitamin D None.
Vitamin E 0.19 mg.
Vitamin B1 0.12 mg.
Vitamin B2 0.31 mg.
Niacin 13.52 mg.
Vitamin B6 0.21 mg.
Vitamin B12 1.3 µg.
Folic acid 16.9 µg.
Pantothenic acid 1.7 mg.
Biotin 3.9 µg.

Don't fry. For example, braise chicken legs in a tomato sauce with herbs. If you eat the skin, the calories and fat increase dramatically.

# Chicken pie

**Portion** Quarter of large pie with pastry top or bottom.
**Weight** 106 g., about 3¾ oz.

**Food Facts**
Energy 358 kcal.
Protein 11.9 g.
Total fat 21.1 g.
Saturated fat Not known.
Polyunsaturated fat Not known.
Carbohydrate 32.2 g.
Sugars Not known.
Fibre 1.4 g.

**Minerals**
Calcium 94 mg.
Iron 1.27 mg.
Zinc 0.85 mg.
Copper 0.12 mg.
Sodium 376 mg.
Potassium 181 mg.
Magnesium 20 mg.
Phosphorus 129 mg.

**Vitamins**
Vitamin A 109 µg.
Vitamin C None.
Vitamin D 0.88 µg.
Vitamin E 0.95 mg.
Vitamin B1 0.13 mg.
Vitamin B2 0.1 mg.
Niacin 5.5 mg.
Vitamin B6 0.13 mg.
Vitamin B12 None.
Folic acid 8.5 µg.
Pantothenic acid 0.5 mg.
Biotin 2.1 µg.

Pastry adds a lot of calories to this low calorie meat. Make a pastry lining of one layer instead of two.

# Chilli con carne

**Portion** About two ladlefuls.

**Weight** 200 g., about 7 oz.

**Food Facts**
Energy 296 kcal.
Protein 22.2 g.
Total fat 17 g.
Saturated fat Not known.
Polyunsaturated fat Not known.
Carbohydrate 14.8 g.
Sugars 5.4 g.
Fibre 6.4 g.

**Minerals**
Calcium 72 mg.
Iron 6.2 mg.
Zinc 4.6 mg.
Copper 0.42 mg.
Sodium 476 mg.
Potassium 888 mg.
Magnesium 76 mg.
Phosphorus 262 mg.

**Vitamins**
Vitamin A 250 µg.
Vitamin C 10 mg.
Vitamin D None.
Vitamin E 1.2 mg.
Vitamin B1 0.18 mg.
Vitamin B2 0.28 mg.
Niacin 3.6 mg.
Vitamin B6 0.5 mg.
Vitamin B12 2 µg.
Folic acid 40 µg.
Pantothenic acid 0.8 mg.
Biotin 2 µg.

This dish tastes just as good
without the meat. The protein in
the beans complements that in
the rice.

# Cockles

**Portion** Six cockles cooked in
salt water.

**Weight** 25 g., about 1 oz.

**Food Facts**
Energy 12 kcal.
Protein 2.8 g.
Total fat 0.08 g.
Saturated fat Not known.
Polyunsaturated fat Not known.
Carbohydrate None.
Sugars None.
Fibre None.

**Minerals**
Calcium 32 mg.
Iron 6.5 mg.
Zinc 0.3 mg.
Copper 0.07 mg.
Sodium 880 mg.
Potassium 10.7 mg.
Magnesium 12.7 mg.
Phosphorus 50 mg.

**Vitamins**
Vitamin A None..
Vitamin C None.
Vitamin D None.
Vitamin E Not known.
Vitamin B1 Not known.
Vitamin B2 Not known.
Niacin 0.6 mg.
Vitamin B6 Not known.
Vitamin B12 None.
Folic acid Not known.
Pantothenic acid Not known.
Biotin Not known.

Cockles are very low in calories and
naturally rich in iron. Try them in a
seafood salad.

# Cod in-a-bag

**Portion** One portion of cod with sauce.
**Weight** 150 g., about 5¼ oz.

**Food Facts**
**Energy** 168 kcal.
**Protein** 24.4 g.
**Total fat** 5.9 g.
**Saturated fat** 3.5 g.
**Polyunsaturated fat** 0.9 g.
**Carbohydrate** 4.9 g.
**Sugars** 2.3 g.
**Fibre** 0.1 g.

**Minerals**
**Calcium** 86 mg.
**Iron** 0.55 mg.
**Zinc** 0.7 mg.
**Copper** 0.09 mg.
**Sodium** 541 mg.
**Potassium** 439 mg.
**Magnesium** 34.5 mg.
**Phosphorus** 249 mg.

**Vitamins**
**Vitamin A** 46 µg.
**Vitamin C** None.
**Vitamin D** 0.28 µg.
**Vitamin E** 0.93 mg.
**Vitamin B1** 0.1 mg.
**Vitamin B2** 0.15 mg.
**Niacin** 6.52 mg.
**Vitamin B6** 0.42 mg.
**Vitamin B12** 2.1 µg.
**Folic acid** 14.4 µg.
**Pantothenic acid** 0.3 mg.
**Biotin** 4 µg.

Most of the fat and a third of the calories in this dish come from the sauce.

# Cod, grilled

**Portion** Half a cod fillet.
**Weight** 175 g., about 6¼ oz.

**Food Facts**
**Energy** 166 kcal.
**Protein** 36.4 g.
**Total fat** 2.3 g.
**Saturated fat** 0.4 g.
**Polyunsaturated fat** 0.89 g.
**Carbohydrate** None.
**Sugars** None.
**Fibre** None.

**Minerals**
**Calcium** 17.5 mg.
**Iron** 0.7 mg.
**Zinc** 0.87 mg.
**Copper** 0.12 mg.
**Sodium** 159 mg.
**Potassium** 665 mg.
**Magnesium** 45 mg.
**Phosphorus** 350 mg.

**Vitamins**
**Vitamin A** None.
**Vitamin C** None.
**Vitamin D** None.
**Vitamin E** 1.05 mg.
**Vitamin B1** 0.14 mg.
**Vitamin B2** 0.1 mg.
**Niacin** 10.15 mg.
**Vitamin B6** 0.72 mg.
**Vitamin B12** 3.5 µg.
**Folic acid** 17.5 µg.
**Pantothenic acid** 0.4 mg.
**Biotin** 5.2 µg.

As well as grilling, white fish such as cod can also be baked in the oven, or poached in fish stock, wine or cider for special occasions.

# Cod in batter

**Portion** Average portion from fish and chip shop.
**Weight** 225 g., about 8 oz.

**Food Facts**
Energy 447 kcal.
Protein 44.1 g.
Total fat 23.2 g.
Saturated fat 16.3 g.
Polyunsaturated fat 1.57 g.
Carbohydrate 16.9 g.
Sugars None.
Fibre None.

**Minerals**
Calcium 180 mg.
Iron 1.1 mg.
Zinc 1.1 mg.
Copper 0.1 mg.
Sodium 225 mg.
Potassium 832 mg.
Magnesium 54 mg.
Phosphorus 450 mg.

**Vitamins**
Vitamin A None.
Vitamin C None.
Vitamin D None.
Vitamin E None.
Vitamin B1 0.16 mg.
Vitamin B2 0.16 mg.
Niacin 12.1 mg.
Vitamin B6 0.85 mg.
Vitamin B12 4.5 µg.
Folic acid 27 µg.
Pantothenic acid 0.4 mg.
Biotin 6.7 µg.

If you like fried fish, try just eating the fish and leaving the batter.
Think of different ways to cook fish.

# Corn oil

**Portion** One tablespoon.

**Weight** 5 g., about ⅕ oz.

**Food Facts**
Energy 44 kcal.
Protein None.
Total fat 5 g.
Saturated fat 0.82 g.
Polyunsaturated fat 2.46 g.
Carbohydrate None.
Sugars None.
Fibre None.

**Minerals**
Calcium None.
Iron None.
Zinc None.
Copper None.
Sodium None.
Potassium None.
Magnesium None.
Phosphorus None.

**Vitamins**
Vitamin A None.
Vitamin C None.
Vitamin D None.
Vitamin E 0.56 mg.
Vitamin B1 None.
Vitamin B2 None.
Niacin None.
Vitamin B6 None.
Vitamin B12 None.
Folic acid None.
Pantothenic acid None.
Biotin None.

If you wish to fry foods, stir-fry or shallow fry, and only use the oil once or twice before throwing it away.

# Corned beef

**Portion** Two slices.

**Weight** 80 g., about 2¾ oz.

**Food Facts**
Energy 173 kcal.
Protein 21.5 g.
Total fat 9.7 g.
Saturated fat 4 g.
Polyunsaturated fat 0.39 g.
Carbohydrate None.
Sugars None.
Fibre None.

**Minerals**
Calcium 11.2 mg.
Iron 2.32 mg.
Zinc 4.48 mg.
Copper 0.19 mg.
Sodium 760 mg.
Potassium 112 mg.
Magnesium 12 mg.
Phosphorus 96 mg.

**Vitamins**
Vitamin A None.
Vitamin C None.
Vitamin D None.
Vitamin E 0.62 mg.
Vitamin B1 None.
Vitamin B2 0.18 mg.
Niacin 7.2 mg.
Vitamin B6 0.05 mg.
Vitamin B12 1.6 µg.
Folic acid 1.6 µg.
Pantothenic acid 0.3 mg.
Biotin 1.6 µg.

Corned beef is not as high in fat as you might think. It does however contain sixteen times as much sodium as roast beef.

# Cornish pastie

**Portion** One Cornish pastie.

**Weight** 238 g., about 8½ oz.

**Food Facts**
Energy 790 kcal.
Protein 19 g.
Total fat 48.6 g.
Saturated fat Not known.
Polyunsaturated fat Not known.
Carbohydrate 74 g.
Sugars None.
Fibre None.

**Minerals**
Calcium 142 mg.
Iron 3.57 mg.
Zinc 2.38 mg.
Copper 0.83 mg.
Sodium 1404 mg.
Potassium 452 mg.
Magnesium 42.8 mg.
Phosphorus 261 mg.

**Vitamins**
Vitamin A None.
Vitamin C None.
Vitamin D None.
Vitamin E 3.09 mg.
Vitamin B1 0.24 mg.
Vitamin B2 0.14 mg.
Niacin 7.85 mg.
Vitamin B6 0.29 mg.
Vitamin B12 2.38 µg.
Folic acid 7.1 µg.
Pantothenic acid 1.4 mg.
Biotin 2.4 µg.

The high calorie, fat and sodium content of pasties means that they should only be eaten very occasionally.

# Cottage cheese

**Portion** One small tub.

**Weight** 112 g., about 4 oz.

**Food Facts**
Energy 107 kcal.
Protein 15.2 g.
Total fat 4.5 g.
Saturated fat 2.6 g.
Polyunsaturated fat 0.12 g.
Carbohydrate 1.6 g.
Sugars None.
Fibre None.

**Minerals**
Calcium 67 mg.
Iron 0.11 mg.
Zinc 0.53 mg.
Copper 0.02 mg.
Sodium 504 mg.
Potassium 60 mg.
Magnesium 6.7 mg.
Phosphorus 156 mg.

**Vitamins**
Vitamin A 30 g.
Vitamin C None.
Vitamin D 0.03 µg.
Vitamin E Not known.
Vitamin B1 0.02 mg.
Vitamin B2 0.21 mg.
Niacin 3.68 mg.
Vitamin B6 0.01 mg.
Vitamin B12 0.56 µg.
Folic acid 10.1 µg.
Pantothenic acid Not known.
Biotin Not known.

Spice up cottage cheese by adding
peppers, spring onions or tomatoes.
Adding black pepper or cayenne
pepper will help.

# Crab

**Portion** White meat, about
two tablespoons or half a tin.

**Weight** 85 g., about 3 oz.

**Food Facts**
Energy 68 kcal.
Protein 15.4 g.
Total fat 0.8 g.
Saturated fat 0.07 g.
Polyunsaturated fat 0.26 g.
Carbohydrate None.
Sugars None.
Fibre None.

**Minerals**
Calcium 102 mg.
Iron 2.38 mg.
Zinc 4.25 mg.
Copper 0.36 mg.
Sodium 467 mg.
Potassium 85 mg.
Magnesium 27 mg.
Phosphorus 119 mg.

**Vitamins**
Vitamin A None.
Vitamin C None.
Vitamin D None.
Vitamin E Not known.
Vitamin B1 None.
Vitamin B2 0.04 mg.
Niacin 3.82 mg.
Vitamin B6 Not known.
Vitamin B12 None.
Folic acid 17 µg.
Pantothenic acid Not known.
Biotin None.

For a change, try crab instead of
prawns with an avocado pear. Crab
can also be added to soups such as
Chinese-style crab and sweetcorn.

# Cream cheese

**Portion** Half a small packet.

**Weight** 30 g., about 1 oz.

**Food Facts**
**Energy** 131 kcal.
**Protein** 0.9 g.
**Total fat** 14.2 g.
**Saturated fat** 8.4 g.
**Polyunsaturated fat** 0.39 g.
**Carbohydrate** None.
**Sugars** None.
**Fibre** None.

**Minerals**
**Calcium** 29 mg.
**Iron** 0.04 mg.
**Zinc** 0.14 mg.
**Copper** 0.01 mg.
**Sodium** 90 mg.
**Potassium** 48 mg.
**Magnesium** 3 mg.
**Phosphorus** 30 mg.

**Vitamins**
**Vitamin A** 126 µg.
**Vitamin C** None.
**Vitamin D** 0.08 µg.
**Vitamin E** 0.3 mg.
**Vitamin B1** 0.01 mg.
**Vitamin B2** 0.04 mg.
**Niacin** 0.25 mg.
**Vitamin B6** None.
**Vitamin B12** 0.09 µg.
**Folic acid** 1.5 µg.
**Pantothenic acid** Not known.
**Biotin** Not known.

Try to substitute curd cheese,
cottage cheese or fromage frais
for cream cheese when using it for
cooking.

# Cream, double

**Portion** One tablespoon.

**Weight** 20 g., about ⅔ oz.

**Food Facts**
**Energy** 89 kcal.
**Protein** 0.3 g.
**Total fat** 9.6 g.
**Saturated fat** 5.7 g.
**Polyunsaturated fat** 0.26 g.
**Carbohydrate** 0.4 g.
**Sugars** 0.4 g.
**Fibre** None.

**Minerals**
**Calcium** 10 mg.
**Iron** 0.04 mg.
**Zinc** 0.03 mg.
**Copper** 0.03 mg.
**Sodium** 5.4 mg.
**Potassium** 15.8 mg.
**Magnesium** 0.8 mg.
**Phosphorus** 4.2 mg.

**Vitamins**
**Vitamin A** 71.3 µg.
**Vitamin C** 0.16 mg.
**Vitamin D** 0.04 µg.
**Vitamin E** 0.18 mg.
**Vitamin B1** None.
**Vitamin B2** 0.02 mg.
**Niacin** 0.08 mg.
**Vitamin B6** None.
**Vitamin B12** 0.02 µg.
**Folic acid** 0.4 µg.
**Pantothenic acid** None.
**Biotin** 0.2 µg.

Use cream as little as possible
when cooking, particularly double
cream, which has twice the calories
and fat of single cream.

# Cream, single

**Portion** One tablespoon.

**Weight** 20 g., about ⅔ oz.

**Food Facts**
**Energy** 42 kcal.
**Protein** 0.5 g.
**Total fat** 4.2 g.
**Saturated fat** 2.53 g.
**Polyunsaturated fat** 0.11 g.
**Carbohydrate** 0.6 g.
**Sugars** 0.6 g.
**Fibre** None.

**Minerals**
**Calcium** 15.8 mg.
**Iron** 0.06 mg.
**Zinc** 0.05 mg.
**Copper** 0.04 mg.
**Sodium** 8.4 mg.
**Potassium** 24 mg.
**Magnesium** 1.2 mg.
**Phosphorus** 8.8 mg.

**Vitamins**
**Vitamin A** 31.3 µg.
**Vitamin C** 0.24 mg.
**Vitamin D** 0.02 µg.
**Vitamin E** 0.08 mg.
**Vitamin B1** 0.01 mg.
**Vitamin B2** 0.02 mg.
**Niacin** 0.13 mg.
**Vitamin B6** 0.01 mg.
**Vitamin B12** 0.04 µg.
**Folic acid** 0.8 µg.
**Pantothenic acid** 0.1 mg.
**Biotin** 0.3 µg.

Remember that sour cream will also contain a similar amount of calories. Try using low fat plain yoghurt in cooking or as a topping for puddings.

# Duck

**Portion** Two to three large slices, roasted without skin.

**Weight** 120 g., about 4¼ oz.

**Food Facts**
**Energy** 226 kcal.
**Protein** 30.4 g.
**Total fat** 11.6 g.
**Saturated fat** 3.1 g.
**Polyunsaturated fat** 1.39 g.
**Carbohydrate** None.
**Sugars** None.
**Fibre** None.

**Minerals**
**Calcium** 15.6 mg.
**Iron** 3.24 mg.
**Zinc** 3.12 mg.
**Copper** 0.37 mg.
**Sodium** 115 mg.
**Potassium** 324 mg.
**Magnesium** 24 mg.
**Phosphorus** 240 mg.

**Vitamins**
**Vitamin A** None.
**Vitamin C** None.
**Vitamin D** None.
**Vitamin E** 0.02 mg.
**Vitamin B1** 0.31 mg.
**Vitamin B2** 0.56 mg.
**Niacin** 12.6 mg.
**Vitamin B6** 0.3 mg.
**Vitamin B12** 3.6 µg.
**Folic acid** 12 µg.
**Pantothenic acid** 1.8 mg.
**Biotin** 4.8 µg.

Duck makes a change from chicken but remember it contains more fat, especially in the skin.

# Duck's egg

**Portion** One egg boiled.

**Weight** 70 g., about 2½ oz.

**Food Facts**
Energy 131 kcal.
Protein 9.2 g.
Total fat 9.9 g.
Saturated fat Not known.
Polyunsaturated fat Not known.
Carbohydrate 0.49 g.
Sugars None.
Fibre None.

**Minerals**
Calcium 44 mg.
Iron 2.5 mg.
Zinc 0.56 mg.
Copper Not known.
Sodium 133 mg.
Potassium 180 mg.
Magnesium Not known.
Phosphorus Not known.

**Vitamins**
Vitamin A 280 μg.
Vitamin C None.
Vitamin D Not known.
Vitamin E Not known.
Vitamin B1 0.11 mg.
Vitamin B2 0.28 mg.
Niacin 2.24 mg.
Vitamin B6 Not known.
Vitamin B12 3.15 μg.
Folic acid 11.9 μg.
Pantothenic acid Not known.
Biotin Not known.

**Duck's eggs are higher in calories than a hen's egg and contain more vitamin A. Otherwise they are very similar.**

# Edam cheese

**Portion** One matchbox sized cube.

**Weight** 30 g., about 1 oz.

**Food Facts**
Energy 91 kcal.
Protein 7.3 g.
Total fat 6.9 g.
Saturated fat 4.1 g.
Polyunsaturated fat 0.18 g.
Carbohydrate None.
Sugars None.
Fibre None.

**Minerals**
Calcium 222 mg.
Iron 0.06 mg.
Zinc 1.2 mg.
Copper 0.01 mg.
Sodium 294 mg.
Potassium 48 mg.
Magnesium 8.4 mg.
Phosphorus 156 mg.

**Vitamins**
Vitamin A 71 μg.
Vitamin C None.
Vitamin D 0.05 μg.
Vitamin E 0.24 mg.
Vitamin B1 0.01 mg.
Vitamin B2 0.12 mg.
Niacin 1.74 mg.
Vitamin B6 0.02 mg.
Vitamin B12 0.42 μg.
Folic acid 6 μg.
Pantothenic acid 0.1 mg.
Biotin 0.4 μg.

**This is another cheese that is lower in fat than cheddar. A similar cheese, Gouda, is not as low in fat or calories as Edam.**

# Eel

# Egg, boiled

**Portion** Two slices ½ in. thick, stewed.
**Weight** 40 g., about 1½ oz.

**Portion** One size two egg without shell.
**Weight** 65 g., about 2¼ oz.

**Food Facts**
**Energy** 80 kcal.
**Protein** 8.2 g.
**Total fat** 5.3 g.
**Saturated fat** Not known.
**Polyunsaturated fat** Not known.
**Carbohydrate** None.
**Sugars** None.
**Fibre** None.

**Food Facts**
**Energy** 95 kcal.
**Protein** 8 g.
**Total fat** 7.1 g.
**Saturated fat** 2.2 g.
**Polyunsaturated fat** 0.76 g.
**Carbohydrate** None.
**Sugars** None.
**Fibre** None.

**Minerals**
**Calcium** 8.4 mg.
**Iron** 0.36 mg.
**Zinc** 0.24 mg.
**Copper** 0.02 mg.
**Sodium** 33.6 mg.
**Potassium** 100 mg.
**Magnesium** 8 mg.
**Phosphorus** 92 mg.

**Minerals**
**Calcium** 33.8 mg.
**Iron** 1.3 mg.
**Zinc** 0.97 mg.
**Copper** 0.06 mg.
**Sodium** 91 mg.
**Potassium** 91 mg.
**Magnesium** 7.8 mg.
**Phosphorus** 143 mg.

**Vitamins**
**Vitamin A** 760 µg.
**Vitamin C** None.
**Vitamin D** Not known.
**Vitamin E** Not known.
**Vitamin B1** 0.05 mg.
**Vitamin B2** 0.16 mg.
**Niacin** 2.68 mg.
**Vitamin B6** 0.1 mg.
**Vitamin B12** 0.4 µg.
**Folic acid** Not known.
**Pantothenic acid** 0.1 mg.
**Biotin** Not known.

**Vitamins**
**Vitamin A** 91 µg.
**Vitamin C** None.
**Vitamin D** 1.14 µg.
**Vitamin E** 1.04 mg.
**Vitamin B1** 0.05 mg.
**Vitamin B2** 0.29 mg.
**Niacin** 2.39 mg.
**Vitamin B6** 0.06 mg.
**Vitamin B12** 1.1 µg.
**Folic acid** 14.3 µg.
**Pantothenic acid** 1 mg.
**Biotin** 16.3 µg.

Eel is quite high in calories. A large conger eel steak could contain 400 calories or more.

Although eggs contain cholesterol, having one a day will not be harmful unless you have been put on a special low cholesterol diet.

# Egg, fried

# Egg omelette

**Portion** One size two egg fried in corn oil.
**Weight** 55 g., about 2 oz.

**Portion** Two size two eggs with added salt and fat.
**Weight** 130 g., about 4½ oz.

## Food Facts
**Energy** 127 kcal.
**Protein** 7.8 g.
**Total fat** 10.7 g.
**Saturated fat** 2.8 g.
**Polyunsaturated fat** 2.5 g.
**Carbohydrate** None.
**Sugars** None.
**Fibre** None.

## Food Facts
**Energy** 247 kcal.
**Protein** 15.2 g.
**Total fat** 21.2 g.
**Saturated fat** 6.6 g.
**Polyunsaturated fat** 1.4 g.
**Carbohydrate** None.
**Sugars** None.
**Fibre** None.

## Minerals
**Calcium** 35.2 mg.
**Iron** 1.37 mg.
**Zinc** 0.99 mg.
**Copper** 0.07 mg.
**Sodium** 121 mg.
**Potassium** 99 mg.
**Magnesium** 7.7 mg.
**Phosphorus** 143 mg.

## Minerals
**Calcium** 61.1 mg.
**Iron** 2.21 mg.
**Zinc** 1.69 mg.
**Copper** 0.11 mg.
**Sodium** 1,339 mg.
**Potassium** 156 mg.
**Magnesium** 23.4 mg.
**Phosphorus** 247 mg.

## Vitamins
**Vitamin A** 77 µg.
**Vitamin C** None.
**Vitamin D** 0.96 µg.
**Vitamin E** 0.88 mg.
**Vitamin B1** 0.04 mg.
**Vitamin B2** 0.23 mg.
**Niacin** 2.32 mg.
**Vitamin B6** 0.05 mg.
**Vitamin B12** 0.93 µg.
**Folic acid** 9.3 µg.
**Pantothenic acid** 0.8 mg.
**Biotin** 13.8 µg.

## Vitamins
**Vitamin A** 255 µg.
**Vitamin C** None.
**Vitamin D** 2 µg.
**Vitamin E** 1.95 mg.
**Vitamin B1** 0.09 mg.
**Vitamin B2** 0.41 mg.
**Niacin** 4.12 mg.
**Vitamin B6** 0.1 mg.
**Vitamin B12** 1.95 µg.
**Folic acid** 19.5 µg.
**Pantothenic acid** 1.6 mg.
**Biotin** 28.6 µg.

If you like fried eggs, use a non stick pan with the lid on and hardly any oil. Alternatively try poaching.

If you want to keep the calorie and fat content of an omelette down, add tomatoes, mushrooms or onions instead of cheese or bacon.

# Feta cheese

**Portion** One matchbox sized cube.
**Weight** 30 g., about 1 oz.

**Food Facts**
**Energy** 73 kcal.
**Protein** 4.95 g.
**Total fat** 5.9 g.
**Saturated fat** Not known.
**Polyunsaturated fat** Not known.
**Carbohydrate** None.
**Sugars** None.
**Fibre** None.

**Minerals**
**Calcium** 115 mg.
**Iron** 0.06 mg.
**Zinc** 0.33 mg.
**Copper** 0.03 mg.
**Sodium** 378 mg.
**Potassium** 21 mg.
**Magnesium** 6 mg.
**Phosphorus** Not known.

**Vitamins**
**Vitamin A** 81 µg.
**Vitamin C** Not known.
**Vitamin D** None.
**Vitamin E** Not known.
**Vitamin B1** None.
**Vitamin B2** 0.03 mg.
**Niacin** 0.06 mg.
**Vitamin B6** Not known.
**Vitamin B12** 0.42 µg.
**Folic acid** 4.5 µg.
**Pantothenic acid** Not known.
**Biotin** Not known.

This is cheese made from goat's milk which weight for weight contains fewer calories than many other cheeses.

# Fish cakes

**Portion** 2 fried fish cakes.

**Weight** 100 g., about 3½ oz.

**Food Facts**
**Energy** 188 kcal.
**Protein** 9.1 g.
**Total fat** 10.5 g.
**Saturated fat** Not known.
**Polyunsaturated fat** Not known.
**Carbohydrate** 15.1 g.
**Sugars** None.
**Fibre** None.

**Minerals**
**Calcium** 70 mg.
**Iron** 1 mg.
**Zinc** 0.4 mg.
**Copper** 0.13 mg.
**Sodium** 500 mg.
**Potassium** 260 mg.
**Magnesium** 18 mg.
**Phosphorus** 110 mg.

**Vitamins**
**Vitamin A** None.
**Vitamin C** None.
**Vitamin D** None.
**Vitamin E** Not known.
**Vitamin B1** 0.06 mg.
**Vitamin B2** 0.06 mg.
**Niacin** 2.8 mg.
**Vitamin B6** Not known.
**Vitamin B12** Not known.
**Folic acid** Not known.
**Pantothenic acid** Not known.
**Biotin** Not known.

Try making your own fish cakes, using salmon or tuna for a change, and baking or grilling them.

# Fish fingers

**Portion** Four fried fish fingers.

**Weight** 90 g., about 3¼ oz.

**Food Facts**
**Energy** 209 kcal.
**Protein** 12.1 g.
**Total fat** 11.4 g.
**Saturated fat** Not known.
**Polyunsaturated fat** Not known.
**Carbohydrate** 15.5 g.
**Sugars** None.
**Fibre** None.

**Minerals**
**Calcium** 40 mg.
**Iron** 0.63 mg.
**Zinc** 0.36 mg.
**Copper** 0.07 mg.
**Sodium** 315 mg.
**Potassium** 234 mg.
**Magnesium** 17 mg.
**Phosphorus** 198 mg.

**Vitamins**
**Vitamin A** None.
**Vitamin C** None.
**Vitamin D** None.
**Vitamin E** Not known.
**Vitamin B1** 0.07 mg.
**Vitamin B2** 0.06 mg.
**Niacin** 3.51 mg.
**Vitamin B6** 0.19 mg.
**Vitamin B12** 1.8 µg.
**Folic acid** 14.4 µg.
**Pantothenic acid** Not known.
**Biotin** Not known.

Fish fingers taste just as good grilled rather than fried which reduces the calories significantly. Many fish fingers are now additive-free.

# Fish paste

**Portion** Half a small jar.

**Weight** 37 g., about 1¼ oz.

**Food Facts**
**Energy** 62 kcal.
**Protein** 5.7 g.
**Total fat** 3.8 g.
**Saturated fat** Not known.
**Polyunsaturated fat** Not known.
**Carbohydrate** 1.4 g.
**Sugars** None.
**Fibre** None.

**Minerals**
**Calcium** 103 mg.
**Iron** 3.3 mg.
**Zinc** 0.52 mg.
**Copper** 0.14 mg.
**Sodium** 222 mg.
**Potassium** 111 mg.
**Magnesium** 12.2 mg.
**Phosphorus** 114 mg.

**Vitamins**
**Vitamin A** None.
**Vitamin C** None.
**Vitamin D** Not known.
**Vitamin E** 0.31 mg.
**Vitamin B1** 0.01 mg.
**Vitamin B2** 0.07 mg.
**Niacin** 2.59 mg.
**Vitamin B6** Not known.
**Vitamin B12** Not known.
**Folic acid** Not known.
**Pantothenic acid** Not known.
**Biotin** Not known.

If you are on a calorie controlled diet, a quarter of a jar of fish paste spread on two dry crispbread will make a tasty low calorie snack.

# Gammon rasher

**Portion** One steak, grilled, (raw weight 7½ oz.).
**Weight** 150 g., about 5⅓ oz.

## Food Facts
**Energy** 342 kcal.
**Protein** 44.2 g.
**Total fat** 18.3 g.
**Saturated fat** 3.2 g.
**Polyunsaturated fat** 0.57 g.
**Carbohydrate** None.
**Sugars** None.
**Fibre** None.

## Minerals
**Calcium** 13.5 mg.
**Iron** 2.1 mg.
**Zinc** 4.8 mg.
**Copper** 0.25 mg.
**Sodium** 3,210 mg.
**Potassium** 720 mg.
**Magnesium** 46.5 mg.
**Phosphorus** 390 mg.

## Vitamins
**Vitamin A** None.
**Vitamin C** None.
**Vitamin D** None.
**Vitamin E** 0.1 mg.
**Vitamin B1** 1.32 mg.
**Vitamin B2** 0.36 mg.
**Niacin** 17.7 mg.
**Vitamin B6** 0.49 mg.
**Vitamin B12** None.
**Folic acid** 3 µg.
**Pantothenic acid** 0.9 mg.
**Biotin** 4.5 µg.

One gammon rasher contains the equivalent of 8¼ grams of salt which is over ¼ ounce.

# Goat's milk

**Portion** ½ pint of fresh goat's milk.
**Weight** 280 g., about 10 oz.

## Food Facts
**Energy** 198 kcal
**Protein** 9.2 g.
**Total fat** 12.6 g.
**Saturated fat** 8.26 g.
**Polyunsaturated fat** 0.39 g.
**Carbohydrate** 12.9 g.
**Sugars** 12.8 g.
**Fibre** None.

## Minerals
**Calcium** 364 mg.
**Iron** 0.11 mg.
**Zinc** 0.84 mg.
**Copper** 0.14 mg.
**Sodium** 112 mg.
**Potassium** 504 mg.
**Magnesium** 56 mg.
**Phosphorus** 308 mg.

## Vitamins
**Vitamin A** 112 µg.
**Vitamin C** 4.2 mg.
**Vitamin D** 0.17 µg.
**Vitamin E** Not known.
**Vitamin B1** 0.11 mg.
**Vitamin B2** 0.42 mg.
**Niacin** 2.72 mg.
**Vitamin B6** 0.11 mg.
**Vitamin B12** None.
**Folic acid** 2.8 µg.
**Pantothenic acid** 1 mg.
**Biotin** 5.6 µg.

You should never give a baby or young child goat's milk unless advised to do so by a doctor or dietician.

# Goose

**Portion** Two slices.

**Weight** 120 g., about 4¼ oz.

**Food Facts**
**Energy** 382 kcal.
**Protein** 35.2 g.
**Total fat** 26.9 g.
**Saturated fat** Not known.
**Polyunsaturated fat** Not known.
**Carbohydrate** None.
**Sugars** None.
**Fibre** None.

**Minerals**
**Calcium** 12 mg.
**Iron** 5.52 mg.
**Zinc** Not known.
**Copper** 0.59 mg.
**Sodium** 180 mg.
**Potassium** 492 mg.
**Magnesium** 37.2 mg.
**Phosphorus** 324 mg.

**Vitamins**
**Vitamin A** None.
**Vitamin C** Not known.
**Vitamin D** None.
**Vitamin E** Not known.
**Vitamin B1** Not known.
**Vitamin B2** Not known.
**Niacin** 6.6 mg.
**Vitamin B6** 0.52 mg.
**Vitamin B12** Not known.
**Folic acid** Not known.
**Pantothenic acid** Not known.
**Biotin** Not known.

**Some people have goose as an alternative to turkey at Christmas. However, goose is very high in fat so not a very healthy substitute.**

# Ham

**Portion** Two thin slices.

**Weight** 50 g., about 2 oz.

**Food Facts**
**Energy** 60 kcal.
**Protein** 9.2 g.
**Total fat** 2.5 g.
**Saturated fat** 0.9 g.
**Polyunsaturated fat** 0.24 g.
**Carbohydrate** None.
**Sugars** None.
**Fibre** None.

**Minerals**
**Calcium** 4.5 mg.
**Iron** 0.6 mg.
**Zinc** 1.15 mg.
**Copper** 0.11 mg.
**Sodium** 625 mg.
**Potassium** 140 mg.
**Magnesium** 9 mg.
**Phosphorus** 140 mg.

**Vitamins**
**Vitamin A** None.
**Vitamin C** None.
**Vitamin D** None.
**Vitamin E** 0.04 mg.
**Vitamin B1** 0.26 mg.
**Vitamin B2** 0.12 mg.
**Niacin** 3.45 mg.
**Vitamin B6** 0.11 mg.
**Vitamin B12** None.
**Folic acid** None.
**Pantothenic acid** 0.3 mg.
**Biotin** 0.5 µg.

**Ham is low in calories and fat and although it has a high sodium content, makes an excellent sandwich-filling.**

# Heart

# Herring, grilled

**Portion** One lamb's heart, roast or stewed.
**Weight** 80 g., about 2¾ oz.

**Portion** One filleted herring.
**Weight** 119 g., about 4¼ oz.

**Food Facts**
**Energy** 189 kcal.
**Protein** 20.9 g.
**Total fat** 11.8 g.
**Saturated fat** 4.5 g.
**Polyunsaturated fat** 1.12 g.
**Carbohydrate** None.
**Sugars** None.
**Fibre** None.

**Food Facts**
**Energy** 236 kcal.
**Protein** 24.3 g.
**Total fat** 15.5 g.
**Saturated fat** 3 g.
**Polyunsaturated fat** 2.7 g.
**Carbohydrate** None.
**Sugars** None.
**Fibre** None.

**Minerals**
**Calcium** 8 mg.
**Iron** 6.48 mg.
**Zinc** Not known.
**Copper** Not known.
**Sodium** 120 mg.
**Potassium** 296 mg.
**Magnesium** 28 mg.
**Phosphorus** 312 mg.

**Minerals**
**Calcium** 39 mg.
**Iron** 1.19 mg.
**Zinc** 0.59 mg.
**Copper** 0.13 mg.
**Sodium** 202 mg.
**Potassium** 440 mg.
**Magnesium** 38 mg.
**Phosphorus** 285 mg.

**Vitamins**
**Vitamin A** None.
**Vitamin C** 8.8 mg.
**Vitamin D** None.
**Vitamin E** 0.56 mg.
**Vitamin B1** 0.36 mg.
**Vitamin B2** 1.2 mg.
**Niacin** 11.7 mg.
**Vitamin B6** 0.3 mg.
**Vitamin B12** 11.2 µg.
**Folic acid** 3.2 µg.
**Pantothenic acid** 3 mg.
**Biotin** 6.4 µg.

**Vitamins**
**Vitamin A** 58.3 µg.
**Vitamin C** None.
**Vitamin D** 29.7 µg.
**Vitamin E** 0.36 mg.
**Vitamin B1** None.
**Vitamin B2** 0.21 mg.
**Niacin** 9.28 mg.
**Vitamin B6** 0.68 mg.
**Vitamin B12** 13.0 µg.
**Folic acid** 11.9 µg.
**Pantothenic acid** 1 mg.
**Biotin** 11.9 µg.

**Although heart can contain quite a lot of fat, it is a rich source of iron and some B vitamins.**

**Compared to other fatty fish, herring does not contain much polyunsaturated fat.**

# Herring, pickled

# Hot dog sausages

**Portion** One pickled roll-mop herring.

**Weight** 90 g., about 3¼ oz.

**Food Facts**
**Energy** 210 kcal.
**Protein** 15.1 g.
**Total fat** 16.6 g.
**Saturated fat** 3.3 g.
**Polyunsaturated fat** 2.9 g.
**Carbohydrate** None.
**Sugars** None.
**Fibre** None.

**Minerals**
**Calcium** 29.7 mg.
**Iron** 0.72 mg.
**Zinc** 0.45 mg.
**Copper** 0.11 mg.
**Sodium** 60.3 mg.
**Potassium** 306 mg.
**Magnesium** 26.1 mg.
**Phosphorus** 189 mg.

**Vitamins**
**Vitamin A** 40.5 µg.
**Vitamin C** None.
**Vitamin D** 20.25 µg.
**Vitamin E** 0.19 mg.
**Vitamin B1** None.
**Vitamin B2** 0.16 mg.
**Niacin** 6.48 mg.
**Vitamin B6** 0.4 mg.
**Vitamin B12** 5.4 µg.
**Folic acid** 4.5 µg.
**Pantothenic acid** 0.9 mg.
**Biotin** 9 µg.

Roll-mop herrings are a tasty alternative to salmon, pilchards or sardines. The above amounts are the same as for raw herring.

**Portion** Three frankfurters.

**Weight** 66 g., about 2¼ oz.

**Food Facts**
**Energy** 180 kcal.
**Protein** 6.3 g.
**Total fat** 16.5 g.
**Saturated fat** 6.5 g.
**Polyunsaturated fat** 1.2 g.
**Carbohydrate** 2 g.
**Sugars** None.
**Fibre** None.

**Minerals**
**Calcium** 22.4 mg.
**Iron** 0.99 mg.
**Zinc** 0.92 mg.
**Copper** 0.16 mg.
**Sodium** 646 mg.
**Potassium** 64 mg.
**Magnesium** 5.9 mg.
**Phosphorus** 85 mg.

**Vitamins**
**Vitamin A** None.
**Vitamin C** None.
**Vitamin D** None.
**Vitamin E** 0.16 mg.
**Vitamin B1** 0.05 mg.
**Vitamin B2** 0.08 mg.
**Niacin** 1.98 mg.
**Vitamin B6** 0.02 mg.
**Vitamin B12** 0.66 µg.
**Folic acid** 0.7 µg.
**Pantothenic acid** 0.3 mg.
**Biotin** 1.3 µg.

Compared to ordinary sausages, these do not provide very much protein but are surprisingly high in fat.

# Kidney

**Portion** One lamb's kidney fried in butter.
**Weight** 75 g., about 3 oz. (raw weight 112 g.)

**Food Facts**
**Energy** 115 kcal.
**Protein** 18.4 g.
**Total fat** 4.7 g.
**Saturated fat** 1.1 g.
**Polyunsaturated fat** 0.06 g.
**Carbohydrate** None.
**Sugars** None.
**Fibre** None.

**Minerals**
**Calcium** 9.7 mg.
**Iron** 8.9 mg.
**Zinc** 3 mg.
**Copper** 0.48 mg.
**Sodium** 202 mg.
**Potassium** 254 mg.
**Magnesium** 21.7 mg.
**Phosphorus** 269 mg.

**Vitamins**
**Vitamin A** 119 µg.
**Vitamin C** 7.2 mg.
**Vitamin D** None.
**Vitamin E** 0.3 mg.
**Vitamin B1** 0.42 mg.
**Vitamin B2** 1.72 mg.
**Niacin** 11.1 mg.
**Vitamin B6** 0.22 mg.
**Vitamin B12** 59 µg.
**Folic acid** 59.2 µg.
**Pantothenic acid** 3.8 mg.
**Biotin** 31.4 µg.

**Kidneys are rich in B vitamins and iron, and make a pleasant alternative to liver.**

# Kipper

**Portion** One grilled kipper fillet.
**Weight** 120 g., about 4¼ oz.

**Food Facts**
**Energy** 229 kcal.
**Protein** 28.5 g.
**Total fat** 12.8 g.
**Saturated fat** 2.5 g.
**Polyunsaturated fat** 2.2 g.
**Carbohydrate** None.
**Sugars** None.
**Fibre** None.

**Minerals**
**Calcium** 72 mg.
**Iron** 1.56 mg.
**Zinc** 0.56 mg.
**Copper** Not known.
**Sodium** 1,108 mg.
**Potassium** 582 mg.
**Magnesium** 53.6 mg.
**Phosphorus** 481 mg.

**Vitamins**
**Vitamin A** 51.8 µg.
**Vitamin C** None.
**Vitamin D** 28 µg.
**Vitamin E** 0.33 mg.
**Vitamin B1** None.
**Vitamin B2** 0.2 mg.
**Niacin** 9.8 mg.
**Vitamin B6** 0.64 mg.
**Vitamin B12** 12.3 µg.
**Folic acid** 11.2 µg.
**Pantothenic acid** 0.96 mg.
**Biotin** 11.2 µg.

**Kippers contain over six times more sodium than fresh herrings. Try poaching them in milk or water to lose some of this sodium.**

# Lamb chop

## Lamb leg, roasted

**Portion** Grilled lamb chop, lean meat only.
**Weight** 85 g., about 3 oz.

**Portion** Two slices including fat.
**Weight** 120 g., about 4¼ oz.

**Food Facts**
Energy 188 kcal.
Protein 23.6 g.
Total fat 10.5 g.
Saturated fat 5 g.
Polyunsaturated fat 0.49 g.
Carbohydrate None.
Sugars None.
Fibre None.

**Food Facts**
Energy 319 kcal.
Protein 31.3 g.
Total fat 21.5 g.
Saturated fat 10.4 g.
Polyunsaturated fat 1.0 g.
Carbohydrate None.
Sugars None.
Fibre None.

**Minerals**
Calcium 7.6 mg.
Iron 1.78 mg.
Zinc 3.48 mg.
Copper 0.16 mg.
Sodium 63 mg.
Potassium 323 mg.
Magnesium 23 mg.
Phosphorus 204 mg.

**Minerals**
Calcium 9.6 mg.
Iron 3 mg.
Zinc 5.52 mg.
Copper 0.34 mg.
Sodium 78 mg.
Potassium 372 mg.
Magnesium 30 mg.
Phosphorus 240 mg.

**Vitamins**
Vitamin A None.
Vitamin C None.
Vitamin D None.
Vitamin E 0.08 mg.
Vitamin B1 0.13 mg.
Vitamin B2 0.25 mg.
Niacin 11.13 mg.
Vitamin B6 0.19 mg.
Vitamin B12 1.7 µg.
Folic acid 3.4 µg.
Pantothenic acid 0.6 mg.
Biotin 1.7 µg.

**Vitamins**
Vitamin A None.
Vitamin C None.
Vitamin D None.
Vitamin E 0.13 mg.
Vitamin B1 0.14 mg.
Vitamin B2 0.37 mg.
Niacin 13.2 mg.
Vitamin B6 0.22 mg.
Vitamin B12 2.4 µg.
Folic acid 3.6 µg.
Pantothenic acid 0.7 mg.
Biotin 1.2 µg.

**Although lamb chops look small, they have a surprising amount of meat on them.**

**Cut all the visible fat from lamb and pot roast it instead of roasting it in the normal way.**

# Lamb shoulder, roasted

**Portion** Two slices including fat.
**Weight** 120 g., about 4¼ oz.

**Food Facts**
**Energy** 379 kcal.
**Protein** 23 g.
**Total fat** 31 g.
**Saturated fat** 15.3 g.
**Polyunsaturated fat** 1.46 g.
**Carbohydrate** None.
**Sugars** None.
**Fibre** None.

**Minerals**
**Calcium** 10.8 mg.
**Iron** 1.92 mg.
**Zinc** 5.16 mg.
**Copper** 0.18 mg.
**Sodium** 73 mg.
**Potassium** 312 mg.
**Magnesium** 22 mg.
**Phosphorus** 180 mg.

**Vitamins**
**Vitamin A** None.
**Vitamin C** None.
**Vitamin D** None.
**Vitamin E** 0.14 mg.
**Vitamin B1** 0.08 mg.
**Vitamin B2** 0.24 mg.
**Niacin** 8.76 mg.
**Vitamin B6** 0.19 mg.
**Vitamin B12** 2.4 µg.
**Folic acid** 3.6 µg.
**Pantothenic acid** 0.6 mg.
**Biotin** 1.2 µg.

Not only is lamb quite high in fat, but also half of that fat is saturated fat.

# Lard

**Portion** One tablespoon.
**Weight** 25 g., about 1 oz.

**Food Facts**
**Energy** 222 kcal.
**Protein** None.
**Total fat** 24.7 g.
**Saturated fat** 10.4 g.
**Polyunsaturated fat** 2.24 g.
**Carbohydrate** None.
**Sugars** None.
**Fibre** None.

**Minerals**
**Calcium** 0.2 mg.
**Iron** 0.02 mg.
**Zinc** None.
**Copper** None.
**Sodium** 0.5 mg.
**Potassium** 0.2 mg.
**Magnesium** 0.2 mg.
**Phosphorus** 0.7 mg.

**Vitamins**
**Vitamin A** None.
**Vitamin C** None.
**Vitamin D** None.
**Vitamin E** None.
**Vitamin B1** None.
**Vitamin B2** None.
**Niacin** None.
**Vitamin B6** None.
**Vitamin B12** None.
**Folic acid** None.
**Pantothenic acid** None.
**Biotin** None.

Not only do you often have to use more lard than oil, but it is also very high in saturated fat.

# Lasagne

**Portion** Half a plateful.

**Weight** 300 g., about 10½ oz.

**Food Facts**
Energy 453 kcal.
Protein 20.4 g.
Total fat 25.8 g.
Saturated fat Not known.
Polyunsaturated fat Not known.
Carbohydrate 37.5 g.
Sugars 5.1 g.
Fibre 1.2 g.

**Minerals**
Calcium 294 mg.
Iron 2.4 mg.
Zinc 3.3 mg.
Copper 0.24 mg.
Sodium 891 mg.
Potassium 510 mg.
Magnesium 48 mg.
Phosphorus 309 mg.

**Vitamins**
Vitamin A 472 µg.
Vitamin C None.
Vitamin D 0.57 µg.
Vitamin E 1.8 mg.
Vitamin B1 0.12 mg.
Vitamin B2 0.36 mg.
Niacin 6.6 mg.
Vitamin B6 0.21 mg.
Vitamin B12 None.
Folic acid 18 µg.
Pantothenic acid 0.6 mg.
Biotin 3 µg.

Instead of using meat, make
lasagne with lentils or spinach.
Make the sauce with skimmed milk
to reduce the fat content.

# Liver, lamb's, fried

**Portion** Three thin fried slices.
(raw weight 130 g.)
**Weight** 105 g., about 3¾ oz.

**Food Facts**
Energy 243 kcal.
Protein 24 g.
Total fat 14.7 g.
Saturated fat 3.3 g.
Polyunsaturated fat 1.5 g.
Carbohydrate 4 g.
Sugars None.
Fibre None.

**Minerals**
Calcium 12.6 mg.
Iron 10.5 mg.
Zinc 46 mg.
Copper 10.3 mg.
Sodium 199 mg.
Potassium 315 mg.
Magnesium 23.1 mg.
Phosphorus 420 mg.

**Vitamins**
Vitamin A 21,640 µg.
Vitamin C 12.6 mg.
Vitamin D 0.52 µg.
Vitamin E 0.33 mg.
Vitamin B1 0.27 mg.
Vitamin B2 4.62 mg.
Niacin 15.9 mg.
Vitamin B6 0.51 mg.
Vitamin B12 85 µg.
Folic acid 252 µg.
Pantothenic acid 7.9 mg.
Biotin 43 µg.

Liver is very rich in most vitamins
and minerals and quite low in fat
unless it is fried. Grill or braise
instead.

# Liver, pig's, braised

**Portion** Three thin braised slices (raw weight 130 g.)
**Weight** 105 g., about 3¾ oz.

## Food Facts
**Energy** 198 kcal.
**Protein** 26.8 g.
**Total fat** 8.4 g.
**Saturated fat** 2.5 g.
**Polyunsaturated fat** 2.2 g.
**Carbohydrate** 3.7 g.
**Sugars** None.
**Fibre** None.

## Minerals
**Calcium** 11.5 mg.
**Iron** 17.8 mg.
**Zinc** 8.6 mg.
**Copper** 2.6 mg.
**Sodium** 136 mg.
**Potassium** 262 mg.
**Magnesium** 23.1 mg.
**Phosphorus** 409 mg.

## Vitamins
**Vitamin A** 12,180 µg.
**Vitamin C** 9.4 mg.
**Vitamin D** 1.19 µg.
**Vitamin E** 0.16 mg.
**Vitamin B1** 0.21 mg.
**Vitamin B2** 3.25 mg.
**Niacin** 17.8 mg.
**Vitamin B6** 0.67 mg.
**Vitamin B12** 27.3 µg.
**Folic acid** 115 µg.
**Pantothenic acid** 4.8 mg.
**Biotin** 35.7 µg.

Instead of frying liver, try it braised or in a casserole. Pig's liver can also be stir-fried and used in Chinese dishes.

# Lobster

**Portion** Two tablespoons.

**Weight** 85 g., about 3 oz.

## Food Facts
**Energy** 101 kcal.
**Protein** 18.7 g.
**Total fat** 2.85 g.
**Saturated fat** 0.34 g.
**Polyunsaturated fat** 1.06 g.
**Carbohydrate** None.
**Sugars** None.
**Fibre** None.

## Minerals
**Calcium** 52.7 mg.
**Iron** 0.68 mg.
**Zinc** 1.5 mg.
**Copper** 1.4 mg.
**Sodium** 280 mg.
**Potassium** 221 mg.
**Magnesium** 28 mg.
**Phosphorus** 238 mg.

## Vitamins
**Vitamin A** None.
**Vitamin C** None.
**Vitamin D** None.
**Vitamin E** 1.27 mg.
**Vitamin B1** 0.06 mg.
**Vitamin B2** 0.04 mg.
**Niacin** 4.76 mg.
**Vitamin B6** Not known.
**Vitamin B12** 0.85 µg.
**Folic acid** 14.4 µg.
**Pantothenic acid** 1.38 mg.
**Biotin** 4.2 µg.

Lobster is something most of us cannot afford to eat. If you get the chance, it is well worth trying it.

# Low fat spread

**Portion** Enough to spread on a slice of bread.
**Weight** 7 g., about ¼ oz.

**Food Facts**
**Energy** 25 kcal.
**Protein** None.
**Total fat** 2.8 g.
**Saturated fat** 0.76 g.
**Polyunsaturated fat** 0.84 g.
**Carbohydrate** None.
**Sugars** None.
**Fibre** None.

**Minerals**
**Calcium** None.
**Iron** None.
**Zinc** None.
**Copper** None.
**Sodium** 48 mg.
**Potassium** None.
**Magnesium** None.
**Phosphorus** None.

**Vitamins**
**Vitamin A** 63 µg.
**Vitamin C** None.
**Vitamin D** 0.56 µg.
**Vitamin E** 0.28 mg.
**Vitamin B1** None.
**Vitamin B2** None.
**Niacin** None.
**Vitamin B6** None.
**Vitamin B12** None.
**Folic acid** None.
**Pantothenic acid** None.
**Biotin** None.

Low fat spreads contain half the calories of butter and all margarines. They are useful if you are unable to spread margarine thinly.

# Luncheon meat

**Portion** Three slices.

**Weight** 56 g., about 2 oz.

**Food Facts**
**Energy** 175 kcal.
**Protein** 7.1 g.
**Total fat** 15.1 g.
**Saturated fat** 5.6 g.
**Polyunsaturated fat** 1.2 g.
**Carbohydrate** 3.1 g.
**Sugars** None.
**Fibre** None.

**Minerals**
**Calcium** 8.4 mg.
**Iron** 0.62 mg.
**Zinc** 1.23 mg.
**Copper** 0.18 mg.
**Sodium** 588 mg.
**Potassium** 78.4 mg.
**Magnesium** 4.5 mg.
**Phosphorus** 112 mg.

**Vitamins**
**Vitamin A** None.
**Vitamin C** None.
**Vitamin D** None.
**Vitamin E** 0.06 mg.
**Vitamin B1** 0.04 mg.
**Vitamin B2** 0.07 mg.
**Niacin** 2.52 mg.
**Vitamin B6** 0.01 mg.
**Vitamin B12** 0.56 µg.
**Folic acid** 0.6 µg.
**Pantothenic acid** 0.3 mg.
**Biotin** None.

Luncheon meat is high in fat and does not provide much iron or vitamins. It is not suitable for a main meal.

# Macaroni cheese

**Portion** One ladleful.

**Weight** 215 g., about 7½ oz.

**Food Facts**
Energy 374 kcal.
Protein 15.9 g.
Total fat 20.9 g.
Saturated fat 10.7 g.
Polyunsaturated fat 1.59 g.
Carbohydrate 32.5 g.
Sugars None.
Fibre None.

**Minerals**
Calcium 387 mg.
Iron 0.86 mg.
Zinc 1.93 mg.
Copper 0.06 mg.
Sodium 602 mg.
Potassium 258 mg.
Magnesium 38.7 mg.
Phosphorus 301 mg.

**Vitamins**
Vitamin A 207 µg.
Vitamin C None.
Vitamin D 0.71 µg.
Vitamin E 0.64 mg.
Vitamin B1 0.06 mg.
Vitamin B2 0.3 mg.
Niacin 3.93 mg.
Vitamin B6 0.06 mg.
Vitamin B12 0.64 µg.
Folic acid 6.4 µg.
Pantothenic acid 0.4 mg.
Biotin 2.1 µg.

If making this dish at home, you can reduce the fat content by using skimmed milk and a small amount of a very strong cheese.

# Mackerel

**Portion** One whole fried mackerel.

**Weight** 220 g., about 7¾ oz.

**Food Facts**
Energy 413 kcal.
Protein 47.3 g.
Total fat 24.9 g.
Saturated fat 8.69 g.
Polyunsaturated fat 8.95 g.
Carbohydrate None.
Sugars None.
Fibre None.

**Minerals**
Calcium 61.6 mg.
Iron 2.64 mg.
Zinc 1.1 mg.
Copper 0.44 mg.
Sodium 330 mg.
Potassium 924 mg.
Magnesium 77 mg.
Phosphorus 616 mg.

**Vitamins**
Vitamin A 114 µg.
Vitamin C None.
Vitamin D 46.4 µg.
Vitamin E Not known.
Vitamin B1 0.2 mg.
Vitamin B2 0.84 mg.
Niacin 27.94 mg.
Vitamin B6 1.85 mg.
Vitamin B12 26.4 µg.
Folic acid Not known.
Pantothenic acid 2.1 mg.
Biotin 17.6 µg.

Although mackerel is quite fatty, over a third of the fat is polyunsaturated. Grill or bake mackerel rather than frying.

# Margarine, hard and soft

**Portion** Enough to spread on one slice of bread.
**Weight** 7 g., about ¼ oz.

**Food Facts**
**Energy** 51 kcal.
**Protein** None.
**Total fat** 5.7 g.
**Saturated fat** 1.91 g.
**Polyunsaturated fat** 1 g.
**Carbohydrate** None.
**Sugars** None.
**Fibre** None.

**Minerals**
**Calcium** 0.3 mg.
**Iron** 0.02 mg.
**Zinc** Not known.
**Copper** None.
**Sodium** 56 mg.
**Potassium** 0.3 mg.
**Magnesium** 0.1 mg.
**Phosphorus** 0.8 mg.

**Vitamins**
**Vitamin A** 63 µg.
**Vitamin C** None.
**Vitamin D** 0.56 µg.
**Vitamin E** 0.56 mg.
**Vitamin B1** None.
**Vitamin B2** None.
**Niacin** None.
**Vitamin B6** None.
**Vitamin B12** None.
**Folic acid** None.
**Pantothenic acid** None.
**Biotin** None.

**There is no difference in the fat content of soft or hard margarine. They also contain similar amounts of polyunsaturated fat.**

# Margarine, polyunsaturated

**Portion** Enough to spread on a slice of bread.
**Weight** 7 g., about ¼ oz.

**Food Facts**
**Energy** 51 kcal.
**Protein** None.
**Total fat** 5.7 g.
**Saturated fat** 1.3 g.
**Polyunsaturated fat** 4.2 g.
**Carbohydrate** None.
**Sugars** None.
**Fibre** None.

**Minerals**
**Calcium** 0.3 mg.
**Iron** 0.02 mg.
**Zinc** Not known.
**Copper** None.
**Sodium** 56 mg.
**Potassium** 0.3 mg.
**Magnesium** 0.1 mg.
**Phosphorus** 0.8 mg.

**Vitamins**
**Vitamin A** 63 µg.
**Vitamin C** None.
**Vitamin D** 0.56 µg.
**Vitamin E** 0.56 µg.
**Vitamin B1** None.
**Vitamin B2** None.
**Niacin** None.
**Vitamin B6** None.
**Vitamin B12** None.
**Folic acid** None.
**Pantothenic acid** None.
**Biotin** None.

**Only margarine labelled 'high in polyunsaturated fat' contains more than other margarines. The calorie value is still as high as butter.**

# Meat pie

# Milk, condensed

**Portion** One individual meat pie.
**Weight** 154 g., about 5½ oz.

**Portion** One tablespoon.
**Weight** 25 g., about 1 oz.

**Food Facts**
**Energy** 603 kcal.
**Protein** 12 g.
**Total fat** 36.9 g.
**Saturated fat** Not known.
**Polyunsaturated fat** Not known.
**Carbohydrate** 59.4 g.
**Sugars** 1.2 g.
**Fibre** 2.4 g.

**Food Facts**
**Energy** 80 kcal.
**Protein** 2.1 g.
**Total fat** 2.2 g.
**Saturated fat** 1.3 g.
**Polyunsaturated fat** 0.06 g.
**Carbohydrate** 13.9 g.
**Sugars** 13.8 g.
**Fibre** None.

**Minerals**
**Calcium** 123 mg.
**Iron** 2.4 mg.
**Zinc** 1.38 mg.
**Copper** 0.18 mg.
**Sodium** 699 mg.
**Potassium** 203 mg.
**Magnesium** 24.6 mg.
**Phosphorus** 118 mg.

**Minerals**
**Calcium** 70 mg.
**Iron** 0.05 mg.
**Zinc** 0.25 mg.
**Copper** 0.01 mg.
**Sodium** 32.5 mg.
**Potassium** 97.5 mg.
**Magnesium** 6.7 mg.
**Phosphorus** 55 mg.

**Vitamins**
**Vitamin A** 300 µg.
**Vitamin C** None.
**Vitamin D** 1.4 µg.
**Vitamin E** 1.54 mg.
**Vitamin B1** 0.2 mg.
**Vitamin B2** 0.06 mg.
**Niacin** 4.62 mg.
**Vitamin B6** 0.15 mg.
**Vitamin B12** None.
**Folic acid** 10.7 µg.
**Pantothenic acid** 0.3 mg.
**Biotin** 1.54 µg.

**Vitamins**
**Vitamin A** 26.7 µg.
**Vitamin C** 0.5 mg.
**Vitamin D** 0.02 µg.
**Vitamin E** 0.1 mg.
**Vitamin B1** 0.02 mg.
**Vitamin B2** 0.12 mg.
**Niacin** 0.54 mg.
**Vitamin B6** None.
**Vitamin B12** 0.12 µg.
**Folic acid** 2 µg.
**Pantothenic acid** 0.2 mg.
**Biotin** 0.7 µg.

**As they are already high in fat and carbohydrate, it would be better to have vegetables with a meat pie, instead of chips.**

**Condensed milk has a lot of added sugar and you should try to avoid using it wherever possible.**

# Milk, evaporated

**Portion** One tablespoon.

**Weight** 20 g., about ⅔ oz.

**Food Facts**
**Energy** 31 kcal.
**Protein** 1.7 g.
**Total fat** 1.8 g.
**Saturated fat** 1.07 g.
**Polyunsaturated fat** 0.05 g.
**Carbohydrate** 2.3 g.
**Sugars** 2.3 g.
**Fibre** None.

**Minerals**
**Calcium** 56 mg.
**Iron** 0.04 mg.
**Zinc** 0.22 mg.
**Copper** 0.01 mg.
**Sodium** 36 mg.
**Potassium** 78 mg.
**Magnesium** 5.6 mg.
**Phosphorus** 50 mg.

**Vitamins**
**Vitamin A** 18.4 µg.
**Vitamin C** 0.2 mg.
**Vitamin D** 0.02 µg.
**Vitamin E** 0.11 mg.
**Vitamin B1** 0.01 mg.
**Vitamin B2** 0.1 mg.
**Niacin** 0.46 mg.
**Vitamin B6** 0.01 mg.
**Vitamin B12** None.
**Folic acid** 1.4 µg.
**Pantothenic acid** 0.2 mg.
**Biotin** 0.6 µg.

Evaporated milk is lower in calories and fat than single cream. It is better to use fresh milk where possible.

# Milk, fresh whole

**Portion** ½ pint of fresh silver top.

**Weight** 280 g., about 10 oz.

**Food Facts**
**Energy** 182 kcal.
**Protein** 9.2 g.
**Total fat** 10.6 g.
**Saturated fat** 6.3 g.
**Polyunsaturated fat** 0.28 g.
**Carbohydrate** 13.2 g.
**Sugars** 13.2 g.
**Fibre** None.

**Minerals**
**Calcium** 336 mg.
**Iron** 0.14 mg.
**Zinc** 0.98 mg.
**Copper** 0.06 mg.
**Sodium** 140 mg.
**Potassium** 420 mg.
**Magnesium** 33 mg.
**Phosphorus** 266 mg.

**Vitamins**
**Vitamin A** 78.4 µg.
**Vitamin C** 4.2 mg.
**Vitamin D** 0.04 µg.
**Vitamin E** 0.2 mg.
**Vitamin B1** 0.11 mg.
**Vitamin B2** 0.53 mg.
**Niacin** 2.41 mg.
**Vitamin B6** 0.11 mg.
**Vitamin B12** 0.84 µg.
**Folic acid** 14 µg.
**Pantothenic acid** 1 mg.
**Biotin** 5.6 µg.

Reduce the calories by pouring off the cream from the top. Sterilised, UHT and homogenised milk have the same calories as fresh milk.

# Milk, semi-skimmed

**Portion** ½ pint fresh milk (red and silver striped top).
**Weight** 280 g., about 10 oz.

**Food Facts**
Energy 126 kcal.
Protein 9.5 g.
Total fat 4.48 g.
Saturated fat 2.64 g.
Polyunsaturated fat 0.01 g.
Carbohydrate 13.2 g.
Sugars 13.2 g.
Fibre None.

**Minerals**
Calcium 350 mg.
Iron 0.14 mg.
Zinc 1.02 mg.
Copper 0.05 mg.
Sodium 145 mg.
Potassium 441 mg.
Magnesium 35.2 mg.
Phosphorus 279 mg.

**Vitamins**
Vitamin A 47.6 µg.
Vitamin C 4.2 mg.
Vitamin D 0.02 µg.
Vitamin E 0.1 mg.
Vitamin B1 0.11 mg.
Vitamin B2 0.53 mg.
Niacin 2.41 mg.
Vitamin B6 0.11 mg.
Vitamin B12 0.84 µg.
Folic acid 14 µg.
Pantothenic acid 1 mg.
Biotin 5.6 µg.

**Semi-skimmed milk is often the most acceptable and suitable milk for all the family, except children under five.**

# Milk, skimmed

**Portion** ½ pint fresh skimmed milk (blue top).
**Weight** 280 g., about 10 oz.

**Food Facts**
Energy 92 kcal.
Protein 9.5 g.
Total fat 0.3 g.
Saturated fat 0.11 g.
Polyunsaturated fat None.
Carbohydrate 14 g.
Sugars 14 g.
Fibre None.

**Minerals**
Calcium 364 mg.
Iron 0.14 mg.
Zinc 1.01 mg.
Copper 0.06 mg.
Sodium 145 mg.
Potassium 420 mg.
Magnesium 33 mg.
Phosphorus 280 mg.

**Vitamins**
Vitamin A None.
Vitamin C 4.48 mg.
Vitamin D None.
Vitamin E None.
Vitamin B1 0.11 mg.
Vitamin B2 0.56 mg.
Niacin 2.46 mg.
Vitamin B6 0.11 mg.
Vitamin B12 0.84 µg.
Folic acid 14 µg.
Pantothenic acid 1 mg.
Biotin 5.6 µg.

**Skimmed milk is ideal for slimmers but not suitable for children. It takes time to get used to, so persevere.**

# Milk, skimmed, powder

**Portion** Three tablespoons to make ½ pint with water.
**Weight** 28 g., about 1 oz.

**Food Facts**
Energy 99 kcal.
Protein 10.2 g.
Total fat 0.4 g.
Saturated fat 0.2 g.
Polyunsaturated fat 0.01 g.
Carbohydrate 14.8 g.
Sugars 14.7 g.
Fibre None.

**Minerals**
Calcium 333 mg.
Iron 0.11 mg.
Zinc 1.15 mg.
Copper 0.06 mg.
Sodium 154 mg.
Potassium 462 mg.
Magnesium 32.6 mg.
Phosphorus 266 mg.

**Vitamins**
Vitamin A None.
Vitamin C 1.6 mg.
Vitamin D None.
Vitamin E None.
Vitamin B1 0.12 mg.
Vitamin B2 0.45 mg.
Niacin 2.73 mg.
Vitamin B6 0.07 mg.
Vitamin B12 0.84 µg.
Folic acid 5.9 µg.
Pantothenic acid 1 mg.
Biotin 4.5 µg.

**Many milk powders have added vegetable fat, which makes them as high in calories as fresh milk.**

# Mussels

**Portion** Five mussels.

**Weight** 40 g., about 1½ oz.

**Food Facts**
Energy 34 kcal.
Protein 6.9 g.
Total fat 0.8 g.
Saturated fat 0.14 g.
Polyunsaturated fat 0.22 g.
Carbohydrate None.
Sugars None.
Fibre None.

**Minerals**
Calcium 80 mg.
Iron 3.08 mg.
Zinc 0.84 mg.
Copper 0.19 mg.
Sodium 84 mg.
Potassium 36.8 mg.
Magnesium 10 mg.
Phosphorus 132 mg.

**Vitamins**
Vitamin A None.
Vitamin C None.
Vitamin D None.
Vitamin E 0.48 mg.
Vitamin B1 Not known.
Vitamin B2 Not known.
Niacin 1.48 mg.
Vitamin B6 Not known.
Vitamin B12 Not known.
Folic acid Not known.
Pantothenic acid Not known.
Biotin Not known.

**Fresh mussels can be bought in the winter and take very little time to prepare and cook. Add them to rice and pasta dishes.**

# Olive oil

**Portion** One tablespoon.

**Weight** 5 g., about ⅕ oz.

**Food Facts**
**Energy** 44 kcal.
**Protein** None.
**Total fat** 5 g.
**Saturated fat** 0.7 g.
**Polyunsaturated fat** 0.55 g.
**Carbohydrate** None.
**Sugars** None.
**Fibre** None.

**Minerals**
**Calcium** None.
**Iron** None.
**Zinc** None.
**Copper** None.
**Sodium** None.
**Potassium** None.
**Magnesium** None.
**Phosphorus** None.

**Vitamins**
**Vitamin A** None.
**Vitamin C** None.
**Vitamin D** None.
**Vitamin E** 0.25 mg.
**Vitamin B1** None.
**Vitamin B2** None.
**Niacin** None.
**Vitamin B6** None.
**Vitamin B12** None.
**Folic acid** None.
**Pantothenic acid** None.
**Biotin** None.

All oils contain the same amount of calories. Mono-unsaturated fat is included in the total fat figure.

# Oysters

**Portion** Four oysters.

**Weight** 40 g., about 1½ oz.

**Food Facts**
**Energy** 20 kcal.
**Protein** 4.3 g.
**Total fat** 0.4 g.
**Saturated fat** 0.08 g.
**Polyunsaturated fat** 0.11 g.
**Carbohydrate** None.
**Sugars** None.
**Fibre** None.

**Minerals**
**Calcium** 76 mg.
**Iron** 2.4 mg.
**Zinc** 18 mg.
**Copper** 3.04 mg.
**Sodium** 204 mg.
**Potassium** 104 mg.
**Magnesium** 16.8 mg.
**Phosphorus** 108 mg.

**Vitamins**
**Vitamin A** 30 µg.
**Vitamin C** None.
**Vitamin D** None.
**Vitamin E** 0.34 mg.
**Vitamin B1** 0.04 mg.
**Vitamin B2** 0.08 mg.
**Niacin** 1.52 mg..
**Vitamin B6** 0.01 mg.
**Vitamin B12** 6 µg.
**Folic acid** Not known.
**Pantothenic acid** 0.2 mg.
**Biotin** 4 µg.

Oysters used to be a very common snack food sold by street vendors in Dickens' time.

# Parmesan cheese     Pâté

**Portion** One tablespoon of grated cheese.
**Weight** 5 g., about ⅕ oz.

**Portion** Two 1 in. squares to spread on two cream crackers.
**Weight** 20 g., about ⅔ oz.

**Food Facts**
**Energy** 20 kcal.
**Protein** 1.8 g.
**Total fat** 1.5 g.
**Saturated fat** 0.8 g.
**Polyunsaturated fat** 0.04 g.
**Carbohydrate** None.
**Sugars** None.
**Fibre** None.

**Food Facts**
**Energy** 69 kcal.
**Protein** 2.7 g.
**Total fat** 6.3 g.
**Saturated fat** Not known.
**Polyunsaturated fat** Not known.
**Carbohydrate** 0.3 g.
**Sugars** 0.14 g.
**Fibre** None.

**Minerals**
**Calcium** 61 mg.
**Iron** 0.02 mg.
**Zinc** 0.2 mg.
**Copper** Not known.
**Sodium** 38 mg.
**Potassium** 7.5 mg.
**Magnesium** 2.5 mg.
**Phosphorus** 38.5 mg.

**Minerals**
**Calcium** 2.8 mg.
**Iron** 1.6 mg.
**Zinc** 0.6 mg.
**Copper** 0.1 mg.
**Sodium** 152 mg.
**Potassium** 30 mg.
**Magnesium** 2.4 mg.
**Phosphorus** 92 mg.

**Vitamins**
**Vitamin A** 17.9 µg.
**Vitamin C** None.
**Vitamin D** 0.01 µg.
**Vitamin E** 0.04 mg.
**Vitamin B1** None.
**Vitamin B2** 0.02 mg.
**Niacin** 0.43 mg.
**Vitamin B6** None.
**Vitamin B12** 0.07 µg.
**Folic acid** 1 µg.
**Pantothenic acid** None.
**Biotin** 0.1 µg.

**Vitamins**
**Vitamin A** 1,318 µg.
**Vitamin C** None.
**Vitamin D** 0.12 µg.
**Vitamin E** 0.06 mg.
**Vitamin B1** 0.02 mg.
**Vitamin B2** 0.26 mg.
**Niacin** 0.82 mg.
**Vitamin B6** 0.06 mg.
**Vitamin B12** 1.66 µg.
**Folic acid** 32 µg.
**Pantothenic acid** 0.5 mg.
**Biotin** 2.6 µg.

**Although Parmesan has quite a high fat content, the amount you would normally add to foods is so small, it will not greatly increase the calories.**

**Pâté is usually very high in fat and not a very suitable sandwich filling.**

# Pilchards

**Portion** Two pilchards canned in tomato sauce.
**Weight** 180 g., about 6½ oz.

**Food Facts**
**Energy** 226 kcal.
**Protein** 33.8 g.
**Total fat** 9.7 g.
**Saturated fat** 3 g.
**Polyunsaturated fat** 3.3 g.
**Carbohydrate** 1.3 g.
**Sugars** None.
**Fibre** None.

**Minerals**
**Calcium** 540 mg.
**Iron** 4.86 mg.
**Zinc** 2.88 mg.
**Copper** 0.34 mg.
**Sodium** 666 mg.
**Potassium** 756 mg.
**Magnesium** 70.2 mg.
**Phosphorus** 630 mg.

**Vitamins**
**Vitamin A** None.
**Vitamin C** None.
**Vitamin D** 14.4 µg.
**Vitamin E** 1.26 mg.
**Vitamin B1** 0.04 mg.
**Vitamin B2** 0.52 mg.
**Niacin** 19.98 mg.
**Vitamin B6** Not known.
**Vitamin B12** 21.6 µg.
**Folic acid** Not known.
**Pantothenic acid** Not known.
**Biotin** Not known.

**One pilchard on toast makes a substantial lunch time snack that is quite low in calories.**

# Plaice in breadcrumbs

**Portion** One fillet fried in corn oil.
**Weight** 180 g., about 6½ oz.

**Food Facts**
**Energy** 410 kcal.
**Protein** 32.4 g.
**Total fat** 24.7 g.
**Saturated fat** 3.5 g.
**Polyunsaturated fat** 10.5 g.
**Carbohydrate** 15.5 g.
**Sugars** None.
**Fibre** None.

**Minerals**
**Calcium** 120 mg.
**Iron** 1.4 mg.
**Zinc** 1.26 mg.
**Copper** 0.36 mg.
**Sodium** 396 mg.
**Potassium** 504 mg.
**Magnesium** 43 mg.
**Phosphorus** 324 mg.

**Vitamins**
**Vitamin A** None.
**Vitamin C** None.
**Vitamin D** None.
**Vitamin E** Not known.
**Vitamin B1** 0.41 mg.
**Vitamin B2** 0.32 mg.
**Niacin** 11.34 mg.
**Vitamin B6** 0.65 mg.
**Vitamin B12** 1.8 µg.
**Folic acid** 30.6 µg.
**Pantothenic acid** Not known.
**Biotin** Not known.

**Cooking plaice in this way greatly increases its fat and calorie value. If you buy fish already prepared in breadcrumbs, bake it instead.**

# Plaice, steamed

**Portion** One fillet.

**Weight** 136 g., about 4¾ oz.

## Food Facts
**Energy** 126 kcal.
**Protein** 25.7 g.
**Total fat** 2.6 g.
**Saturated fat** 0.4 g.
**Polyunsaturated fat** 0.61 g.
**Carbohydrate** None.
**Sugars** None.
**Fibre** None.

## Minerals
**Calcium** 51.7 mg.
**Iron** 0.8 mg.
**Zinc** 0.68 mg.
**Copper** 0.07 mg.
**Sodium** 163 mg.
**Potassium** 380 mg.
**Magnesium** 32 mg.
**Phosphorus** 340 mg.

## Vitamins
**Vitamin A** None.
**Vitamin C** None.
**Vitamin D** None.
**Vitamin E** Not known.
**Vitamin B1** 0.41 mg.
**Vitamin B2** 0.15 mg.
**Niacin** 9.11 mg.
**Vitamin B6** 0.64 mg.
**Vitamin B12** 2.72 µg.
**Folic acid** 15 µg.
**Pantothenic acid** 1 mg.
**Biotin** Not known.

The delicate flavour of plaice makes it ideally suited to this method of cooking. It needs no sauce, just a squeeze of lemon juice.

# Pork chop

**Portion** One grilled pork chop, lean meat only.

**Weight** 135 g., about 5 oz.

## Food Facts
**Energy** 305 kcal.
**Protein** 43.6 g.
**Total fat** 14.4 g.
**Saturated fat** 5.7 g.
**Polyunsaturated fat** 1.12 g.
**Carbohydrate** None.
**Sugars** None.
**Fibre** None.

## Minerals
**Calcium** 12.1 mg.
**Iron** 1.62 mg.
**Zinc** 4.72 mg.
**Copper** 0.22 mg.
**Sodium** 113 mg.
**Potassium** 567 mg.
**Magnesium** 39 mg.
**Phosphorus** 351 mg.

## Vitamins
**Vitamin A** None.
**Vitamin C** None.
**Vitamin D** None.
**Vitamin E** None.
**Vitamin B1** 1.19 mg.
**Vitamin B2** 0.35 mg.
**Niacin** 18.36 mg.
**Vitamin B6** 0.55 mg.
**Vitamin B12** 2.7 µg.
**Folic acid** 9.4 µg.
**Pantothenic acid** 1.8 mg.
**Biotin** 4 µg.

If you cut the fat off a pork chop and grill or braise it, the calorie value is acceptable for someone on a reducing diet.

# Pork leg, roasted

**Portion** Three slices including fat.
**Weight** 120 g., about 4¼ oz.

**Food Facts**
**Energy** 343 kcal.
**Protein** 32.3 g.
**Total fat** 23.8 g.
**Saturated fat** 9.4 g.
**Polyunsaturated fat** 1.8 g.
**Carbohydrate** None.
**Sugars** None.
**Fibre** None.

**Minerals**
**Calcium** 12 mg.
**Iron** 1.56 mg.
**Zinc** 3.48 mg.
**Copper** 0.3 mg.
**Sodium** 94.8 mg.
**Potassium** 420 mg.
**Magnesium** 26.4 mg.
**Phosphorus** 240 mg.

**Vitamins**
**Vitamin A** None.
**Vitamin C** None.
**Vitamin D** None.
**Vitamin E** 0.04 mg.
**Vitamin B1** 0.78 mg.
**Vitamin B2** 0.32 mg.
**Niacin** 12 mg.
**Vitamin B6** 0.37 mg.
**Vitamin B12** 1.2 µg.
**Folic acid** 7.2 µg.
**Pantothenic acid** 1.2 mg.
**Biotin** 2.4 µg.

**Leave the crackling and fat of your roast pork on your plate if you want to cut down on calories and fat.**

# Pork pie

**Portion** One individual pork pie.
**Weight** 145 g., about 5 oz.

**Food Facts**
**Energy** 545 kcal.
**Protein** 14.2 g.
**Total fat** 39.1 g.
**Saturated fat** Not known.
**Polyunsaturated fat** Not known.
**Carbohydrate** 36.1 g.
**Sugars** Not known.
**Fibre** Not known.

**Minerals**
**Calcium** 68.1 mg.
**Iron** 2.03 mg.
**Zinc** 1.45 mg.
**Copper** 0.46 mg.
**Sodium** 1,044 mg.
**Potassium** 217 mg.
**Magnesium** 23.2 mg.
**Phosphorus** 174 mg.

**Vitamins**
**Vitamin A** None.
**Vitamin C** None.
**Vitamin D** None.
**Vitamin E** 0.62 mg.
**Vitamin B1** 0.23 mg.
**Vitamin B2** 0.13 mg.
**Niacin** 5.65 mg.
**Vitamin B6** 0.09 mg.
**Vitamin B12** 1.45 µg.
**Folic acid** 4.3 µg.
**Pantothenic acid** 0.9 mg.
**Biotin** 1.4 µg.

**The fat content of a pork pie makes it one of the most unacceptable of all meat products.**

# Prawns

**Portion** Thirteen shelled prawns.
**Weight** 25 g., about 1 oz.

**Food Facts**
**Energy** 26 kcal.
**Protein** 5.6 g.
**Total fat** 0.4 g.
**Saturated fat** 0.05 g.
**Polyunsaturated fat** 0.16 g.
**Carbohydrate** None.
**Sugars** None.
**Fibre** None.

**Minerals**
**Calcium** 37.5 mg.
**Iron** 0.27 mg.
**Zinc** 0.4 mg.
**Copper** 0.17 mg.
**Sodium** 397 mg.
**Potassium** 65 mg.
**Magnesium** 10.5 mg.
**Phosphorus** 87.5 mg.

**Vitamins**
**Vitamin A** None.
**Vitamin C** None.
**Vitamin D** None.
**Vitamin E** Not known.
**Vitamin B1** Not known.
**Vitamin B2** Not known.
**Niacin** 1.05 mg.
**Vitamin B6** Not known.
**Vitamin B12** Not known.
**Folic acid** Not known.
**Pantothenic acid** Not known.
**Biotin** Not known.

If making avocado prawns or a prawn cocktail, substitute plain yoghurt for some of the mayonnaise.

# Quiche

**Portion** One slice, about ⅙ of whole quiche.
**Weight** 70 g., about 2½ oz.

**Food Facts**
**Energy** 273 kcal.
**Protein** 10.2 g.
**Total fat** 19.6 g.
**Saturated fat** 8.75 g.
**Polyunsaturated fat** 1.6 g.
**Carbohydrate** 14.7 g.
**Sugars** None.
**Fibre** Not known.

**Minerals**
**Calcium** 182 mg.
**Iron** 0.91 mg.
**Zinc** 1.26 mg.
**Copper** 0.07 mg.
**Sodium** 427 mg.
**Potassium** 133 mg.
**Magnesium** 14.7 mg.
**Phosphorus** 168 mg.

**Vitamins**
**Vitamin A** 117 µg.
**Vitamin C** None.
**Vitamin D** 0.61 µg.
**Vitamin E** 0.63 mg.
**Vitamin B1** 0.09 mg.
**Vitamin B2** 0.16 mg.
**Niacin** 3.09 mg..
**Vitamin B6** 0.07 mg.
**Vitamin B12** 0.56 µg.
**Folic acid** 5.6 µg.
**Pantothenic acid** 0.35 mg.
**Biotin** 4.9 µg.

When making the pastry use half or all wholemeal flour to increase the fibre content.

# Rabbit

**Portion** One small ladleful.

**Weight** 110 g., about 4 oz.

**Food Facts**
Energy 196 kcal.
Protein 30 g.
Total fat 8.5 g.
Saturated fat 3.4 g.
Polyunsaturated fat 2.7 g.
Carbohydrate None.
Sugars None.
Fibre None.

**Minerals**
Calcium 12.1 mg.
Iron 2.09 mg.
Zinc Not known.
Copper Not known.
Sodium 35 mg.
Potassium 231 mg.
Magnesium 24.2 mg.
Phosphorus 220 mg.

**Vitamins**
Vitamin A None.
Vitamin C None.
Vitamin D None.
Vitamin E Not known.
Vitamin B1 0.08 mg.
Vitamin B2 0.31 mg.
Niacin 14.96 mg.
Vitamin B6 0.55 mg.
Vitamin B12 13.2 µg.
Folic acid 4.4 µg.
Pantothenic acid 0.9 mg.
Biotin 1.1 µg.

**Rabbit ranks with chicken as being a good low fat substitute for red meat.**

# Safflower seed oil

**Portion** One tablespoon.

**Weight** 5 g., about ⅕ oz.

**Food Facts**
Energy 44 kcal.
Protein None.
Total fat 5 g.
Saturated fat 0.51 g.
Polyunsaturated fat 3.6 g.
Carbohydrate None.
Sugars None.
Fibre None.

**Minerals**
Calcium None.
Iron None.
Zinc None.
Copper None.
Sodium None.
Potassium None.
Magnesium None.
Phosphorus None.

**Vitamins**
Vitamin A None.
Vitamin C None.
Vitamin D None.
Vitamin E 1.93 mg.
Vitamin B1 None.
Vitamin B2 None.
Niacin None.
Vitamin B6 None.
Vitamin B12 None.
Folic acid None.
Pantothenic acid None.
Biotin None.

**Safflower seed oil contains the most polyunsaturated fat of all the oils.**

# Salami

**Portion** 4 slices.

**Weight** 56 g., about 2 oz.

**Food Facts**
**Energy** 275 kcal.
**Protein** 30.8 g.
**Total fat** 25.3 g.
**Saturated fat** 10 g.
**Polyunsaturated fat** 1.96 g.
**Carbohydrate** 1.1 g.
**Sugars** None.
**Fibre** None.

**Minerals**
**Calcium** 5.6 mg.
**Iron** 0.56 mg.
**Zinc** 0.95 mg.
**Copper** 0.13 mg.
**Sodium** 1,036 mg.
**Potassium** 89.6 mg.
**Magnesium** 5.6 mg.
**Phosphorus** 89.6 mg.

**Vitamins**
**Vitamin A** None.
**Vitamin C** None.
**Vitamin D** None.
**Vitamin E** 0.16 mg.
**Vitamin B1** 0.12 mg.
**Vitamin B2** 0.13 mg.
**Niacin** 4.59 mg.
**Vitamin B6** 0.08 mg.
**Vitamin B12** 0.56 µg.
**Folic acid** 1.7 µg.
**Pantothenic acid** 0.4 mg.
**Biotin** 1.7 µg.

**Salami is half fat, a substantial amount of which is saturated fat. It is best avoided except in very small amounts.**

# Salmon, tinned

**Portion** Half a large tin of salmon.

**Weight** 105 g., about 3¾ oz.

**Food Facts**
**Energy** 162 kcal.
**Protein** 21.3 g.
**Total fat** 8.6 g.
**Saturated fat** 2.13 g.
**Polyunsaturated fat** 2.19 g.
**Carbohydrate** None.
**Sugars** None.
**Fibre** None.

**Minerals**
**Calcium** 97 mg.
**Iron** 1.47 mg.
**Zinc** 0.94 mg.
**Copper** 0.09 mg.
**Sodium** 598 mg.
**Potassium** 315 mg.
**Magnesium** 31 mg.
**Phosphorus** 252 mg.

**Vitamins**
**Vitamin A** 94.5 µg.
**Vitamin C** None.
**Vitamin D** 13.13 µg.
**Vitamin E** 1.57 mg.
**Vitamin B1** 0.04 mg.
**Vitamin B2** 0.19 mg.
**Niacin** 11.34 mg.
**Vitamin B6** 0.47 mg.
**Vitamin B12** 4.2 µg.
**Folic acid** 12.6 µg.
**Pantothenic acid** 0.5 mg.
**Biotin** 5.2 µg.

**Many people keep tinned salmon to eat with salad. It can also be put into quiches or used instead of white fish to make a more exotic fish pie.**

# Salmon, fresh

**Portion** One poached salmon steak, flesh only.
**Weight** 110 g., about 4 oz.

## Food Facts
**Energy** 216 kcal.
**Protein** 22.1 g.
**Total fat** 14.3 g.
**Saturated fat** 3.54 g.
**Polyunsaturated fat** 3.64 g.
**Carbohydrate** None.
**Sugars** None.
**Fibre** Not known.

## Minerals
**Calcium** 31.9 mg.
**Iron** 0.88 mg.
**Zinc** 0.99 mg.
**Copper** Not known.
**Sodium** 121 mg.
**Potassium** 363 mg.
**Magnesium** 31.9 mg.
**Phosphorus** 330 mg.

## Vitamins
**Vitamin A** 94.5 µg.
**Vitamin C** None.
**Vitamin D** 13.13 µg.
**Vitamin E** Not known.
**Vitamin B1** 0.22 mg.
**Vitamin B2** 0.12 mg.
**Niacin** 11.88 mg.
**Vitamin B6** 0.91 mg.
**Vitamin B12** 6.6 µg.
**Folic acid** 31.9 µg.
**Pantothenic acid** 1.98 mg.
**Biotin** 4.4 µg.

Fresh salmon is a treat which is becoming more popular and less expensive due to fish farming.

# Sardines

**Portion** Four sardines tinned in oil.
**Weight** 100 g., about 3½ oz.

## Food Facts
**Energy** 217 kcal.
**Protein** 23.7 g.
**Total fat** 13.6 g.
**Saturated fat** 2.66 g.
**Polyunsaturated fat** 2.69 g.
**Carbohydrate** None.
**Sugars** None.
**Fibre** None.

## Minerals
**Calcium** 550 mg.
**Iron** 2.9 mg.
**Zinc** 3 mg.
**Copper** 0.19 mg.
**Sodium** 650 mg.
**Potassium** 430 mg.
**Magnesium** 52 mg.
**Phosphorus** 520 mg.

## Vitamins
**Vitamin A** None.
**Vitamin C** None.
**Vitamin D** 7.5 µg.
**Vitamin E** 0.3 mg.
**Vitamin B1** 0.04 mg.
**Vitamin B2** 0.36 mg.
**Niacin** 12.6 mg.
**Vitamin B6** 0.48 mg.
**Vitamin B12** 28 µg.
**Folic acid** 8 µg.
**Pantothenic acid** 0.5 mg.
**Biotin** 5 µg.

Try to buy sardines in tomato sauce instead of oil where possible.

# Sausages, beef, grilled

**Portion** Three large grilled sausages (2 oz. each raw).
**Weight** 126 g., about 4½ oz.

**Food Facts**
**Energy** 333 kcal.
**Protein** 16.4 g.
**Total fat** 21.8 g.
**Saturated fat** 9.2 g.
**Polyunsaturated fat** 1 g.
**Carbohydrate** 19.2 g.
**Sugars** None.
**Fibre** None.

**Minerals**
**Calcium** 92 mg.
**Iron** 2.14 mg.
**Zinc** 2.14 mg.
**Copper** 0.38 mg.
**Sodium** 1,386 mg.
**Potassium** 239 mg.
**Magnesium** 21.4 mg.
**Phosphorus** 264 mg.

**Vitamins**
**Vitamin A** None.
**Vitamin C** None.
**Vitamin D** None.
**Vitamin E** 0.28 mg.
**Vitamin B1** None.
**Vitamin B2** 0.18 mg.
**Niacin** 10.33 mg.
**Vitamin B6** 0.09 mg.
**Vitamin B12** 1.26 µg.
**Folic acid** 5 µg.
**Pantothenic acid** 0.6 mg.
**Biotin** 2.5 µg.

**Beef sausages have fewer calories than pork sausages because they have a lower fat content.**

# Sausages, pork, grilled

**Portion** Three large grilled sausages (2 oz. each raw).
**Weight** 126 g., about 4½ oz.

**Food Facts**
**Energy** 400 kcal.
**Protein** 16.8 g.
**Total fat** 31 g.
**Saturated fat** 12.2 g.
**Polyunsaturated fat** 2.4 g.
**Carbohydrate** 14.5 g.
**Sugars** None.
**Fibre** None.

**Minerals**
**Calcium** 66.8 mg.
**Iron** 1.89 mg.
**Zinc** 2.02 mg.
**Copper** 0.43 mg.
**Sodium** 1,260 mg.
**Potassium** 252 mg.
**Magnesium** 18.9 mg.
**Phosphorus** 277 mg.

**Vitamins**
**Vitamin A** None.
**Vitamin C** None.
**Vitamin D** None.
**Vitamin E** 0.28 mg.
**Vitamin B1** 0.03 mg.
**Vitamin B2** 0.19 mg.
**Niacin** 8.57 mg.
**Vitamin B6** 0.08 mg.
**Vitamin B12** 1.26 µg.
**Folic acid** 3.8 µg.
**Pantothenic acid** 0.8 mg.
**Biotin** 3.8 µg.

**If you eat sausages regularly always grill them or cook in a casserole. Good quality sausages will cost more but contain less fat.**

# Sausages, pork, fried

**Portion** Three large fried sausages (2 oz. each raw).
**Weight** 151 g., about 5½ oz.

## Food Facts
Energy 478 kcal.
Protein 20.8 g.
Total fat 37 g.
Saturated fat 14.5 g.
Polyunsaturated fat 2.8 g.
Carbohydrate 16.6 g.
Sugars None.
Fibre None.

## Minerals
Calcium 83 mg.
Iron 2.26 mg.
Zinc 2.57 mg.
Copper 0.56 mg.
Sodium 1,585 mg.
Potassium 302 mg.
Magnesium 22.6 mg.
Phosphorus 317 mg.

## Vitamins
Vitamin A None.
Vitamin C None.
Vitamin D None.
Vitamin E 0.42 mg.
Vitamin B1 0.02 mg.
Vitamin B2 0.24 mg.
Niacin 11.02 mg.
Vitamin B6 0.11 mg.
Vitamin B12 1.51 µg.
Folic acid 3 µg.
Pantothenic acid 0.9 mg.
Biotin 4.5 µg.

**Avoid frying anything that already contains a lot of fat. Also avoid cooking methods that add fat such as sausages fried in batter.**

# Sausage roll

**Portion** One sausage roll.
**Weight** 58 g., about 2 oz.

## Food Facts
Energy 277 kcal.
Protein 4.2 g.
Total fat 21 g.
Saturated fat 8.2 g.
Polyunsaturated fat 2.3 g.
Carbohydrate 19.2 g.
Sugars None.
Fibre None.

## Minerals
Calcium 40 mg.
Iron 0.75 mg.
Zinc 0.41 mg.
Copper 0.1 mg.
Sodium 319 mg.
Potassium 63 mg.
Magnesium 7.5 mg.
Phosphorus 56.3 mg.

## Vitamins
Vitamin A 72.5 µg.
Vitamin C None.
Vitamin D 0.64 µg.
Vitamin E 0.75 mg.
Vitamin B1 0.06 mg.
Vitamin B2 0.02 mg.
Niacin 1.91 mg..
Vitamin B6 0.03 mg.
Vitamin B12 None.
Folic acid 2.3 µg.
Pantothenic acid 0.1 mg.
Biotin 0.6 µg.

**If you are trying to lose weight avoid sausage rolls and similar snacks at parties. They can be very expensive on calories.**

# Saveloy

**Portion** One saveloy.

**Weight** 80 g., about 2¾ oz.

**Food Facts**
**Energy** 209 kcal.
**Protein** 7.9 g.
**Total fat** 16.4 g.
**Saturated fat** Not known.
**Polyunsaturated fat** Not known.
**Carbohydrate** 8.1 g.
**Sugars** None.
**Fibre** None.

**Minerals**
**Calcium** 18.4 mg.
**Iron** 1.2 mg.
**Zinc** 1.12 mg.
**Copper** 0.22 mg.
**Sodium** 712 mg.
**Potassium** 128 mg.
**Magnesium** 7.2 mg.
**Phosphorus** 168 mg.

**Vitamins**
**Vitamin A** None.
**Vitamin C** None.
**Vitamin D** None.
**Vitamin E** 0.06 mg.
**Vitamin B1** 0.11 mg.
**Vitamin B2** 0.07 mg.
**Niacin** 3.04 mg.
**Vitamin B6** 0.05 mg.
**Vitamin B12** None.
**Folic acid** 0.8 µg.
**Pantothenic acid** 0.3 mg.
**Biotin** None.

Saveloys contain the same amount
of fat and starch as ordinary
sausages but a lot less protein.

# Scampi

**Portion** Twelve breadcrumbed
scampi, fried.

**Weight** 100 g., about 3½ oz.

**Food Facts**
**Energy** 316 kcal.
**Protein** 12.2 g.
**Total fat** 17.6 g.
**Saturated fat** Not known.
**Polyunsaturated fat** Not known.
**Carbohydrate** 28.9 g.
**Sugars** Not known.
**Fibre** Not known.

**Minerals**
**Calcium** 99 mg.
**Iron** 1.1 mg.
**Zinc** 0.6 mg.
**Copper** 0.22 mg.
**Sodium** 380 mg.
**Potassium** 390 mg.
**Magnesium** 30 mg.
**Phosphorus** 310 mg.

**Vitamins**
**Vitamin A** None.
**Vitamin C** None.
**Vitamin D** None.
**Vitamin E** Not known.
**Vitamin B1** 0.08 mg.
**Vitamin B2** 0.05 mg.
**Niacin** 3.6 mg.
**Vitamin B6** Not known.
**Vitamin B12** Not known.
**Folic acid** Not known.
**Pantothenic acid** Not known.
**Biotin** Not known.

Prawns are relatively low in fat and
calories, so fried is not the best way
to eat them.

# Scotch egg

**Portion** One scotch egg.

**Weight** 112 g., about 4 oz.

**Food Facts**
Energy 312 kcal.
Protein 13 g.
Total fat 23.4 g.
Saturated fat 8.76 g.
Polyunsaturated fat 2 g.
Carbohydrate 13.2 g.
Sugars None.
Fibre None.

**Minerals**
Calcium 62.7 mg.
Iron 1.9 mg.
Zinc 1.46 mg.
Copper 0.22 mg.
Sodium 537 mg.
Potassium 168 mg.
Magnesium 14.6 mg.
Phosphorus 212 mg.

**Vitamins**
Vitamin A 67 µg.
Vitamin C None.
Vitamin D 0.84 µg.
Vitamin E 0.9 mg.
Vitamin B1 0.07 mg.
Vitamin B2 0.25 mg.
Niacin 4.97 mg.
Vitamin B6 0.08 mg.
Vitamin B12 1.34 µg.
Folic acid 9 µg.
Pantothenic acid 0.9 mg.
Biotin 13.4 µg.

**Making an egg into a scotch egg adds a lot of calories. it is often thought to be a low calorie food as it is traditionally associated with salad.**

# Shepherds pie

**Portion** Two tablespoons or an individual frozen portion.

**Weight** 175 g., about 6¼ oz.

**Food Facts**
Energy 208 kcal.
Protein 13.3 g.
Total fat 10.7 g.
Saturated fat 4.3 g.
Polyunsaturated fat 0.7 g.
Carbohydrate 15.6 g.
Sugars None.
Fibre None.

**Minerals**
Calcium 26.2 mg.
Iron 1.92 mg.
Zinc 3.32 mg.
Copper 0.23 mg.
Sodium 787 mg.
Potassium 420 mg.
Magnesium 28 mg.
Phosphorus 120 mg.

**Vitamins**
Vitamin A 24.5 µg.
Vitamin C 3.5 mg.
Vitamin D 0.24 µg.
Vitamin E 0.49 mg.
Vitamin B1 0.07 mg.
Vitamin B2 0.21 mg.
Niacin 5.6 mg.
Vitamin B6 0.3 mg.
Vitamin B12 1.75 µg.
Folic acid 12.2 µg.
Pantothenic acid 0.5 mg.
Biotin None.

**Shepherds pie is quite a healthy way of serving mince. It is probably one of the better meals to eat in a pub or cafe.**

# Smoked haddock

**Portion** One poached fillet.

**Weight** 150 g., about 5¼ oz.

**Food Facts**
**Energy** 151 kcal.
**Protein** 34.9 g.
**Total fat** 1.3 g.
**Saturated fat** 0.25 g.
**Polyunsaturated fat** 0.43 g.
**Carbohydrate** None.
**Sugars** None.
**Fibre** None.

**Minerals**
**Calcium** 87 mg.
**Iron** 1.5 mg.
**Zinc** 0.6 mg.
**Copper** 0.19 mg.
**Sodium** 1,830 mg.
**Potassium** 435 mg.
**Magnesium** 37.5 mg.
**Phosphorus** 375 mg.

**Vitamins**
**Vitamin A** None.
**Vitamin C** None.
**Vitamin D** None.
**Vitamin E** Not known.
**Vitamin B1** 0.15 mg.
**Vitamin B2** 0.16 mg.
**Niacin** 9.15 mg.
**Vitamin B6** 0.52 mg.
**Vitamin B12** 4.5 µg.
**Folic acid** 7.5 µg.
**Pantothenic acid** 0.3 mg.
**Biotin** 4.5 µg.

If you are making fish pâté, smoked haddock makes a less rich and fatty pâté than mackerel. Smoked haddock may contain artificial colouring.

# Smoked salmon

**Portion** One thin piece, size of slice of bread.

**Weight** 56 g., about 2 oz.

**Food Facts**
**Energy** 79 kcal.
**Protein** 14.2 g.
**Total fat** 2.5 g.
**Saturated fat** 0.6 g.
**Polyunsaturated fat** 0.6 g.
**Carbohydrate** None.
**Sugars** None.
**Fibre** None.

**Minerals**
**Calcium** 10.6 mg.
**Iron** 0.34 mg.
**Zinc** 0.22 mg.
**Copper** 0.05 mg.
**Sodium** 1,052 mg.
**Potassium** 235 mg.
**Magnesium** 17.9 mg.
**Phosphorus** 140 mg.

**Vitamins**
**Vitamin A** None.
**Vitamin C** None.
**Vitamin D** None.
**Vitamin E** Not known.
**Vitamin B1** 0.09 mg.
**Vitamin B2** 0.1 mg.
**Niacin** 7.56 mg.
**Vitamin B6** Not known.
**Vitamin B12** Not known.
**Folic acid** Not known.
**Pantothenic acid** Not known.
**Biotin** Not known.

Smoked salmon is a tasty delicacy that is not too high in calories. Serve on canapes instead of pâté or cream cheese.

# Spaghetti bolognaise

**Portion** 100 g. boiled spaghetti; 130 g. minced meat (no fat).
**Weight** 230 g., about 8¼ oz.

## Food Facts
**Energy** 287 kcal.
**Protein** 21.2 g.
**Total fat** 8.6 g.
**Saturated fat** 3.5 g.
**Polyunsaturated fat** 0.3 g.
**Carbohydrate** 33.3 g.
**Sugars** 0.8 g.
**Fibre** 1.5 g.

## Minerals
**Calcium** 35.6 mg.
**Iron** 1.96 mg.
**Zinc** 2.9 mg.
**Copper** 0.21 mg.
**Sodium** 408 mg.
**Potassium** 308 mg.
**Magnesium** 29.2 mg.
**Phosphorus** 152 mg.

## Vitamins
**Vitamin A** None.
**Vitamin C** None.
**Vitamin D** None.
**Vitamin E** 0.13 mg.
**Vitamin B1** 0.07 mg.
**Vitamin B2** 0.18 mg.
**Niacin** 7.31 mg.
**Vitamin B6** 0.18 mg.
**Vitamin B12** 1.3 µg.
**Folic acid** 7.2 µg.
**Pantothenic acid** 0.4 mg.
**Biotin** None.

**Use wholewheat spaghetti to increase the fibre content of this dish and use more vegetables and less meat. Skim off fat to reduce calories.**

# Squid

**Portion** Four raw squid (cooked weight 65 g.).
**Weight** 130 g., about 4½ oz.

## Food Facts
**Energy** 97 kcal.
**Protein** 19.8 g.
**Total fat** 1.04 g.
**Saturated fat** Not known.
**Polyunsaturated fat** Not known.
**Carbohydrate** 0.91 g.
**Sugars** None.
**Fibre** None.

## Minerals
**Calcium** 19.5 mg.
**Iron** 1.3 mg.
**Zinc** Not known.
**Copper** Not known.
**Sodium** 228 mg.
**Potassium** 345 mg.
**Magnesium** Not known.
**Phosphorus** Not known.

## Vitamins
**Vitamin A** 19.5 µg.
**Vitamin C** None.
**Vitamin D** Not known.
**Vitamin E** Not known.
**Vitamin B1** 0.03 mg.
**Vitamin B2** 0.1 mg.
**Niacin** 6.8 mg.
**Vitamin B6** Not known.
**Vitamin B12** 1.69 µg.
**Folic acid** 16.9 µg.
**Pantothenic acid** Not known.
**Biotin** Not known.

**People are becoming more familiar with squid (calamares). Squid loses half its weight when cooked.**

# Steak, grilled

**Portion** Grilled rump steak, lean only.
**Weight** 130 g., about 4½ oz. (raw weight 225 g.)
**Food Facts**
**Energy** 218 kcal.
**Protein** 37.2 g.
**Total fat** 7.7 g.
**Saturated fat** 3.2 g.
**Polyunsaturated fat** 0.3 g.
**Carbohydrate** None.
**Sugars** None.
**Fibre** None.

**Minerals**
**Calcium** 9.1 mg.
**Iron** 4.5 mg.
**Zinc** 6.8 mg.
**Copper** 0.23 mg.
**Sodium** 72 mg.
**Potassium** 520 mg.
**Magnesium** 33.7 mg.
**Phosphorus** 298 mg.

**Vitamins**
**Vitamin A** None.
**Vitamin C** None.
**Vitamin D** None.
**Vitamin E** 0.37 mg.
**Vitamin B1** 0.11 mg.
**Vitamin B2** 0.47 mg.
**Niacin** 16.2 mg.
**Vitamin B6** 0.4 mg.
**Vitamin B12** 2.5 µg.
**Folic acid** 22 µg.
**Pantothenic acid** 1.1 mg.
**Biotin** None.

**Make steak an occasional treat and try to eat less red meat.**

# Steak pudding

**Portion** One individual pudding.
**Weight** 154 g., about 5½ oz.

**Food Facts**
**Energy** 343 kcal.
**Protein** 16.6 g.
**Total fat** 18.6 g.
**Saturated fat** 9.4 g.
**Polyunsaturated fat** 0.55 g.
**Carbohydrate** 29.1 g.
**Sugars** None.
**Fibre** None.

**Minerals**
**Calcium** 169 mg.
**Iron** 2.31 mg.
**Zinc** 2.77 mg.
**Copper** 0.17 mg.
**Sodium** 554 mg.
**Potassium** 277 mg.
**Magnesium** 23 mg.
**Phosphorus** 215 mg.

**Vitamins**
**Vitamin A** None.
**Vitamin C** None.
**Vitamin D** None.
**Vitamin E** 0.31 mg.
**Vitamin B1** 0.12 mg.
**Vitamin B2** 0.14 mg.
**Niacin** 3.7 mg..
**Vitamin B6** 0.2 mg.
**Vitamin B12** 1.54 µg.
**Folic acid** 7.7 µg.
**Pantothenic acid** 0.5 mg.
**Biotin** None.

**Weight for weight, a steak pudding contains fewer calories and less fat than a pie.**

# Steak and kidney pie

**Portion** Quarter large pie, pastry top and bottom.
**Weight** 106 g., about 3¾ oz.

**Food Facts**
**Energy** 342 kcal.
**Protein** 9.6 g.
**Total fat** 22.5 g.
**Saturated fat** 9.4 g.
**Polyunsaturated fat** 2.33 g.
**Carbohydrate** 27.1 g.
**Sugars** None.
**Fibre** None.

**Minerals**
**Calcium** 56.2 mg.
**Iron** 2.65 mg.
**Zinc** 1.27 mg.
**Copper** 0.11 mg.
**Sodium** 540 mg.
**Potassium** 148 mg.
**Magnesium** 19.1 mg.
**Phosphorus** 116 mg.

**Vitamins**
**Vitamin A** 106 µg.
**Vitamin C** None.
**Vitamin D** None.
**Vitamin E** Not known.
**Vitamin B1** 0.13 mg.
**Vitamin B2** 0.16 mg.
**Niacin** 3.6 mg.
**Vitamin B6** 0.06 mg.
**Vitamin B12** 2.12 µg.
**Folic acid** 8.5 µg.
**Pantothenic acid** 0.3 mg.
**Biotin** 1.1 µg.

If you want to cut down on calories, cook the steak and kidney first, then remove your portion before making the rest into a pie.

# Stilton cheese

**Portion** One matchbox sized cube.
**Weight** 30 g., about 1 oz.

**Food Facts**
**Energy** 138 kcal.
**Protein** 7.7 g.
**Total fat** 12 g.
**Saturated fat** 7.1 g.
**Polyunsaturated fat** 0.3 g.
**Carbohydrate** None.
**Sugars** None.
**Fibre** None.

**Minerals**
**Calcium** 108 mg.
**Iron** 0.14 mg.
**Zinc** Not known.
**Copper** 0.01 mg.
**Sodium** 345 mg.
**Potassium** 48 mg.
**Magnesium** 8.1 mg.
**Phosphorus** 90 mg.

**Vitamins**
**Vitamin A** 122 µg.
**Vitamin C** None.
**Vitamin D** 0.09 µg.
**Vitamin E** 0.3 mg.
**Vitamin B1** 0.02 mg.
**Vitamin B2** 0.09 mg.
**Niacin** 1.81 mg.
**Vitamin B6** Not known.
**Vitamin B12** Not known.
**Folic acid** Not known.
**Pantothenic acid** Not known.
**Biotin** Not known.

Stilton is one of the highest calorie cheeses with the most fat. Reserve for special occasions.

# Sunflower seed oil

**Portion** One tablespoon.

**Weight** 5 g., about ⅕ oz.

**Food Facts**
**Energy** 44 kcal.
**Protein** None.
**Total fat** 5 g.
**Saturated fat** 0.65 g.
**Polyunsaturated fat** 2.49 g.
**Carbohydrate** None.
**Sugars** None.
**Fibre** None.

**Minerals**
**Calcium** None.
**Iron** None.
**Zinc** None.
**Copper** None.
**Sodium** None.
**Potassium** None.
**Magnesium** None.
**Phosphorus** None.

**Vitamins**
**Vitamin A** None.
**Vitamin C** None.
**Vitamin D** None.
**Vitamin E** 2.43 mg.
**Vitamin B1** None.
**Vitamin B2** None.
**Niacin** None.
**Vitamin B6** None.
**Vitamin B12** None.
**Folic acid** None.
**Pantothenic acid** None.
**Biotin** None.

**Foods fried in oil are high in calories despite their proportions of saturated, polyunsaturated and mono-unsaturated fat. Grill or bake.**

# Taramasalata

**Portion** One tablespoon.

**Weight** 15 g., about ½ oz.

**Food Facts**
**Energy** 66 kcal.
**Protein** 0.48 g.
**Total fat** 6.96 g.
**Saturated fat** Not known.
**Polyunsaturated fat** Not known.
**Carbohydrate** 0.6 g.
**Sugars** Not known.
**Fibre** Not known.

**Minerals**
**Calcium** 3.15 mg.
**Iron** 0.06 mg.
**Zinc** 0.06 mg.
**Copper** 0.87 mg.
**Sodium** 97 mg.
**Potassium** 9 mg.
**Magnesium** 0.9 mg.
**Phosphorus** Not known.

**Vitamins**
**Vitamin A** Not known.
**Vitamin C** 0.13 mg.
**Vitamin D** Not known.
**Vitamin E** Not known.
**Vitamin B1** 0.01 mg.
**Vitamin B2** 0.01 mg.
**Niacin** 0.04 mg.
**Vitamin B6** Not known.
**Vitamin B12** 0.4 µg.
**Folic acid** 0.6 µg.
**Pantothenic acid** Not known.
**Biotin** Not known.

**If used sparingly taramasalata can be a useful spread for those trying to lose weight. However, it is easy to eat more than you realise.**

# Tripe, stewed

**Portion** One serving, about half a plateful.
**Weight** 150 g., about 5¼ oz.

**Food Facts**
**Energy** 150 kcal.
**Protein** 22.2 g.
**Total fat** 6.7 g.
**Saturated fat** 3.18 g.
**Polyunsaturated fat** 0.1 g.
**Carbohydrate** None.
**Sugars** None.
**Fibre** None.

**Minerals**
**Calcium** 225 mg.
**Iron** 1.05 mg.
**Zinc** 3.45 mg.
**Copper** 0.21 mg.
**Sodium** 109 mg.
**Potassium** 150 mg.
**Magnesium** 22.5 mg.
**Phosphorus** 135 mg.

**Vitamins**
**Vitamin A** None.
**Vitamin C** 4.5 mg.
**Vitamin D** None.
**Vitamin E** 0.13 mg.
**Vitamin B1** None.
**Vitamin B2** 0.12 mg.
**Niacin** 4.83 mg.
**Vitamin B6** 0.03 mg.
**Vitamin B12** None.
**Folic acid** 1.5 μg.
**Pantothenic acid** 0.3 mg.
**Biotin** 3 μg.

**Tripe is low in fat and could be eaten more regularly as an alternative to other offal dishes.**

# Trout

**Portion** One trout grilled without head and bones.
**Weight** 180 g., about 6½ oz.

**Food Facts**
**Energy** 243 kcal.
**Protein** 42 g.
**Total fat** 8.1 g.
**Saturated fat** Not known.
**Polyunsaturated fat** Not known.
**Carbohydrate** None.
**Sugars** None.
**Fibre** None.

**Minerals**
**Calcium** 64 mg.
**Iron** 1.8 mg.
**Zinc** Not known.
**Copper** Not known.
**Sodium** 158 mg.
**Potassium** 666 mg.
**Magnesium** 55 mg.
**Phosphorus** 486 mg.

**Vitamins**
**Vitamin A** None.
**Vitamin C** None.
**Vitamin D** Not known.
**Vitamin E** Not known.
**Vitamin B1** Not known.
**Vitamin B2** Not known.
**Niacin** 7.92 mg.
**Vitamin B6** Not known.
**Vitamin B12** Not known.
**Folic acid** Not known.
**Pantothenic acid** Not known.
**Biotin** Not known.

**Trout is less fatty than mackerel and is more readily available and cheaper, since rainbow trout farms have come into existence.**

# Tuna fish tinned in oil

**Portion** Half a large tin.

**Weight** 92 g., about 3¼ oz.

## Food Facts
**Energy** 265 kcal.
**Protein** 21 g.
**Total fat** 20.2 g.
**Saturated fat** 3.6 g.
**Polyunsaturated fat** 7.3 g.
**Carbohydrate** None.
**Sugars** None.
**Fibre** None.

## Minerals
**Calcium** 6.4 mg.
**Iron** 1.01 mg.
**Zinc** 0.74 mg.
**Copper** 0.08 mg.
**Sodium** 386 mg.
**Potassium** 257 mg.
**Magnesium** 25.8 mg.
**Phosphorus** 174 mg.

## Vitamins
**Vitamin A** None.
**Vitamin C** None.
**Vitamin D** 5.3 µg.
**Vitamin E** 5.8 mg.
**Vitamin B1** 0.04 mg.
**Vitamin B2** 0.1 mg.
**Niacin** 15.8 mg.
**Vitamin B6** 0.4 mg.
**Vitamin B12** 4.6 µg.
**Folic acid** 13.8 µg.
**Pantothenic acid** 0.4 mg.
**Biotin** 2.8 µg.

Tuna fish is very versatile and is good in pasta dishes. Not as strongly flavoured as other fatty fish, it is more popular with children.

# Turkey, roast

**Portion** Two slices, meat without skin.

**Weight** 120 g., about 4¼ oz.

## Food Facts
**Energy** 168 kcal.
**Protein** 34.6 g.
**Total fat** 3.2 g.
**Saturated fat** 1.1 g.
**Polyunsaturated fat** 1 g.
**Carbohydrate** None.
**Sugars** None.
**Fibre** None.

## Minerals
**Calcium** 10.8 mg.
**Iron** 1.08 mg.
**Zinc** 2.88 mg.
**Copper** 0.18 mg.
**Sodium** 68 mg.
**Potassium** 372 mg.
**Magnesium** 32 mg.
**Phosphorus** 264 mg.

## Vitamins
**Vitamin A** None.
**Vitamin C** None.
**Vitamin D** None.
**Vitamin E** None.
**Vitamin B1** 0.08 mg.
**Vitamin B2** 0.25 mg.
**Niacin** 16.68 mg.
**Vitamin B6** 0.38 mg.
**Vitamin B12** 2.4 µg.
**Folic acid** 18 µg.
**Pantothenic acid** 1 mg.
**Biotin** 2.4 µg.

Compared to other meats, turkey usually contains the least amount of fat. It makes a good alternative to chicken.

# Veal fillet

**Portion** One thin fillet, grilled or roasted.
**Weight** 112 g., about 4 oz.

**Food Facts**
**Energy** 257 kcal.
**Protein** 35.4 g.
**Total fat** 12.9 g.
**Saturated fat** 5.3 g.
**Polyunsaturated fat** 0.5 g.
**Carbohydrate** None.
**Sugars** None.
**Fibre** None.

**Minerals**
**Calcium** 15.7 mg.
**Iron** 1.79 mg.
**Zinc** 4.5 mg.
**Copper** Not known.
**Sodium** 108 mg.
**Potassium** 481 mg.
**Magnesium** 31.4 mg.
**Phosphorus** 403 mg.

**Vitamins**
**Vitamin A** None.
**Vitamin C** None.
**Vitamin D** None.
**Vitamin E** Not known.
**Vitamin B1** 0.07 mg.
**Vitamin B2** 0.3 mg.
**Niacin** 15.34 mg.
**Vitamin B6** 0.36 mg.
**Vitamin B12** 1.12 µg.
**Folic acid** 4.5 µg.
**Pantothenic acid** 0.6 mg.
**Biotin** None.

**Eat veal plainly cooked and avoid breaded and fried veal escalopes.**

# Venison

**Portion** Three small slices.

**Weight** 96 g., about 3½ oz.

**Food Facts**
**Energy** 190 kcal.
**Protein** 33.6 g.
**Total fat** 6.1 g.
**Saturated fat** Not known.
**Polyunsaturated fat** Not known.
**Carbohydrate** None.
**Sugars** None.
**Fibre** None.

**Minerals**
**Calcium** 27.8 mg.
**Iron** 7.49 mg.
**Zinc** Not known.
**Copper** Not known.
**Sodium** 82.6 mg.
**Potassium** 345 mg.
**Magnesium** 31.7 mg.
**Phosphorus** 278 mg.

**Vitamins**
**Vitamin A** None.
**Vitamin C** None.
**Vitamin D** None.
**Vitamin E** Not known.
**Vitamin B1** 0.21 mg.
**Vitamin B2** Not known.
**Niacin** 6.24 mg.
**Vitamin B6** Not known.
**Vitamin B12** Not known.
**Folic acid** Not known.
**Pantothenic acid** Not known.
**Biotin** Not known.

**Venison is not commonly eaten in the UK. Like other game, it is low in fat.**

# Whelks

# Whitebait

**Portion** Four whelks.

**Weight** 30 g., about 1 oz.

## Food Facts
**Energy** 26 kcal.
**Protein** 5.5 g.
**Total fat** 0.6 g.
**Saturated fat** Not known.
**Polyunsaturated fat** Not known.
**Carbohydrate** None.
**Sugars** None.
**Fibre** None.

## Minerals
**Calcium** 16.2 mg.
**Iron** 1.86 mg.
**Zinc** 2.16 mg.
**Copper** 2.16 mg.
**Sodium** 81 mg.
**Potassium** 96 mg.
**Magnesium** 48 mg.
**Phosphorus** 69 mg.

## Vitamins
**Vitamin A** None.
**Vitamin C** None.
**Vitamin D** None.
**Vitamin E** 0.24 mg.
**Vitamin B1** Not known.
**Vitamin B2** Not known.
**Niacin** 1.2 mg.
**Vitamin B6** Not known.
**Vitamin B12** Not known.
**Folic acid** Not known.
**Pantothenic acid** Not known.
**Biotin** Not known.

**Most seafood goes well with pasta cooked in a tomato sauce.**

**Portion** Twenty fried whitebait.

**Weight** 60 g., about 2¼ oz.

## Food Facts
**Energy** 315 kcal.
**Protein** 11.7 g.
**Total fat** 28.5 g.
**Saturated fat** Not known.
**Polyunsaturated fat** Not known.
**Carbohydrate** 3.2 g.
**Sugars** None.
**Fibre** None.

## Minerals
**Calcium** 516 mg.
**Iron** 3.06 mg.
**Zinc** Not known.
**Copper** Not known.
**Sodium** 138 mg.
**Potassium** 66 mg.
**Magnesium** 30 mg.
**Phosphorus** 516 mg.

## Vitamins
**Vitamin A** None.
**Vitamin C** None.
**Vitamin D** Not known.
**Vitamin E** Not known.
**Vitamin B1** Not known.
**Vitamin B2** Not known.
**Niacin** 2.16 mg.
**Vitamin B6** Not known.
**Vitamin B12** Not known.
**Folic acid** Not known.
**Pantothenic acid** Not known.
**Biotin** Not known.

**A normal restaurant serving could be twice as much, which makes fried whitebait a very high fat, high calorie starter.**

# Yoghurt, fruit

**Portion** One carton low-fat fruit yoghurt.
**Weight** 150 g., about 5¼ oz.

**Food Facts**
**Energy** 142 kcal.
**Protein** 7.2 g.
**Total fat** 1.5 g.
**Saturated fat** 0.9 g.
**Polyunsaturated fat** 0.03 g.
**Carbohydrate** 26.8 g.
**Sugars** 26.8 g.
**Fibre** None.

**Minerals**
**Calcium** 240 mg.
**Iron** 0.36 mg.
**Zinc** 0.94 mg.
**Copper** 0.1 mg.
**Sodium** 96 mg.
**Potassium** 330 mg.
**Magnesium** 25 mg.
**Phosphorus** 210 mg.

**Vitamins**
**Vitamin A** 18.7 µg.
**Vitamin C** 2.7 mg.
**Vitamin D** None.
**Vitamin E** 0.1 mg.
**Vitamin B1** 0.07 mg.
**Vitamin B2** 0.34 mg.
**Niacin** 1.68 mg.
**Vitamin B6** 0.06 mg.
**Vitamin B12** None.
**Folic acid** 4.5 µg.
**Pantothenic acid** Not known.
**Biotin** Not known.

**Most low fat fruit yoghurts contain added sugar. Look at the label.**

# Yoghurt, plain

**Portion** One carton plain low-fat yoghurt.
**Weight** 150 g., about 5¼ oz.

**Food Facts**
**Energy** 78 kcal.
**Protein** 7.5 g.
**Total fat** 1.5 g.
**Saturated fat** 0.9 g.
**Polyunsaturated fat** 0.03 g.
**Carbohydrate** 9.3 g.
**Sugars** 9.3 g.
**Fibre** None.

**Minerals**
**Calcium** 270 mg.
**Iron** 0.13 mg.
**Zinc** 0.9 mg.
**Copper** 0.06 mg.
**Sodium** 114 mg.
**Potassium** 360 mg.
**Magnesium** 25 mg.
**Phosphorus** 210 mg.

**Vitamins**
**Vitamin A** 13.5 µg.
**Vitamin C** 0.6 mg.
**Vitamin D** None.
**Vitamin E** 0.04 mg.
**Vitamin B1** 0.07 mg.
**Vitamin B2** 0.39 mg.
**Niacin** 1.74 mg.
**Vitamin B6** 0.06 mg.
**Vitamin B12** None.
**Folic acid** 3 µg.
**Pantothenic acid** Not known.
**Biotin** Not known.

**There are now plain yoghurts which are full fat. The Greek variety often made from sheep or goat's milk are particularly high in calories.**

# 7

# Fruit, vegetables and nuts

It is important to eat fruit and vegetables regularly. This chapter gives the vitamin and mineral content of fresh and tinned foods sold by most greengrocers and supermarkets together with their calories and essential fibre. The sugar found in fruit is a different type than that normally added to processed food – for an explanation see page 12.

# Almonds

**Portion** Six whole almonds.

**Weight** 10 g., about ⅓ oz.

**Food Facts**
**Energy** 56 kcal.
**Protein** 1.7 g.
**Total fat** 5.3 g.
**Saturated fat** 0.4 g.
**Polyunsaturated fat** 1 g.
**Carbohydrate** 0.4 g.
**Sugars** 0.4 g.
**Fibre** 1.4 g.

**Minerals**
**Calcium** 25 mg.
**Iron** 0.42 mg.
**Zinc** 0.31 mg.
**Copper** 0.01 mg.
**Sodium** 0.6 mg.
**Potassium** 86 mg.
**Magnesium** 26 mg.
**Phosphorus** 44 mg.

**Vitamins**
**Vitamin A** None.
**Vitamin C** None.
**Vitamin D** None.
**Vitamin E** 2 mg.
**Vitamin B1** 0.02 mg.
**Vitamin B2** 0.09 mg.
**Niacin** 0.47 mg.
**Vitamin B6** 0.01 mg.
**Vitamin B12** None.
**Folic acid** 9.6 μg.
**Pantothenic acid** None.
**Biotin** None.

Almonds are high in calories but a few will add texture to puddings and cereals.

# Apple

**Portion** One eating apple without core.

**Weight** 100 g., about 3½ oz.

**Food Facts**
**Energy** 46 kcal.
**Protein** 0.3 g.
**Total fat** None.
**Saturated fat** None.
**Polyunsaturated fat** None.
**Carbohydrate** 11.9 g.
**Sugars** 11.8 g.
**Fibre** 2.0 g.

**Minerals**
**Calcium** 4 mg.
**Iron** 0.3 mg.
**Zinc** 0.1 mg.
**Copper** 0.04 mg.
**Sodium** 2 mg.
**Potassium** 120 mg.
**Magnesium** 5 mg.
**Phosphorus** 8 mg.

**Vitamins**
**Vitamin A** 5 μg.
**Vitamin C** 3 mg.
**Vitamin D** None.
**Vitamin E** 0.2 mg.
**Vitamin B1** 0.04 mg.
**Vitamin B2** 0.02 mg.
**Niacin** 0.1 mg.
**Vitamin B6** 0.03 mg.
**Vitamin B12** None.
**Folic acid** 5 μg.
**Pantothenic acid** 0.1 mg.
**Biotin** 0.3 μg.

Wash an apple and do not peel it before eating. Apples are filling without being high in calories.

# Apple, baked

**Portion** One medium-sized without core or sugar.
**Weight** 180 g., about 6½ oz.

**Food Facts**
**Energy** 55 kcal.
**Protein** 0.5 g.
**Total fat** None.
**Saturated fat** None.
**Polyunsaturated fat** None.
**Carbohydrate** 14.4 g.
**Sugars** 13.9 g.
**Fibre** 3.6 g.

**Minerals**
**Calcium** 5.4 mg.
**Iron** 0.36 mg.
**Zinc** 0.18 mg.
**Copper** 0.13 mg.
**Sodium** 3.6 mg.
**Potassium** 180 mg.
**Magnesium** 3.6 mg.
**Phosphorus** 23.4 mg.

**Vitamins**
**Vitamin A** 6.3 µg.
**Vitamin C** 18 mg.
**Vitamin D** None.
**Vitamin E** 0.18 mg.
**Vitamin B1** 0.05 mg.
**Vitamin B2** 0.02 mg.
**Niacin** 0.18 mg.
**Vitamin B6** 0.02 mg.
**Vitamin B12** None.
**Folic acid** 3.6 µg.
**Pantothenic acid** 0.1 mg.
**Biotin** 0.4 µg.

Instead of having apple pie try a baked apple with natural yoghurt. Jazz it up with a little dried fruit or nuts.

# Apricot

**Portion** One fresh apricot without stone.
**Weight** 65 g., about 2¼ oz.

**Food Facts**
**Energy** 18 kcal.
**Protein** 0.4 g.
**Total fat** None.
**Saturated fat** None.
**Polyunsaturated fat** None.
**Carbohydrate** 4.4 g.
**Sugars** 4.4 g.
**Fibre** 1.4 g.

**Minerals**
**Calcium** 11 mg.
**Iron** 0.26 mg.
**Zinc** 0.06 mg.
**Copper** 0.08 mg.
**Sodium** None.
**Potassium** 208 mg.
**Magnesium** 7.8 mg.
**Phosphorus** 13.6 mg.

**Vitamins**
**Vitamin A** 162 µg.
**Vitamin C** 4.5 mg.
**Vitamin D** None.
**Vitamin E** Not known.
**Vitamin B1** 0.03 mg.
**Vitamin B2** 0.03 mg.
**Niacin** 0.39 mg.
**Vitamin B6** 0.05 mg.
**Vitamin B12** None.
**Folic acid** 3.2 µg.
**Pantothenic acid** 0.2 mg.
**Biotin** Not known.

In the summer fresh apricots make a nice change from plums or peaches. A good snack for slimmers.

# Artichoke

**Portion** One globe artichoke heart.
**Weight** 50 g., about 2 oz.

**Food Facts**
**Energy** 7 kcal.
**Protein** 0.5 g.
**Total fat** None.
**Saturated fat** None.
**Polyunsaturated fat** None.
**Carbohydrate** 1.3 g.
**Sugars** Not known.
**Fibre** Not known.

**Minerals**
**Calcium** 22 mg.
**Iron** 0.25 mg.
**Zinc** Not known.
**Copper** 0.04 mg.
**Sodium** 7.5 mg.
**Potassium** 165 mg.
**Magnesium** 13.5 mg.
**Phosphorus** 20 mg.

**Vitamins**
**Vitamin A** 7.5 µg.
**Vitamin C** 4 mg.
**Vitamin D** None.
**Vitamin E** Not known.
**Vitamin B1** 0.03 mg.
**Vitamin B2** 0.01 mg.
**Niacin** 0.55 mg.
**Vitamin B6** 0.03 mg.
**Vitamin B12** None.
**Folic acid** 15 µg.
**Pantothenic acid** 0.1 mg.
**Biotin** 2 µg.

**A good low-calorie starter ideal with a low-fat dressing such as plain yoghurt.**

# Asparagus

**Portion** Five spears.

**Weight** 125 g., about 5 oz.

**Food Facts**
**Energy** 22 kcal.
**Protein** 4.2 g.
**Total fat** None.
**Saturated fat** None.
**Polyunsaturated fat** None.
**Carbohydrate** 1.4 g.
**Sugars** 1.4 g.
**Fibre** 1.9 g.

**Minerals**
**Calcium** 32.5 mg.
**Iron** 1.12 mg.
**Zinc** 0.37 mg.
**Copper** 0.25 mg.
**Sodium** 2.5 mg.
**Potassium** 300 mg.
**Magnesium** 12.5 mg.
**Phosphorus** 106 mg.

**Vitamins**
**Vitamin A** 104 µg.
**Vitamin C** 25 mg.
**Vitamin D** None.
**Vitamin E** 3.12 mg.
**Vitamin B1** 0.12 mg.
**Vitamin B2** 0.1 mg.
**Niacin** 1.75 mg.
**Vitamin B6** 0.05 mg.
**Vitamin B12** None.
**Folic acid** 37.5 µg.
**Pantothenic acid** 0.2 mg.
**Biotin** 0.5 µg.

**Asparagus is very high in many minerals and vitamins. In season it turns an ordinary meal into something special.**

# Aubergine

**Portion** Half including skin cooked without added fat.
**Weight** 130 g., about 4½ oz.

**Food Facts**
**Energy** 18 kcal.
**Protein** 0.9 g.
**Total fat** None.
**Saturated fat** None.
**Polyunsaturated fat** None.
**Carbohydrate** 4 g.
**Sugars** 3.8 g.
**Fibre** 3.2 g.

**Minerals**
**Calcium** 13 mg.
**Iron** 0.52 mg.
**Zinc** Not known.
**Copper** 0.1 mg.
**Sodium** 3.9 mg.
**Potassium** 312 mg.
**Magnesium** 13 mg.
**Phosphorus** 15.6 mg.

**Vitamins**
**Vitamin A** None.
**Vitamin C** 6.5 mg.
**Vitamin D** None.
**Vitamin E** Not known.
**Vitamin B1** 0.06 mg.
**Vitamin B2** 0.04 mg.
**Niacin** 1.17 mg.
**Vitamin B6** 0.1 mg.
**Vitamin B12** None.
**Folic acid** 26 µg.
**Pantothenic acid** 0.3 mg.
**Biotin** Not known.

Aubergine is very low in calories but unfortunately people fry it. Try baking it in the oven stuffed with meat, beans or lentils.

# Avocado Pear

**Portion** Half an avocado pear without stone.
**Weight** 75 g., about 2¾ oz.

**Food Facts**
**Energy** 167 kcal.
**Protein** 3.1 g.
**Total fat** 16.6 g.
**Saturated fat** 1.9 g.
**Polyunsaturated fat** 1.4 g.
**Carbohydrate** 1.3 g.
**Sugars** 1.3 g.
**Fibre** 1.5 g.

**Minerals**
**Calcium** 11.2 mg.
**Iron** 1.12 mg.
**Zinc** 0.32 mg.
**Copper** 0.16 mg.
**Sodium** 1.5 mg.
**Potassium** 300 mg.
**Magnesium** 21.7 mg.
**Phosphorus** 23.2 mg.

**Vitamins**
**Vitamin A** 12.4 µg.
**Vitamin C** 11.2 mg.
**Vitamin D** Not known.
**Vitamin E** 2.4 mg.
**Vitamin B1** 0.07 mg.
**Vitamin B2** 0.07 mg.
**Niacin** 1.35 mg.
**Vitamin B6** 0.31 mg.
**Vitamin B12** None.
**Folic acid** 49.5 µg.
**Pantothenic acid** 0.8 mg.
**Biotin** 2.4 µg.

The high calorie and fat content of avocado pears makes them unsuitable for people trying to lose weight.

# Baked beans

**Portion** Half a medium sized tin.
**Weight** 225 g., about 8 oz.

**Food Facts**
**Energy** 144 kcal.
**Protein** 11.5 g.
**Total fat** 1.1 g.
**Saturated fat** Not known.
**Polyunsaturated fat** Not known.
**Carbohydrate** 23.1 g.
**Sugars** 11.7 g.
**Fibre** 16.4 g.

**Minerals**
**Calcium** 101 mg.
**Iron** 3.15 mg.
**Zinc** 1.57 mg.
**Copper** 0.47 mg.
**Sodium** 1,080 mg.
**Potassium** 675 mg.
**Magnesium** 69.7 mg.
**Phosphorus** 204 mg.

**Vitamins**
**Vitamin A** None.
**Vitamin C** None.
**Vitamin D** None.
**Vitamin E** 1.35 mg.
**Vitamin B1** 0.16 mg.
**Vitamin B2** 0.11 mg.
**Niacin** 2.92 mg.
**Vitamin B6** 0.27 mg.
**Vitamin B12** None.
**Folic acid** 65.2 µg.
**Pantothenic acid** Not known.
**Biotin** Not known.

Baked beans are a very good source of fibre and protein but try to buy ones which contain less sugar and salt.

# Banana

**Portion** One medium-sized without skin.
**Weight** 120 g., about 4¼ oz.

**Food Facts**
**Energy** 94 kcal.
**Protein** 1.3 g.
**Total fat** 0.4 g.
**Saturated fat** Not known.
**Polyunsaturated fat** Not known.
**Carbohydrate** 23 g.
**Sugars** 19.4 g.
**Fibre** 4.1 g.

**Minerals**
**Calcium** 8.4 mg.
**Iron** 0.48 mg.
**Zinc** 0.24 mg.
**Copper** 0.19 mg.
**Sodium** 1.2 mg.
**Potassium** 420 mg.
**Magnesium** 50.4 mg.
**Phosphorus** 33.6 mg.

**Vitamins**
**Vitamin A** 40.2 µg.
**Vitamin C** 12 mg.
**Vitamin D** None.
**Vitamin E** 0.24 mg.
**Vitamin B1** 0.05 mg.
**Vitamin B2** 0.08 mg.
**Niacin** 0.96 mg.
**Vitamin B6** 0.61 mg.
**Vitamin B12** None.
**Folic acid** 26.4 µg.
**Pantothenic acid** 0.3 mg.
**Biotin** Not known.

Bananas are filling and high in fibre. They also contain twice as many calories as other fruits, so slimmers beware.

# Beansprouts

**Portion** Two tablespoons.

**Weight** 70 g., about 2½ oz.

## Food Facts
**Energy** 6 kcal.
**Protein** 1.1 g.
**Total fat** None.
**Saturated fat** None.
**Polyunsaturated fat** None.
**Carbohydrate** 0.6 g.
**Sugars** 0.3 g.
**Fibre** 2.1 g.

## Minerals
**Calcium** 9.1 mg.
**Iron** 0.7 mg.
**Zinc** 0.56 mg.
**Copper** 0.06 mg.
**Sodium** 56 mg.
**Potassium** 25 mg.
**Magnesium** 7 mg.
**Phosphorus** 14 mg.

## Vitamins
**Vitamin A** None.
**Vitamin C** 0.7 mg.
**Vitamin D** None.
**Vitamin E** Not known.
**Vitamin B1** 0.01 mg.
**Vitamin B2** 0.02 mg.
**Niacin** 0.35 mg.
**Vitamin B6** 0.02 mg.
**Vitamin B12** None.
**Folic acid** 8.4 µg.
**Pantothenic acid** Not known.
**Biotin** Not known.

**Try raw beansprouts in salads or add to stir-fried vegetables cooked in a small amount of oil.**

# Beetroot

**Portion** One small whole beetroot.

**Weight** 35 g., about 1¼ oz.

## Food Facts
**Energy** 15 kcal.
**Protein** 0.6 g.
**Total fat** None.
**Saturated fat** None.
**Polyunsaturated fat** None.
**Carbohydrate** 3.5 g.
**Sugars** 3.5 g.
**Fibre** 0.9 g.

## Minerals
**Calcium** 10.5 mg.
**Iron** 0.14 mg.
**Zinc** 0.14 mg.
**Copper** 0.03 mg.
**Sodium** 22.4 mg.
**Potassium** 122.5 mg.
**Magnesium** 5.9 mg.
**Phosphorus** 12.6 mg.

## Vitamins
**Vitamin A** None.
**Vitamin C** 1.75 mg.
**Vitamin D** None.
**Vitamin E** None.
**Vitamin B1** 0.01 mg.
**Vitamin B2** 0.01 mg.
**Niacin** 0.14 mg.
**Vitamin B6** 0.01 mg.
**Vitamin B12** None.
**Folic acid** 17.5 µg.
**Pantothenic acid** None.
**Biotin** None.

**Although beetroot is a starchy vegetable, a few slices in a salad will add colour but not many calories.**

# Blackberries

**Portion** Eighteen blackberries.

**Weight** 90 g., about 3 oz.

**Food Facts**
**Energy** 26 kcal.
**Protein** 1.2 g.
**Total fat** None.
**Saturated fat** None.
**Polyunsaturated fat** None.
**Carbohydrate** 5.8 g.
**Sugars** 5.8 g.
**Fibre** 6.6 g.

**Minerals**
**Calcium** 56.7 mg.
**Iron** 0.8 mg.
**Zinc** Not known.
**Copper** 0.11 mg.
**Sodium** 3.6 mg.
**Potassium** 189 mg.
**Magnesium** 27 mg.
**Phosphorus** 21.6 mg.

**Vitamins**
**Vitamin A** 30 µg.
**Vitamin C** 18 mg.
**Vitamin D** None.
**Vitamin E** 0.73 mg.
**Vitamin B1** 0.03 mg.
**Vitamin B2** 0.04 mg.
**Niacin** 0.54 mg.
**Vitamin B6** 0.04 mg.
**Vitamin B12** None.
**Folic acid** Not known.
**Pantothenic acid** 0.2 mg.
**Biotin** 0.4 µg.

**Blackberries are not only low in calories, but very high in fibre. Use them to make fruit salad and crumbles more interesting.**

# Blackcurrants

**Portion** One heaped tablespoon, stewed, no sugar.

**Weight** 75 g., about 3 oz.

**Food Facts**
**Energy** 18 kcal.
**Protein** 0.6 g.
**Total fat** None.
**Saturated fat** None.
**Polyunsaturated fat** None.
**Carbohydrate** 4.2 g.
**Sugars** 4.2 g.
**Fibre** 5.5 g.

**Minerals**
**Calcium** 38 mg.
**Iron** 0.82 mg.
**Zinc** Not known.
**Copper** 0.09 mg.
**Sodium** 2.2 mg.
**Potassium** 240 mg.
**Magnesium** 12 mg.
**Phosphorus** 27.7 mg.

**Vitamins**
**Vitamin A** 21.4 µg.
**Vitamin C** 112 mg.
**Vitamin D** None.
**Vitamin E** 0.67 mg.
**Vitamin B1** 0.02 mg.
**Vitamin B2** 0.04 mg.
**Niacin** 0.3 mg.
**Vitamin B6** 0.04 mg.
**Vitamin B12** None.
**Folic acid** Not known.
**Pantothenic acid** 0.2 mg.
**Biotin** 1.6 µg.

**When cooking blackcurrants don't add too much sugar. A tart sauce makes an ideal topping for puddings. Full of vitamin C.**

# Brazil nuts

**Portion** Three brazil nuts.

**Weight** 10 g., about ⅓ oz.

**Food Facts**
**Energy** 61 kcal.
**Protein** 1.2 g.
**Total fat** 6.1 g.
**Saturated fat** 1.57 g.
**Polyunsaturated fat** 2.3 g.
**Carbohydrate** 0.4 g.
**Sugars** 0.2 g.
**Fibre** 0.9 g.

**Minerals**
**Calcium** 18 mg.
**Iron** 0.28 mg.
**Zinc** 0.42 mg.
**Copper** 0.11 mg.
**Sodium** 0.2 mg.
**Potassium** 76 mg.
**Magnesium** 41 mg.
**Phosphorus** 59 mg.

**Vitamins**
**Vitamin A** None.
**Vitamin C** None.
**Vitamin D** None.
**Vitamin E** 0.65 mg.
**Vitamin B1** 0.1 mg.
**Vitamin B2** 0.01 mg.
**Niacin** 0.42 mg.
**Vitamin B6** 0.02 mg.
**Vitamin B12** None.
**Folic acid** 0.4 µg.
**Pantothenic acid** None.
**Biotin** Not known.

**Many muesli-type cereals are high in calories because they contain a lot of dried fruit and nuts such as brazil nuts.**

# Broad beans

**Portion** Two tablespoons, cooked.

**Weight** 120 g., about 4 oz.

**Food Facts**
**Energy** 57 kcal.
**Protein** 4.9 g.
**Total fat** 0.7 g.
**Saturated fat** Not known.
**Polyunsaturated fat** Not known.
**Carbohydrate** 8.5 g.
**Sugars** 0.7 g.
**Fibre** 5 g.

**Minerals**
**Calcium** 25.2 mg.
**Iron** 1.2 mg.
**Zinc** Not known.
**Copper** 0.52 mg.
**Sodium** 24 mg.
**Potassium** 276 mg.
**Magnesium** 33.6 mg.
**Phosphorus** 118.8 mg.

**Vitamins**
**Vitamin A** 49.8 µg.
**Vitamin C** 18 mg.
**Vitamin D** None.
**Vitamin E** None.
**Vitamin B1** 0.12 mg.
**Vitamin B2** 0.05 mg.
**Niacin** 4.44 mg.
**Vitamin B6** Not known.
**Vitamin B12** None.
**Folic acid** Not known.
**Pantothenic acid** 4.6 mg.
**Biotin** 2.5 µg.

**Try using cooked or tinned broad beans in salads. In the summer fresh broad beans make a pleasant change from peas.**

# Broccoli

**Portion** One boiled spear.

**Weight** 45 g., about 1½ oz.

**Food Facts**
Energy 8 kcal.
Protein 1.4 g.
Total fat None.
Saturated fat None.
Polyunsaturated fat None.
Carbohydrate 0.7 g.
Sugars 0.7 g.
Fibre 1.8 g.

**Minerals**
Calcium 34.2 mg.
Iron 0.45 mg.
Zinc 0.18 mg.
Copper 0.04 mg.
Sodium 2.7 mg.
Potassium 99 mg.
Magnesium 5.4 mg.
Phosphorus 27 mg.

**Vitamins**
Vitamin A 187 µg.
Vitamin C 15.3 mg.
Vitamin D None.
Vitamin E 0.49 mg.
Vitamin B1 0.03 mg.
Vitamin B2 0.09 mg.
Niacin 0.54 mg.
Vitamin B6 0.06 mg.
Vitamin B12 None.
Folic acid 49.5 µg.
Pantothenic acid 0.3 mg.
Biotin 0.1 µg.

**Broccoli is easily overcooked so try steaming it or cooking in a microwave oven.**

# Brussels sprouts

**Portion** Average serving of nine prepared boiled sprouts.

**Weight** 120 g., about 4¼ oz.

**Food Facts**
Energy 21 kcal.
Protein 3.4 g.
Total fat None.
Saturated fat None.
Polyunsaturated fat None.
Carbohydrate 2 g.
Sugars 1.9 g.
Fibre 3.5 g.

**Minerals**
Calcium 30 mg.
Iron 0.6 mg.
Zinc 0.48 mg.
Copper 0.06 mg.
Sodium 2.4 mg.
Potassium 288 mg.
Magnesium 15.6 mg.
Phosphorus 61.2 mg.

**Vitamins**
Vitamin A 79.8 µg.
Vitamin C 48 mg.
Vitamin D None.
Vitamin E 1.08 mg.
Vitamin B1 0.07 mg.
Vitamin B2 0.12 mg.
Niacin 1.08 mg.
Vitamin B6 0.2 mg.
Vitamin B12 None.
Folic acid 104 µg.
Pantothenic acid 0.3 mg.
Biotin 0.4 µg.

**Brussels sprouts have an abundance of vitamins. Try to conserve them by storing away from the light and steaming them.**

# Cabbage, red raw

**Portion** One sixth of a small raw cabbage.
**Weight** 90 g., about 3 oz.

**Food Facts**
**Energy** 18 kcal.
**Protein** 1.5 g.
**Total fat** None.
**Saturated fat** None.
**Polyunsaturated fat** None.
**Carbohydrate** 3.1 g.
**Sugars** 3.1 g.
**Fibre** 3 g.

**Minerals**
**Calcium** 47 mg.
**Iron** 0.5 mg.
**Zinc** 0.27 mg.
**Copper** 0.08 mg.
**Sodium** 28 mg.
**Potassium** 270 mg.
**Magnesium** 15.3 mg.
**Phosphorus** 28.8 mg.

**Vitamins**
**Vitamin A** 2.9 µg.
**Vitamin C** 49 mg.
**Vitamin D** None.
**Vitamin E** 0.18 mg.
**Vitamin B1** 0.05 mg.
**Vitamin B2** 0.04 mg.
**Niacin** 0.27 mg.
**Vitamin B6** 0.18 mg.
**Vitamin B12** None.
**Folic acid** 81 µg.
**Pantothenic acid** 0.28 mg.
**Biotin** 0.09 µg.

Red cabbage makes a colourful change. Try to eat it raw in salads as it is high in vitamin C.

# Cabbage, white cooked

**Portion** One sixth of a small boiled cabbage.
**Weight** 90 g., about 3 oz.

**Food Facts**
**Energy** 13 kcal.
**Protein** 1.5 g.
**Total fat** None.
**Saturated fat** None.
**Polyunsaturated fat** None.
**Carbohydrate** 2.1 g.
**Sugars** 2 g.
**Fibre** 2.5 g.

**Minerals**
**Calcium** 34.2 mg.
**Iron** 0.36 mg.
**Zinc** 0.18 mg.
**Copper** 0.03 mg.
**Sodium** 3.6 mg.
**Potassium** 144 mg.
**Magnesium** 7.2 mg.
**Phosphorus** 30 mg.

**Vitamins**
**Vitamin A** 45 µg.
**Vitamin C** 18 mg.
**Vitamin D** None.
**Vitamin E** 0.18 mg.
**Vitamin B1** 0.03 mg.
**Vitamin B2** 0.03 mg.
**Niacin** 0.45 mg.
**Vitamin B6** 0.09 mg.
**Vitamin B12** None.
**Folic acid** 31.5 µg.
**Pantothenic acid** 0.1 mg.
**Biotin** None.

Cook white cabbage in a very small amount of water and serve while it is still crisp as nutrients are lost through cooking.

# Carrot, raw

# Carrot, boiled

**Portion** One medium sized
raw carrot.
**Weight** 60 g., about 2 oz.

**Food Facts**
**Energy** 13 kcal.
**Protein** 0.4 g.
**Total fat** None.
**Saturated fat** None.
**Polyunsaturated fat** None.
**Carbohydrate** 3.2 g.
**Sugars** 3.2 g.
**Fibre** 1.7 g.

**Minerals**
**Calcium** 28.8 mg.
**Iron** 0.36 mg.
**Zinc** 0.24 mg.
**Copper** 0.05 mg.
**Sodium** 57 mg.
**Potassium** 132 mg.
**Magnesium** 7.2 mg.
**Phosphorus** 12.6 mg.

**Vitamins**
**Vitamin A** 1,200 µg.
**Vitamin C** 3.6 mg.
**Vitamin D** None.
**Vitamin E** 0.3 mg.
**Vitamin B1** 0.03 mg.
**Vitamin B2** 0.03 mg.
**Niacin** 0.42 mg.
**Vitamin B6** 0.09 mg.
**Vitamin B12** None.
**Folic acid** 9 µg.
**Pantothenic acid** 0.15 mg.
**Biotin** 0.35 µg.

**If you are trying to lose weight,
keep some scrubbed raw carrots
handy to nibble on inbetween
meals.**

**Portion** One medium sized
boiled carrot.
**Weight** 60 g., about 2 oz.

**Food Facts**
**Energy** 12 kcal.
**Protein** 0.39 g.
**Total fat** None.
**Saturated fat** None.
**Polyunsaturated fat** None.
**Carbohydrate** 2.8 g.
**Sugars** 2.7 g.
**Fibre** 1.7 g.

**Minerals**
**Calcium** 24 mg.
**Iron** 0.26 mg.
**Zinc** 0.19 mg.
**Copper** 0.5 mg.
**Sodium** 32 mg.
**Potassium** 56 mg.
**Magnesium** 3.9 mg.
**Phosphorus** 11 mg.

**Vitamins**
**Vitamin A** 1,200 µg.
**Vitamin C** 2.6 mg.
**Vitamin D** None.
**Vitamin E** 0.3 mg.
**Vitamin B1** 0.03 mg.
**Vitamin B2** 0.02 mg.
**Niacin** 0.26 mg.
**Vitamin B6** 0.05 mg.
**Vitamin B12** None.
**Folic acid** 5.2 µg.
**Pantothenic acid** 0.11 mg.
**Biotin** 0.26 µg.

**Carrots contain a lot of vitamin A.
Steamed carrots taste better than
boiled ones.**

# Cashew nuts

## Cauliflower

**Portion** One small bag, about 24 unsalted nuts.
**Weight** 40 g., about 1½ oz.

**Portion** One serving of eight cauliflower florets.
**Weight** 80 g., about 2¾ oz.

### Food Facts
**Energy** 224 kcal.
**Protein** 6.8 g.
**Total fat** 18.2 g.
**Saturated fat** 3.6 g.
**Polyunsaturated fat** 2.9 g.
**Carbohydrate** 11.1 g.
**Sugars** Not known.
**Fibre** 0.5 g.

### Food Facts
**Energy** 7 kcal.
**Protein** 1.3 g.
**Total fat** None.
**Saturated fat** None.
**Polyunsaturated fat** None.
**Carbohydrate** 0.6 g.
**Sugars** 0.6 g.
**Fibre** 1.4 g.

### Minerals
**Calcium** 15.2 mg.
**Iron** 1.5 mg.
**Zinc** Not known.
**Copper** Not known.
**Sodium** 6 mg.
**Potassium** 185 mg.
**Magnesium** 106 mg.
**Phosphorus** Not known.

### Minerals
**Calcium** 14.4 mg.
**Iron** 0.32 mg.
**Zinc** 0.16 mg.
**Copper** 0.02 mg.
**Sodium** 3.2 mg.
**Potassium** 144 mg.
**Magnesium** 6.4 mg.
**Phosphorus** 25.6 mg.

### Vitamins
**Vitamin A** 4 µg.
**Vitamin C** None.
**Vitamin D** None.
**Vitamin E** Not known.
**Vitamin B1** 0.17 mg.
**Vitamin B2** 0.1 mg.
**Niacin** 0.72 mg.
**Vitamin B6** Not known.
**Vitamin B12** None.
**Folic acid** 27.2 µg.
**Pantothenic acid** Not known.
**Biotin** Not known.

### Vitamins
**Vitamin A** 4 µg.
**Vitamin C** 16 mg.
**Vitamin D** None.
**Vitamin E** 0.08 mg.
**Vitamin B1** 0.05 mg.
**Vitamin B2** 0.05 mg.
**Niacin** 0.64 mg.
**Vitamin B6** 0.1 mg.
**Vitamin B12** None.
**Folic acid** 39.2 µg.
**Pantothenic acid** 0.3 mg.
**Biotin** 0.8 µg.

**Because of their high protein content, cashew and other nuts are useful in vegetarian dishes with pulses and cereals.**

**Cauliflower is a good very low calorie vegetable to cook or eat raw in salads. Try to include as much of the stalk as possible.**

# Celery

**Portion** One stick.

**Weight** 45 g., about 1½ oz.

**Food Facts**
Energy 3 kcal.
Protein 0.4 g.
Total fat None.
Saturated fat None.
Polyunsaturated fat None.
Carbohydrate 0.6 g.
Sugars 0.5 g.
Fibre 0.8 g.

**Minerals**
Calcium 23.4 mg.
Iron 0.27 mg.
Zinc 0.04 mg.
Copper 0.05 mg.
Sodium 63 mg.
Potassium 126 mg.
Magnesium 4.5 mg.
Phosphorus 14.4 mg.

**Vitamins**
Vitamin A None.
Vitamin C 3.15 mg.
Vitamin D None.
Vitamin E 0.09 mg.
Vitamin B1 0.01 mg.
Vitamin B2 0.01 mg.
Niacin 0.13 mg.
Vitamin B6 0.04 mg.
Vitamin B12 None.
Folic acid 5.4 µg.
Pantothenic acid 0.18 mg.
Biotin 0.4 µg.

**Celery is one of the best natural slimming aids. Try a stick spread thinly with cottage cheese to stave off hunger pangs.**

# Cherries

**Portion** Six cherries without stones.

**Weight** 60 g., about 2 oz.

**Food Facts**
Energy 28 kcal.
Protein 0.4 g.
Total fat None.
Saturated fat None.
Polyunsaturated fat None.
Carbohydrate 7.1 g.
Sugars 7.1 g.
Fibre 1 g.

**Minerals**
Calcium 9.6 mg.
Iron 0.24 mg.
Zinc 0.06 mg.
Copper 0.04 mg.
Sodium 1.8 mg.
Potassium 168 mg.
Magnesium 6 mg.
Phosphorus 10.2 mg.

**Vitamins**
Vitamin A 12 µg.
Vitamin C 3 mg.
Vitamin D None.
Vitamin E 0.06 mg.
Vitamin B1 0.03 mg.
Vitamin B2 0.04 mg.
Niacin 0.24 mg.
Vitamin B6 0.03 mg.
Vitamin B12 None.
Folic acid 4.8 µg.
Pantothenic acid 0.2 mg.
Biotin 0.2 µg.

**Treat yourself to some cherries instead of sweets. A quarter of a pound will only contain as many calories as an apple.**

# Chestnuts

# Chickpeas

**Portion** Five chestnuts peeled.

**Weight** 50 g., about 2 oz.

**Portion** Two to three tablespoons cooked.

**Weight** 200 g., about 7 oz.

## Food Facts
**Energy** 85 kcal.
**Protein** 1 g.
**Total fat** 1.35 g.
**Saturated fat** 0.24 g.
**Polyunsaturated fat** 0.56 g.
**Carbohydrate** 18.3 g.
**Sugars** 3.5 g.
**Fibre** 3.4 g.

## Food Facts
**Energy** 288 kcal.
**Protein** 16 g.
**Total fat** 6.6 g.
**Saturated fat** Not known.
**Polyunsaturated fat** Not known.
**Carbohydrate** 44 g.
**Sugars** 10.4 g.
**Fibre** 12 g.

## Minerals
**Calcium** 23 mg.
**Iron** 0.45 mg.
**Zinc** Not known.
**Copper** 0.11 mg.
**Sodium** 5.5 mg.
**Potassium** 250 mg.
**Magnesium** 16.5 mg.
**Phosphorus** 37 mg.

## Minerals
**Calcium** 128 mg.
**Iron** 6.2 mg.
**Zinc** 2.8 mg.
**Copper** 0.66 mg.
**Sodium** 1,700 mg.
**Potassium** 800 mg.
**Magnesium** 134 mg.
**Phosphorus** 260 mg.

## Vitamins
**Vitamin A** None.
**Vitamin C** None.
**Vitamin D** None.
**Vitamin E** 0.25 mg.
**Vitamin B1** 0.1 mg.
**Vitamin B2** 0.11 mg.
**Niacin** 0.1 mg.
**Vitamin B6** 0.16 mg.
**Vitamin B12** None.
**Folic acid** Not known.
**Pantothenic acid** 0.23 mg.
**Biotin** 0.65 µg.

## Vitamins
**Vitamin A** 174 µg.
**Vitamin C** 6 mg.
**Vitamin D** 0.1 µg.
**Vitamin E** None.
**Vitamin B1** 0.28 mg.
**Vitamin B2** 0.1 mg.
**Niacin** 3.2 mg.
**Vitamin B6** Not known.
**Vitamin B12** None.
**Folic acid** 74 µg.
**Pantothenic acid** Not known.
**Biotin** Not known.

**Chestnuts are lower in calories than other nuts. Try using them in stuffings in place of sausage meat.**

**Chickpeas are very high in fibre but also high in calories so try to eat them as part of your main meal and not as a vegetable.**

# Chicory

**Portion** One head of chicory.

**Weight** 105 g., about 3¾ oz.

**Food Facts**
Energy 9 kcal.
Protein 0.8 g.
Total fat None.
Saturated fat None.
Polyunsaturated fat None.
Carbohydrate 1.5 g.
Sugars Not known.
Fibre Not known.

**Minerals**
Calcium 18.9 mg.
Iron 0.73 mg.
Zinc 0.21 mg.
Copper 0.14 mg.
Sodium 7.3 mg.
Potassium 189 mg.
Magnesium 13.6 mg.
Phosphorus 22 mg.

**Vitamins**
Vitamin A None.
Vitamin C 4.2 mg.
Vitamin D None.
Vitamin E Not known.
Vitamin B1 0.05 mg.
Vitamin B2 0.05 mg.
Niacin 0.52 mg.
Vitamin B6 0.05 mg.
Vitamin B12 None.
Folic acid 54 µg.
Pantothenic acid Not known.
Biotin Not known.

**Chicory makes an ideal low calorie addition to salads.**

# Chillies

**Portion** One raw chilli.

**Weight** 5 g., about ⅙ oz.

**Food Facts**
Energy 5.8 kcal.
Protein 0.3 g.
Total fat 0.07 g.
Saturated fat Not known.
Polyunsaturated fat Not known.
Carbohydrate 0.4 g.
Sugars Not known.
Fibre Not known.

**Minerals**
Calcium 4.3 mg.
Iron 0.18 mg.
Zinc 0.01 mg.
Copper None.
Sodium 1.15 mg.
Potassium 64 mg.
Magnesium 0.9 mg.
Phosphorus Not known.

**Vitamins**
Vitamin A 55 µg.
Vitamin C 4.8 mg.
Vitamin D None.
Vitamin E Not known.
Vitamin B1 0.01 mg.
Vitamin B2 0.02 mg.
Niacin 0.12 mg.
Vitamin B6 Not known.
Vitamin B12 None.
Folic acid 0.8 µg.
Pantothenic acid Not known.
Biotin Not known.

**A small amount of fresh chilli is much more potent than chilli powder. The seeds are the hottest part.**

# Chinese leaves

**Portion** One large leaf.

**Weight** 40 g., about 1½ oz.

**Food Facts**
**Energy** 10.4 kcal.
**Protein** 1.4 g.
**Total fat** 0.04 g.
**Saturated fat** Not known.
**Polyunsaturated fat** Not known.
**Carbohydrate** 1.4 g.
**Sugars** Not known.
**Fibre** Not known.

**Minerals**
**Calcium** 61.6 mg.
**Iron** 1.16 mg.
**Zinc** Not known.
**Copper** 0.14 mg.
**Sodium** Not known.
**Potassium** Not known.
**Magnesium** 64 mg.
**Phosphorus** Not known.

**Vitamins**
**Vitamin A** 436 µg.
**Vitamin C** 9.2 mg.
**Vitamin D** None.
**Vitamin E** Not known.
**Vitamin B1** 0.01 mg.
**Vitamin B2** 0.08 mg.
**Niacin** 0.28 mg.
**Vitamin B6** Not known.
**Vitamin B12** None.
**Folic acid** 34 µg.
**Pantothenic acid** Not known.
**Biotin** Not known.

Chinese leaves contain many
vitamins and minerals and make a
welcome change from lettuce,
particularly in the winter.

# Coleslaw

**Portion** One tablespoon of
shop-bought coleslaw.
**Weight** 75 g., about 2¾ oz.

**Food Facts**
**Energy** 60 kcal.
**Protein** 1.4 g.
**Total fat** 4.1 g.
**Saturated fat** Not known.
**Polyunsaturated fat** Not known.
**Carbohydrate** 4.6 g.
**Sugars** Not known.
**Fibre** 1.6 g.

**Minerals**
**Calcium** 31.5 mg.
**Iron** 0.37 mg.
**Zinc** 0.15 mg.
**Copper** 0.03 mg.
**Sodium** 130 mg.
**Potassium** 180 mg.
**Magnesium** 11.2 mg.
**Phosphorus** 35.2 mg.

**Vitamins**
**Vitamin A** None.
**Vitamin C** 24 mg.
**Vitamin D** None.
**Vitamin E** None.
**Vitamin B1** 0.04 mg.
**Vitamin B2** 0.03 mg.
**Niacin** 0.37 mg.
**Vitamin B6** 0.1 mg.
**Vitamin B12** None.
**Folic acid** 15.7 µg.
**Pantothenic acid** 0.1 mg.
**Biotin** None.

If you are watching your weight,
use lemon juice instead of
mayonnaise in your home-made
coleslaw.

# Courgettes

**Portion** One courgette cooked without fat.
**Weight** 100 g., about 3½ oz.

**Food Facts**
**Energy** 25 kcal.
**Protein** 1.6 g.
**Total fat** 0.4 g.
**Saturated fat** Not known.
**Polyunsaturated fat** Not known.
**Carbohydrate** 4.5 g.
**Sugars** Not known.
**Fibre** Not known.

**Minerals**
**Calcium** 30 mg.
**Iron** 2.4 mg.
**Zinc** Not known.
**Copper** Not known.
**Sodium** 1 mg.
**Potassium** 202 mg.
**Magnesium** 6 mg.
**Phosphorus** Not known.

**Vitamins**
**Vitamin A** 58 µg.
**Vitamin C** 16 mg.
**Vitamin D** None.
**Vitamin E** Not known.
**Vitamin B1** 0.05 mg.
**Vitamin B2** 0.09 mg.
**Niacin** 0.4 mg.
**Vitamin B6** Not known.
**Vitamin B12** None.
**Folic acid** 48 µg.
**Pantothenic acid** Not known.
**Biotin** Not known.

**Courgettes absorb a lot of fat so try steaming them or make a vegetable dish by cooking them with onions and tomatoes.**

# Cucumber

**Portion** One sixth, about 2 in. long, including skin.
**Weight** 80 g., about 2¾ oz.

**Food Facts**
**Energy** 8 kcal.
**Protein** 0.5 g.
**Total fat** 0.1 g.
**Saturated fat** Not known.
**Polyunsaturated fat** Not known.
**Carbohydrate** 1.4 g.
**Sugars** 1.4 g.
**Fibre** 0.3 g.

**Minerals**
**Calcium** 18.4 mg.
**Iron** 0.24 mg.
**Zinc** 0.08 mg.
**Copper** 0.07 mg.
**Sodium** 10.4 mg.
**Potassium** 112 mg.
**Magnesium** 7.2 mg.
**Phosphorus** 19.2 mg.

**Vitamins**
**Vitamin A** None.
**Vitamin C** 6.4 mg.
**Vitamin D** None.
**Vitamin E** None.
**Vitamin B1** 0.03 mg.
**Vitamin B2** 0.03 mg.
**Niacin** 0.24 mg.
**Vitamin B6** 0.03 mg.
**Vitamin B12** None.
**Folic acid** 12.8 µg.
**Pantothenic acid** 0.2 mg.
**Biotin** 0.3 µg.

**Try grated cucumber in plain yoghurt as a low calorie alternative to coleslaw.**

# Dates, dried

**Portion** One dried date.

**Weight** 15 g., about ½ oz.

**Food Facts**
Energy 37 kcal.
Protein 0.3 g.
Total fat None.
Saturated fat None.
Polyunsaturated fat None.
Carbohydrate 9.6 g.
Sugars 9.6 g.
Fibre 1.3 g.

**Minerals**
Calcium 10.2 mg.
Iron 0.24 mg.
Zinc 0.04 mg.
Copper 0.03 mg.
Sodium 0.7 mg.
Potassium 112 mg.
Magnesium 8.8 mg.
Phosphorus 9.6 mg.

**Vitamins**
Vitamin A 1.3 µg.
Vitamin C None.
Vitamin D None.
Vitamin E Not known.
Vitamin B1 0.01 mg.
Vitamin B2 0.01 mg.
Niacin 0.43 mg.
Vitamin B6 0.02 mg.
Vitamin B12 None.
Folic acid 3.1 µg.
Pantothenic acid 0.1 mg.
Biotin Not known.

**Dried dates often have added syrup and it is easy to eat a lot of them. Avoid them if you are trying to lose weight.**

# Figs, dried

**Portion** One dried fig.

**Weight** 20 g., about ⅔ oz.

**Food Facts**
Energy 42 kcal.
Protein 0.7 g.
Total fat None.
Saturated fat None.
Polyunsaturated fat None.
Carbohydrate 10.6 g.
Sugars 10.6 g.
Fibre 3.7 g.

**Minerals**
Calcium 56 mg.
Iron 0.84 mg.
Zinc 0.18 mg.
Copper 0.05 mg.
Sodium 17.4 mg.
Potassium 202 mg.
Magnesium 18.4 mg.
Phosphorus 18.4 mg.

**Vitamins**
Vitamin A 1.7 µg.
Vitamin C None.
Vitamin D None.
Vitamin E Not known.
Vitamin B1 0.02 mg.
Vitamin B2 0.02 mg.
Niacin 0.44 mg.
Vitamin B6 0.04 mg.
Vitamin B12 None.
Folic acid 1.8 µg.
Pantothenic acid 0.1 mg.
Biotin Not known.

**Half of the weight of a dried fig comes from sugars, so although they are high in fibre and iron, they are also high in calories.**

# Figs, fresh

**Portion** One fresh fig.

**Weight** 55 g., about 2 oz.

**Food Facts**
Energy 22.5 kcal.
Protein 0.7 g.
Total fat None.
Saturated fat None.
Polyunsaturated fat None.
Carbohydrate 5.2 g.
Sugars 5.2 g.
Fibre 1.4 g.

**Minerals**
Calcium 18.7 mg.
Iron 0.22 mg.
Zinc 0.16 mg.
Copper 0.03 mg.
Sodium 1.1 mg.
Potassium 1.48 mg.
Magnesium 11 mg.
Phosphorus 17.6 mg.

**Vitamins**
Vitamin A 45 µg.
Vitamin C 1.1 mg.
Vitamin D None.
Vitamin E Not known.
Vitamin B1 0.03 mg.
Vitamin B2 0.02 mg.
Niacin 0.22 mg.
Vitamin B6 0.06 mg.
Vitamin B12 None.
Folic acid Not known.
Pantothenic acid 0.16 mg.
Biotin Not known.

**Fresh figs make a good dessert. Either eat whole or cut up into fruit salads.**

# Garlic

**Portion** One peeled clove.

**Weight** 5 g., about ⅕ oz.

**Food Facts**
Energy 5.8 kcal.
Protein 0.17 g.
Total fat 0.01 g.
Saturated fat Not known.
Polyunsaturated fat Not known.
Carbohydrate 1.3 g.
Sugars Not known.
Fibre Not known.

**Minerals**
Calcium 0.9 mg.
Iron 0.07 mg.
Zinc 0.04 mg.
Copper Not known.
Sodium 0.9 mg.
Potassium 18.6 mg.
Magnesium 0.4 mg.
Phosphorus Not known.

**Vitamins**
Vitamin A None.
Vitamin C 0.5 mg.
Vitamin D None.
Vitamin E Not known.
Vitamin B1 0.01 mg.
Vitamin B2 None.
Niacin 0.02 mg.
Vitamin B6 Not known.
Vitamin B12 None.
Folic acid 0.3 µg.
Pantothenic acid Not known.
Biotin Not known.

**Garlic can be used to flavour low calorie dishes and also helps to make foods taste better if you are adding less salt.**

# Gherkin

# Gooseberries

**Portion** One pickled gherkin about three inches long.
**Weight** 30 g., about 1 oz.

**Portion** Twelve berries stewed without sugar.
**Weight** 112 g., about 4 oz.

**Food Facts**
**Energy** 3.3 kcal.
**Protein** 0.3 g.
**Total fat** Not known.
**Saturated fat** Not known.
**Polyunsaturated fat** Not known.
**Carbohydrate** 0.54 g.
**Sugars** Not known.
**Fibre** 0.33 g.

**Food Facts**
**Energy** 15 kcal.
**Protein** 1 g.
**Total fat** None.
**Saturated fat** None.
**Polyunsaturated fat** None.
**Carbohydrate** 3.2 g.
**Sugars** 3.2 g.
**Fibre** 3 g.

**Minerals**
**Calcium** 7.5 mg.
**Iron** 0.09 mg.
**Zinc** 0.06 mg.
**Copper** 0.04 mg.
**Sodium** 3.3 mg.
**Potassium** 67 mg.
**Magnesium** 4.5 mg.
**Phosphorus** Not known.

**Minerals**
**Calcium** 26.9 mg.
**Iron** 0.34 mg.
**Zinc** 0.11 mg.
**Copper** 0.12 mg.
**Sodium** 2.2 mg.
**Potassium** 201 mg.
**Magnesium** 6.7 mg.
**Phosphorus** 32.5 mg.

**Vitamins**
**Vitamin A** 6.8 µg.
**Vitamin C** 3.3 mg.
**Vitamin D** None.
**Vitamin E** Not known.
**Vitamin B1** None.
**Vitamin B2** 0.01 mg.
**Niacin** 0.06 mg.
**Vitamin B6** Not known.
**Vitamin B12** None.
**Folic acid** 5.4 µg.
**Pantothenic acid** Not known.
**Biotin** Not known.

**Vitamins**
**Vitamin A** 28 µg.
**Vitamin C** 34 mg.
**Vitamin D** None.
**Vitamin E** 0.34 mg.
**Vitamin B1** 0.03 mg.
**Vitamin B2** 0.03 mg.
**Niacin** 0.56 mg.
**Vitamin B6** 0.02 mg.
**Vitamin B12** None.
**Folic acid** Not known.
**Pantothenic acid** 0.1 mg.
**Biotin** 0.4 µg.

**Gherkins can be added in small amounts to cottage cheese to flavour it. They also make sandwiches taste better.**

**Make a low calorie gooseberry fool with a little sugar or artificial sweetener and skimmed milk.**

# Grapefruit

**Portion** Half a grapefruit, flesh only.
**Weight** 80 g., about 2¾ oz.

**Food Facts**
**Energy** 17 kcal.
**Protein** 0.5 g.
**Total fat** None.
**Saturated fat** None.
**Polyunsaturated fat** None.
**Carbohydrate** 4.2 g.
**Sugars** 4.2 g.
**Fibre** 0.5 g.

**Minerals**
**Calcium** 13.6 mg.
**Iron** 0.24 mg.
**Zinc** 0.08 mg.
**Copper** 0.05 mg.
**Sodium** 0.8 mg.
**Potassium** 184 mg.
**Magnesium** 8 mg.
**Phosphorus** 12.8 mg.

**Vitamins**
**Vitamin A** None.
**Vitamin C** 32 mg.
**Vitamin D** None.
**Vitamin E** 0.24 mg.
**Vitamin B1** 0.04 mg.
**Vitamin B2** 0.02 mg.
**Niacin** 0.24 mg.
**Vitamin B6** 0.02 mg.
**Vitamin B12** None.
**Folic acid** 9.6 µg.
**Pantothenic acid** 0.2 mg.
**Biotin** 0.8 µg.

**Although grapefruits do not have any magical slimming powers, they are very low in calories and contain a lot of vitamin C.**

# Grapes, black

**Portion** About 20 peeled grapes.
**Weight** 112 g., about 4 oz.

**Food Facts**
**Energy** 57 kcal.
**Protein** 0.56 g.
**Total fat** None.
**Saturated fat** None.
**Polyunsaturated fat** None.
**Carbohydrate** 14.5 g.
**Sugars** 14.5 g.
**Fibre** 0.3 g.

**Minerals**
**Calcium** 4.4 mg.
**Iron** 0.3 mg.
**Zinc** 0.11 mg.
**Copper** 0.07 mg.
**Sodium** 1.1 mg.
**Potassium** 302 mg.
**Magnesium** 3.3 mg.
**Phosphorus** 15.6 mg.

**Vitamins**
**Vitamin A** None.
**Vitamin C** 3.36 mg.
**Vitamin D** None.
**Vitamin E** Not known.
**Vitamin B1** 0.03 mg.
**Vitamin B2** 0.02 mg.
**Niacin** 0.22 mg.
**Vitamin B6** 0.08 mg.
**Vitamin B12** None.
**Folic acid** 5.6 µg.
**Pantothenic acid** 0.04 mg.
**Biotin** 0.22 µg.

**Black grapes contain slightly fewer calories than white grapes and compared to other fruits provide little fibre.**

# Grapes, white

**Portion** About 20 unpeeled grapes.
**Weight** 112 g., about 4 oz.

**Food Facts**
**Energy** 67 kcal.
**Protein** 0.7 g.
**Total fat** None.
**Saturated fat** None.
**Polyunsaturated fat** None.
**Carbohydrate** 17.1 g.
**Sugars** 17.1 g.
**Fibre** 1 g.

**Minerals**
**Calcium** 20.2 mg.
**Iron** 0.34 mg.
**Zinc** 0.11 mg.
**Copper** 0.11 mg.
**Sodium** 2.2 mg.
**Potassium** 268 mg.
**Magnesium** 6.7 mg.
**Phosphorus** 23.5 mg.

**Vitamins**
**Vitamin A** None.
**Vitamin C** 4.48 mg.
**Vitamin D** None.
**Vitamin E** Not known.
**Vitamin B1** 0.04 mg.
**Vitamin B2** 0.02 mg.
**Niacin** 0.34 mg.
**Vitamin B6** 0.11 mg.
**Vitamin B12** None.
**Folic acid** 6.7 μg.
**Pantothenic acid** 0.05 mg.
**Biotin** 0.3 μg.

**A few grapes added to a winter fruit salad will make it more interesting and colourful. Not a fruit for slimmers.**

# Hazel nuts

**Portion** One handful, about ten hazelnuts.
**Weight** 10 g., about ⅓ oz.

**Food Facts**
**Energy** 38 kcal.
**Protein** 0.8 g.
**Total fat** 3.6 g.
**Saturated fat** 0.2 g.
**Polyunsaturated fat** 0.3 g.
**Carbohydrate** 0.7 g.
**Sugars** 0.5 g.
**Fibre** 0.6 g.

**Minerals**
**Calcium** 4.4 mg.
**Iron** 0.11 mg.
**Zinc** 0.24 mg.
**Copper** 0.02 mg.
**Sodium** 0.1 mg.
**Potassium** 35 mg.
**Magnesium** 5.6 mg.
**Phosphorus** 23 mg.

**Vitamins**
**Vitamin A** None.
**Vitamin C** None.
**Vitamin D** None.
**Vitamin E** 2.1 mg.
**Vitamin B1** 0.04 mg.
**Vitamin B2** Not known.
**Niacin** 0.31 mg.
**Vitamin B6** 0.05 mg.
**Vitamin B12** None.
**Folic acid** 7.2 μg.
**Pantothenic acid** 0.1 mg.
**Biotin** Not known.

**Hazel nuts are lower in calories than other nuts but should still be used sparingly if you wish to lose weight.**

# Kidney beans

**Portion** About two cooked tablespoons. Dried weight 2 oz.
**Weight** 160 g., about 5½ oz.

**Food Facts**
Energy 152 kcal.
Protein 12.4 g.
Total fat 1 g.
Saturated fat Not known.
Polyunsaturated fat Not known.
Carbohydrate 25.2 g.
Sugars 1.7 g.
Fibre 14 g.

**Minerals**
Calcium 78 mg.
Iron 3.75 mg.
Zinc 1.57 mg.
Copper 0.34 mg.
Sodium 22.4 mg.
Potassium 649 mg.
Magnesium 100 mg.
Phosphorus 229 mg.

**Vitamins**
Vitamin A None.
Vitamin C None.
Vitamin D None.
Vitamin E Not known.
Vitamin B1 0.3 mg.
Vitamin B2 0.1 mg.
Niacin 3.08 mg.
Vitamin B6 0.25 mg.
Vitamin B12 None.
Folic acid 72 µg.
Pantothenic acid 0.3 mg.
Biotin Not known.

**Use less meat by replacing it with kidney beans. The protein content will be similar but it will contain less fat.**

# Kiwi fruit

**Portion** One medium sized.

**Weight** 60 g., about 2 oz.

**Food Facts**
Energy 32 kcal.
Protein 0.7 g.
Total fat 0.4 g.
Saturated fat 0.11 g.
Polyunsaturated fat 0.14 g.
Carbohydrate 7.0 g.
Sugars 7.0 g.
Fibre 1.4 g.

**Minerals**
Calcium 15 mg.
Iron 0.2 mg.
Zinc 0.12 mg.
Copper 0.12 mg.
Sodium 1.2 mg.
Potassium 216 mg.
Magnesium 12 mg.
Phosphorus 24 mg.

**Vitamins**
Vitamin A 11 µg.
Vitamin C 60 mg.
Vitamin D None.
Vitamin E 0.1 mg. (estimated)
Vitamin B1 0.01 mg.
Vitamin B2 0.01 mg.
Niacin 0.15 mg.
Vitamin B6 0.06 mg. (estimated)
Vitamin B12 None.
Folic acid 14 µg. (estimated)
Pantothenic acid Not known.
Biotin Not known.

**One kiwi fruit contains almost the same amount of vitamin C as one orange. If you don't like citrus fruit, it is a very nutritious alternative.**

# Leeks

# Lemon

**Portion** One medium sized
boiled leek.
**Weight** 160 g., about 5¾ oz.

**Portion** One average sized
including peel.
**Weight** 100 g., about 3½ oz.

**Food Facts**
**Energy** 38 kcal.
**Protein** 2.9 g.
**Total fat** None.
**Saturated fat** None.
**Polyunsaturated fat** None.
**Carbohydrate** 7.4 g.
**Sugars** 7.4 g.
**Fibre** 6.2 g.

**Food Facts**
**Energy** 15 kcal.
**Protein** 0.8 g.
**Total fat** None.
**Saturated fat** None.
**Polyunsaturated fat** None.
**Carbohydrate** 3.2 g.
**Sugars** 3.2 g.
**Fibre** 5.2 g.

**Minerals**
**Calcium** 97.6 mg.
**Iron** 3.2 mg.
**Zinc** 0.16 mg.
**Copper** 0.14 mg.
**Sodium** 9.6 mg.
**Potassium** 448 mg.
**Magnesium** 20.8 mg.
**Phosphorus** 44.8 mg.

**Minerals**
**Calcium** 110 mg.
**Iron** 0.4 mg.
**Zinc** 0.1 mg.
**Copper** 0.26 mg.
**Sodium** 6 mg.
**Potassium** 160 mg.
**Magnesium** 12 mg.
**Phosphorus** 21 mg.

**Vitamins**
**Vitamin A** 10.4 µg.
**Vitamin C** 24 mg.
**Vitamin D** None.
**Vitamin E** 1.28 mg.
**Vitamin B1** 0.11 mg.
**Vitamin B2** 0.05 mg.
**Niacin** 1.12 mg.
**Vitamin B6** 0.24 mg.
**Vitamin B12** None.
**Folic acid** Not known.
**Pantothenic acid** 0.2 mg.
**Biotin** 1.6 µg.

**Vitamins**
**Vitamin A** None.
**Vitamin C** 80 mg.
**Vitamin D** None.
**Vitamin E** Not known.
**Vitamin B1** 0.05 mg.
**Vitamin B2** 0.04 mg.
**Niacin** 0.3 mg.
**Vitamin B6** 0.11 mg.
**Vitamin B12** None.
**Folic acid** 12 µg.
**Pantothenic acid** 0.2 mg.
**Biotin** 0.5 µg.

**Leeks can make very good salad
vegetables and also well flavoured
home-made soups.**

**A slice of lemon will add taste and
vitamin C squeezed onto foods and
drinks.**

# Lentils

**Portion** One-third cup of raw lentils boiled (raw weight 2 oz.).
**Weight** 120 g., about 4¼ oz.

**Food Facts**
Energy 118 kcal.
Protein 9.1 g.
Total fat 0.6 g.
Saturated fat Not known.
Polyunsaturated fat Not known.
Carbohydrate 20.4 g.
Sugars 0.9 g.
Fibre 4.4 g.

**Minerals**
Calcium 15.6 mg.
Iron 2.8 mg.
Zinc 1.2 mg.
Copper 0.22 mg.
Sodium 14.4 mg.
Potassium 252 mg.
Magnesium 30 mg.
Phosphorus 92 mg.

**Vitamins**
Vitamin A 3.9 μg.
Vitamin C None.
Vitamin D None.
Vitamin E Not known.
Vitamin B1 0.13 mg.
Vitamin B2 0.04 mg.
Niacin 0.4 mg.
Vitamin B6 0.13 mg.
Vitamin B12 None.
Folic acid 6 μg.
Pantothenic acid 0.3 mg.
Biotin Not known.

**Add lentils to stews and use less meat. Lentils also make good main course soups.**

# Lettuce

**Portion** One serving of four small leaves.
**Weight** 20 g., about ⅔ oz.

**Food Facts**
Energy 2 kcal.
Protein 0.2 g.
Total fat 0.1 g.
Saturated fat Not known.
Polyunsaturated fat Not known.
Carbohydrate 0.2 g.
Sugars 0.2 g.
Fibre 0.3 g.

**Minerals**
Calcium 4.6 mg.
Iron 0.18 mg.
Zinc 0.04 mg.
Copper 0.01 mg.
Sodium 1.8 mg.
Potassium 48 mg.
Magnesium 1.6 mg.
Phosphorus 5.4 mg.

**Vitamins**
Vitamin A 33.3 μg.
Vitamin C 3 mg.
Vitamin D None.
Vitamin E 0.1 mg.
Vitamin B1 0.01 mg.
Vitamin B2 0.02 mg.
Niacin 0.08 mg.
Vitamin B6 0.01 mg.
Vitamin B12 None.
Folic acid 6.8 μg.
Pantothenic acid None.
Biotin 0.1 μg.

**Put lettuce in sandwiches to add bulk without adding calories.**

# Lychees

**Portion** One tinned lychee without skin or stone.
**Weight** 13 g., about ½ oz.

**Food Facts**
Energy 8 kcal.
Protein 0.1 g.
Total fat None.
Saturated fat None.
Polyunsaturated fat None.
Carbohydrate 2.3 g.
Sugars 2.3 g.
Fibre 0.1 g.

**Minerals**
Calcium 0.5 mg.
Iron 0.09 mg.
Zinc 0.03 mg.
Copper 0.01 mg.
Sodium 0.3 mg.
Potassium 9.8 mg.
Magnesium 0.8 mg.
Phosphorus 1.6 mg.

**Vitamins**
Vitamin A None.
Vitamin C 1.04 mg.
Vitamin D None.
Vitamin E Not known.
Vitamin B1 None.
Vitamin B2 None.
Niacin 0.04 mg.
Vitamin B6 Not known.
Vitamin B12 None.
Folic acid Not known.
Pantothenic acid Not known.
Biotin Not known.

**Tinned or fresh lychees will enhance fruit salads and other puddings.**

# Mandarin oranges

**Portion** Eighteen segments from a tin.
**Weight** 80 g., about 3 oz.

**Food Facts**
Energy 44 kcal.
Protein 0.5 g.
Total fat None.
Saturated fat None.
Polyunsaturated fat None.
Carbohydrate 11.4 g.
Sugars 11.4 g.
Fibre 0.2 g.

**Minerals**
Calcium 14.4 mg.
Iron 0.32 mg.
Zinc 0.32 mg.
Copper 0.04 mg.
Sodium 7.2 mg.
Potassium 70.4 mg.
Magnesium 7.2 mg.
Phosphorus 9.6 mg.

**Vitamins**
Vitamin A 40 µg.
Vitamin C 11.2 mg.
Vitamin D None.
Vitamin E None.
Vitamin B1 0.06 mg.
Vitamin B2 0.02 mg.
Niacin 0.24 mg.
Vitamin B6 0.02 mg.
Vitamin B12 None.
Folic acid 6.4 µg.
Pantothenic acid 0.12 mg.
Biotin 0.64 µg.

**Try to get mandarin oranges canned in natural juice without sugar added. Use them to decorate trifles and cheesecakes.**

# Mango

**Portion** One medium-sized, fresh, raw mango without stone or peel.
**Weight** 160 g., about 5¾ oz.

**Food Facts**
**Energy** 94 kcal.
**Protein** 0.8 g.
**Total fat** None.
**Saturated fat** None.
**Polyunsaturated fat** None.
**Carbohydrate** 24.5 g.
**Sugars** 24.5 g.
**Fibre** 2.4 g.

**Minerals**
**Calcium** 16 mg.
**Iron** 0.8 mg.
**Zinc** 0.75 mg.
**Copper** 0.19 mg.
**Sodium** 11.2 mg.
**Potassium** 304 mg.
**Magnesium** 28.8 mg.
**Phosphorus** 20.8 mg.

**Vitamins**
**Vitamin A** 320 µg.
**Vitamin C** 48 mg.
**Vitamin D** None.
**Vitamin E** Not known.
**Vitamin B1** 0.05 mg.
**Vitamin B2** 0.06 mg.
**Niacin** 0.64 mg.
**Vitamin B6** Not known.
**Vitamin B12** None.
**Folic acid** 0.3 µg.
**Pantothenic acid** 0.25 mg.
**Biotin** Not known.

The yellow colour of the mango makes it high in vitamin A. It also contains a lot of vitamin C.

# Marrow

**Portion** One quarter with skin, without pips.

**Weight** 170 g., about 6 oz.

**Food Facts**
**Energy** 11 kcal.
**Protein** 0.6 g.
**Total fat** None.
**Saturated fat** None.
**Polyunsaturated fat** None.
**Carbohydrate** 2.3 g.
**Sugars** 2.2 g.
**Fibre** 0.9 g.

**Minerals**
**Calcium** 23.8 mg.
**Iron** 0.3 mg.
**Zinc** 0.3 mg.
**Copper** 0.05 mg.
**Sodium** 1.6 mg.
**Potassium** 142 mg.
**Magnesium** 11.9 mg.
**Phosphorus** 22 mg.

**Vitamins**
**Vitamin A** 8.6 µg.
**Vitamin C** 3.4 mg.
**Vitamin D** None.
**Vitamin E** None.
**Vitamin B1** None.
**Vitamin B2** None.
**Niacin** 0.5 mg.
**Vitamin B6** 0.05 mg.
**Vitamin B12** None.
**Folic acid** 10.1 µg.
**Pantothenic acid** 0.15 mg.
**Biotin** Not known.

Try stuffing marrow with beans or lentils instead of meat.

# Melon, canteloupe

**Portion** One slice without skin.

**Weight** 180 g., about 6½ oz.

**Food Facts**
**Energy** 43 kcal.
**Protein** 1.8 g.
**Total fat** None.
**Saturated fat** None.
**Polyunsaturated fat** None.
**Carbohydrate** 9.5 g.
**Sugars** 9.5 g.
**Fibre** 1.8 g.

**Minerals**
**Calcium** 34 mg.
**Iron** 1.4 mg.
**Zinc** 0.18 mg.
**Copper** 0.07 mg.
**Sodium** 25 mg.
**Potassium** 576 mg.
**Magnesium** 36 mg.
**Phosphorus** 54 mg.

**Vitamins**
**Vitamin A** 599 µg.
**Vitamin C** 45 mg.
**Vitamin D** None.
**Vitamin E** 0.18 mg.
**Vitamin B1** 0.09 mg.
**Vitamin B2** 0.05 mg.
**Niacin** 0.9 mg.
**Vitamin B6** 0.12 mg.
**Vitamin B12** None.
**Folic acid** 54 µg.
**Pantothenic acid** 0.41 mg.
**Biotin** Not known.

**Compared to other melons, the canteloupe contains a lot of vitamin A due to its yellow-coloured flesh. A delicious starter.**

# Melon, honey dew

**Portion** One slice without skin.

**Weight** 180 g., about 6½ oz.

**Food Facts**
**Energy** 37 kcal.
**Protein** 1.1 g.
**Total fat** None.
**Saturated fat** None.
**Polyunsaturated fat** None.
**Carbohydrate** 9 g.
**Sugars** 9 g.
**Fibre** 1.6 g.

**Minerals**
**Calcium** 25.2 mg.
**Iron** 0.36 mg.
**Zinc** 0.18 mg.
**Copper** 0.07 mg.
**Sodium** 36 mg.
**Potassium** 396 mg.
**Magnesium** 23.4 mg.
**Phosphorus** 16.2 mg.

**Vitamins**
**Vitamin A** 29.7 µg.
**Vitamin C** 45 mg.
**Vitamin D** None.
**Vitamin E** 0.18 mg.
**Vitamin B1** 0.09 mg.
**Vitamin B2** 0.05 mg.
**Niacin** 0.9 mg.
**Vitamin B6** 0.13 mg.
**Vitamin B12** None.
**Folic acid** 54 µg.
**Pantothenic acid** 0.4 mg.
**Biotin** Not known.

**Honey dew and canteloupe melons are both high in vitamin C and folic acid. Try mixing different kinds of melon together for an unusual desert.**

# Mixed vegetables

**Portion** One tablespoon from frozen packet, boiled.
**Weight** 80 g., about 2¾ oz.

**Food Facts**
**Energy** 33 kcal.
**Protein** 1.7 g.
**Total fat** 0.2 g.
**Saturated fat** Not known.
**Polyunsaturated fat** Not known.
**Carbohydrate** 6.7 g.
**Sugars** 2.4 g.
**Fibre** 2.9 g.

**Minerals**
**Calcium** 20.8 mg.
**Iron** 0.56 mg.
**Zinc** 0.32 mg.
**Copper** 0.08 mg.
**Sodium** 64 mg.
**Potassium** 124 mg.
**Magnesium** 10.4 mg.
**Phosphorus** 32.8 mg.

**Vitamins**
**Vitamin A** 533 µg.
**Vitamin C** 6.4 mg.
**Vitamin D** None.
**Vitamin E** 0.16 mg.
**Vitamin B1** 0.06 mg.
**Vitamin B2** 0.05 mg.
**Niacin** 0.8 mg.
**Vitamin B6** 0.08 mg.
**Vitamin B12** None.
**Folic acid** 17.6 µg.
**Pantothenic acid** 0.16 mg.
**Biotin** None.

**Frozen mixed vegetables are useful if you are in a hurry.**

# Mushrooms, raw

**Portion** One average serving raw.
**Weight** 60 g., about 2 oz.

**Food Facts**
**Energy** 7 kcal.
**Protein** 1.1 g.
**Total fat** 0.4 g.
**Saturated fat** Not known.
**Polyunsaturated fat** Not known.
**Carbohydrate** None.
**Sugars** None.
**Fibre** 1.5 g.

**Minerals**
**Calcium** 1.8 mg.
**Iron** 0.6 mg.
**Zinc** 0.06 mg.
**Copper** 0.38 mg.
**Sodium** 5.4 mg.
**Potassium** 282 mg.
**Magnesium** 7.8 mg.
**Phosphorus** 84 mg.

**Vitamins**
**Vitamin A** None.
**Vitamin C** 1.8 mg.
**Vitamin D** None.
**Vitamin E** None.
**Vitamin B1** 0.06 mg.
**Vitamin B2** 0.24 mg.
**Niacin** 2.76 mg.
**Vitamin B6** 0.06 mg.
**Vitamin B12** None.
**Folic acid** 13.8 µg.
**Pantothenic acid** 1.2 mg.
**Biotin** Not known.

**Try adding raw mushrooms to salads making sure that they are well washed.**

# Mushrooms, fried

**Portion** One average serving fried in butter.
**Weight** 44 g., about 1½ oz.

## Food Facts
**Energy** 92 kcal.
**Protein** 0.96 g.
**Total fat** 9.8 g.
**Saturated fat** 4.7 g.
**Polyunsaturated fat** 0.22 g.
**Carbohydrate** None.
**Sugars** None.
**Fibre** 1.76 g.

## Minerals
**Calcium** 1.76 mg.
**Iron** 0.57 mg.
**Zinc** 0.04 mg.
**Copper** 0.34 mg.
**Sodium** 4.8 mg.
**Potassium** 250 mg.
**Magnesium** 7 mg.
**Phosphorus** 74 mg.

## Vitamins
**Vitamin A** None.
**Vitamin C** 0.44 mg.
**Vitamin D** None.
**Vitamin E** None.
**Vitamin B1** 0.03 mg.
**Vitamin B2** 0.15 mg.
**Niacin** 1.54 mg.
**Vitamin B6** 0.02 mg.
**Vitamin B12** None.
**Folic acid** 8.8 µg.
**Pantothenic acid** 0.61 mg.
**Biotin** Not known.

**Cook mushrooms in other ways, such as poaching, so they retain their low calorie value. Mushrooms weigh less after cooking.**

# Mustard and cress

**Portion** One quarter of a punnet.
**Weight** 10 g., about ⅓ oz.

## Food Facts
**Energy** 1 kcal.
**Protein** 0.2 g.
**Total fat** None.
**Saturated fat** None.
**Polyunsaturated fat** None.
**Carbohydrate** 0.1 g.
**Sugars** 0.1 g.
**Fibre** 0.4 g.

## Minerals
**Calcium** 6.6 mg.
**Iron** 0.1 mg.
**Zinc** Not known.
**Copper** 0.01 mg.
**Sodium** 1.9 mg.
**Potassium** 34 mg.
**Magnesium** 2.7 mg.
**Phosphorus** 6.6 mg.

## Vitamins
**Vitamin A** 50 µg.
**Vitamin C** 4 mg.
**Vitamin D** None.
**Vitamin E** 0.07 mg.
**Vitamin B1** Not known.
**Vitamin B2** Not known.
**Niacin** 0.03 mg.
**Vitamin B6** Not known.
**Vitamin B12** None.
**Folic acid** Not known.
**Pantothenic acid** Not known.
**Biotin** Not known.

**Useful as a low calorie garnish or additional sandwich filling.**

# Nectarine

**Portion** One medium sized without stone.
**Weight** 110 g., about 4 oz.

**Food Facts**
Energy 55 kcal.
Protein 1 g.
Total fat None.
Saturated fat None.
Polyunsaturated fat None.
Carbohydrate 13.6 g.
Sugars 13.6 g.
Fibre 2.6 g.

**Minerals**
Calcium 4.4 mg.
Iron 0.55 mg.
Zinc 0.11 mg.
Copper 0.07 mg.
Sodium 9.9 mg.
Potassium 297 mg.
Magnesium 14.3 mg.
Phosphorus 26.4 mg.

**Vitamins**
Vitamin A 550 µg.
Vitamin C 8.8 mg.
Vitamin D None.
Vitamin E Not known.
Vitamin B1 0.02 mg.
Vitamin B2 0.05 mg.
Niacin 1.21 mg.
Vitamin B6 0.02 mg.
Vitamin B12 None.
Folic acid 5.5 µg.
Pantothenic acid 0.2 mg.
Biotin Not known.

Nectarines make a pleasant change from peaches. Be sure to eat the skin to increase your fibre intake.

# Okra

**Portion** Twelve medium sized raw okra about 2 in. long.
**Weight** 60 g., about 2 oz.

**Food Facts**
Energy 10 kcal.
Protein 1.2 g.
Total fat None.
Saturated fat None.
Polyunsaturated fat None.
Carbohydrate 1.4 g.
Sugars 1.4 g.
Fibre 1.9 g.

**Minerals**
Calcium 42 mg.
Iron 0.6 mg.
Zinc Not known.
Copper 0.11 mg.
Sodium 4.2 mg.
Potassium 114 mg.
Magnesium 36 mg.
Phosphorus 36 mg.

**Vitamins**
Vitamin A 9 µg.
Vitamin C 15 mg.
Vitamin D None.
Vitamin E Not known.
Vitamin B1 0.06 mg.
Vitamin B2 0.06 mg.
Niacin 0.78 mg.
Vitamin B6 0.05 mg.
Vitamin B12 None.
Folic acid 60 µg.
Pantothenic acid 0.2 mg.
Biotin Not known.

Not a traditional English vegetable but becoming increasingly available. Fry using only a little oil.

# Olives

**Portion** Five black olives without stones in brine.
**Weight** 15 g., about ½ oz.

## Food Facts
**Energy** 15 kcal.
**Protein** 0.1 g.
**Total fat** 1.6 g.
**Saturated fat** Not known.
**Polyunsaturated fat** Not known.
**Carbohydrate** None.
**Sugars** None.
**Fibre** 0.7 g.

## Minerals
**Calcium** 9.1 mg.
**Iron** 0.15 mg.
**Zinc** 0.04 mg.
**Copper** 0.03 mg.
**Sodium** 337 mg.
**Potassium** 13.6 mg.
**Magnesium** 3.3 mg.
**Phosphorus** 2.5 mg.

## Vitamins
**Vitamin A** 4.5 µg.
**Vitamin C** None.
**Vitamin D** None.
**Vitamin E** Not known.
**Vitamin B1** None.
**Vitamin B2** None.
**Niacin** 0.1 mg.
**Vitamin B6** None.
**Vitamin B12** None.
**Folic acid** Not known.
**Pantothenic acid** None.
**Biotin** None.

**Olives are quite low in calories so add them to salads and rice dishes for a different taste.**

# Onion, raw

**Portion** One average sized raw onion.
**Weight** 90 g., about 3 oz.

## Food Facts
**Energy** 20 kcal.
**Protein** 0.8 g.
**Total fat** None.
**Saturated fat** None.
**Polyunsaturated fat** None.
**Carbohydrate** 4.7 g.
**Sugars** 4.7 g.
**Fibre** 1.2 g.

## Minerals
**Calcium** 27.9 mg.
**Iron** 0.27 mg.
**Zinc** 0.09 mg.
**Copper** 0.07 mg.
**Sodium** 9 mg.
**Potassium** 126 mg.
**Magnesium** 7.2 mg.
**Phosphorus** 27 mg.

## Vitamins
**Vitamin A** None.
**Vitamin C** 9 mg.
**Vitamin D** None.
**Vitamin E** Not known.
**Vitamin B1** 0.03 mg.
**Vitamin B2** 0.04 mg.
**Niacin** 0.36 mg.
**Vitamin B6** 0.09 mg.
**Vitamin B12** None.
**Folic acid** 14.4 µg.
**Pantothenic acid** 0.1 mg.
**Biotin** 0.8 µg.

**Add small amounts to cottage cheese or salads to increase the flavour.**

# Onion, fried

**Portion** One average sized
onion fried in butter.
**Weight** 57 g., about 2 oz.

**Food Facts**
**Energy** 196 kcal.
**Protein** 1.02 g.
**Total fat** 18.9 g.
**Saturated fat** 9.3 g.
**Polyunsaturated fat** 0.38 g.
**Carbohydrate** 5.7 g.
**Sugars** 5.7 g.
**Fibre** Not known.

**Minerals**
**Calcium** 34.5 mg.
**Iron** 0.33 mg.
**Zinc** 0.04 mg.
**Copper** 0.09 mg.
**Sodium** 11.4 mg.
**Potassium** 153 mg.
**Magnesium** 8.5 mg.
**Phosphorus** 33.6 mg.

**Vitamins**
**Vitamin A** None.
**Vitamin C** Not known.
**Vitamin D** None.
**Vitamin E** None.
**Vitamin B1** Not known.
**Vitamin B2** Not known.
**Niacin** 0.22 mg.
**Vitamin B6** Not known.
**Vitamin B12** None.
**Folic acid** Not known.
**Pantothenic acid** Not known.
**Biotin** Not known.

Contrast the calorie value and other
nutrients with that of raw onion.
Most vegetables are low in calories
until you fry them.

# Orange

**Portion** One medium sized,
peeled.
**Weight** 140 g., about 5 oz.

**Food Facts**
**Energy** 49 kcal.
**Protein** 1.1 g.
**Total fat** None.
**Saturated fat** None.
**Polyunsaturated fat** None.
**Carbohydrate** 11.9 g.
**Sugars** 11.9 g.
**Fibre** 2.8 g.

**Minerals**
**Calcium** 57.4 mg.
**Iron** 0.42 mg.
**Zinc** 0.28 mg.
**Copper** 0.1 mg.
**Sodium** 4.2 mg.
**Potassium** 280 mg.
**Magnesium** 18.2 mg.
**Phosphorus** 33.6 mg.

**Vitamins**
**Vitamin A** 11.9 µg.
**Vitamin C** 70 mg.
**Vitamin D** None.
**Vitamin E** 0.28 mg.
**Vitamin B1** 0.14 mg.
**Vitamin B2** 0.04 mg.
**Niacin** 0.42 mg.
**Vitamin B6** 0.08 mg.
**Vitamin B12** None.
**Folic acid** 51.8 µg.
**Pantothenic acid** 0.3 mg.
**Biotin** 1.4 µg.

One orange contains twice the UK
recommended daily intake of
vitamin C.

# Parsley

## Parsnips

**Portion** One sprig.

**Weight** 2 g., about ¹⁄₁₄ oz.

**Portion** One medium sized, peeled.

**Weight** 120 g., about 4 oz.

### Food Facts
**Energy** None.
**Protein** 0.1 g.
**Total fat** None.
**Saturated fat** None.
**Polyunsaturated fat** None.
**Carbohydrate** None.
**Sugars** None.
**Fibre** 0.2 g.

### Food Facts
**Energy** 67 kcal.
**Protein** 1.6 g.
**Total fat** None.
**Saturated fat** None.
**Polyunsaturated fat** None.
**Carbohydrate** 16.2 g.
**Sugars** 3.2 g.
**Fibre** 3 g.

### Minerals
**Calcium** 6.6 mg.
**Iron** 0.16 mg.
**Zinc** 0.02 mg.
**Copper** 0.01 mg.
**Sodium** 0.7 mg.
**Potassium** 21.6 mg.
**Magnesium** 1 mg.
**Phosphorus** 2.6 mg.

### Minerals
**Calcium** 43.2 mg.
**Iron** 0.6 mg.
**Zinc** 0.12 mg.
**Copper** 0.12 mg.
**Sodium** 4.8 mg.
**Potassium** 348 mg.
**Magnesium** 15.6 mg.
**Phosphorus** 38.4 mg.

### Vitamins
**Vitamin A** 23 µg.
**Vitamin C** 3 mg.
**Vitamin D** None.
**Vitamin E** 0.04 mg.
**Vitamin B1** None.
**Vitamin B2** 0.01 mg.
**Niacin** 0.04 mg.
**Vitamin B6** None.
**Vitamin B12** None.
**Folic acid** Not known.
**Pantothenic acid** None.
**Biotin** None.

### Vitamins
**Vitamin A** None.
**Vitamin C** 12 mg.
**Vitamin D** None.
**Vitamin E** 1.2 mg.
**Vitamin B1** 0.08 mg.
**Vitamin B2** 0.07 mg.
**Niacin** 1.08 mg.
**Vitamin B6** 0.07 mg.
**Vitamin B12** None.
**Folic acid** 36 µg.
**Pantothenic acid** 0.4 mg.
**Biotin** None.

**Parsley adds colour to many dishes and flavour to sauces.**

**Instead of roasting your parsnips try steaming them next time you have a Sunday roast.**

# Passion Fruit

**Portion** One average sized, flesh and seeds only.
**Weight** 15 g., about ½ oz.

**Food Facts**
**Energy** 5 kcal.
**Protein** 0.4 g.
**Total fat** None.
**Saturated fat** None.
**Polyunsaturated fat** None.
**Carbohydrate** 0.9 g.
**Sugars** 0.9 g.
**Fibre** 2.4 g.

**Minerals**
**Calcium** 2.4 mg.
**Iron** 0.16 mg.
**Zinc** Not known.
**Copper** 0.02 mg.
**Sodium** 4.2 mg.
**Potassium** 52.5 mg.
**Magnesium** 5.8 mg.
**Phosphorus** 8.1 mg.

**Vitamins**
**Vitamin A** 0.2 µg.
**Vitamin C** 3 mg.
**Vitamin D** None.
**Vitamin E** Not known.
**Vitamin B1** None.
**Vitamin B2** 0.01 mg.
**Niacin** 0.28 mg.
**Vitamin B6** Not known.
**Vitamin B12** None.
**Folic acid** Not known.
**Pantothenic acid** Not known.
**Biotin** Not known.

The flesh of a passion fruit is mostly seeds so it is high in fibre. Add just one to any fruit dish for a distinctive flavour.

# Peach, fresh

**Portion** One medium sized without stone.
**Weight** 110 g., about 4 oz.

**Food Facts**
**Energy** 40 kcal.
**Protein** 0.7 g.
**Total fat** None.
**Saturated fat** None.
**Polyunsaturated fat** None.
**Carbohydrate** 10 g.
**Sugars** 10 g.
**Fibre** 1.5 g.

**Minerals**
**Calcium** 5.5 mg.
**Iron** 0.44 mg.
**Zinc** 0.11 mg.
**Copper** 0.05 mg.
**Sodium** 3.3 mg.
**Potassium** 286 mg.
**Magnesium** 8.8 mg.
**Phosphorus** 20.9 mg.

**Vitamins**
**Vitamin A** 91.8 µg.
**Vitamin C** 8.8 mg.
**Vitamin D** None.
**Vitamin E** Not known.
**Vitamin B1** 0.02 mg.
**Vitamin B2** 0.05 mg.
**Niacin** 1.1 mg.
**Vitamin B6** 0.02 mg.
**Vitamin B12** None.
**Folic acid** 3.3 µg.
**Pantothenic acid** 0.2 mg.
**Biotin** 0.2 µg.

In the summer, eat fresh peaches or serve chilled in medium or sweet wine with a spot of honey for extra flavour.

# Peaches, tinned

**Portion** One small bowlful of ten slices.
**Weight** 105 g., about 3¾ oz.

**Food Facts**
**Energy** 91 kcal.
**Protein** 0.4 g.
**Total fat** None.
**Saturated fat** None.
**Polyunsaturated fat** None.
**Carbohydrate** 24 g.
**Sugars** 24 g.
**Fibre** 1 g.

**Minerals**
**Calcium** 4.2 mg.
**Iron** 0.42 mg.
**Zinc** 0.1 mg.
**Copper** 0.06 mg.
**Sodium** 1 mg.
**Potassium** 157 mg.
**Magnesium** 6.3 mg.
**Phosphorus** 10.5 mg.

**Vitamins**
**Vitamin A** 43.6 µg.
**Vitamin C** 4.2 mg.
**Vitamin D** None.
**Vitamin E** Not known.
**Vitamin B1** 0.01 mg.
**Vitamin B2** 0.02 mg.
**Niacin** 0.63 mg.
**Vitamin B6** 0.02 mg.
**Vitamin B12** None.
**Folic acid** 3.1 µg.
**Pantothenic acid** 0.1 mg.
**Biotin** 0.2 µg.

If you eat tinned peaches regularly, try those tinned in natural juice with no added sugar. They cost a few pence more but are much tastier.

# Peanuts, salted

**Portion** One small bag containing about 25 whole nuts.
**Weight** 25 g., about 1 oz.

**Food Facts**
**Energy** 142 kcal.
**Protein** 6.1 g.
**Total fat** 12.2 g.
**Saturated fat** 2.6 g.
**Polyunsaturated fat** 3.4 g.
**Carbohydrate** 2.1 g.
**Sugars** 0.8 g.
**Fibre** 2 g.

**Minerals**
**Calcium** 15.2 mg.
**Iron** 0.5 mg.
**Zinc** 0.75 mg.
**Copper** 0.07 mg.
**Sodium** 110 mg.
**Potassium** 170 mg.
**Magnesium** 45 mg.
**Phosphorus** 92 mg.

**Vitamins**
**Vitamin A** None.
**Vitamin C** None.
**Vitamin D** None.
**Vitamin E** 2.02 mg.
**Vitamin B1** 0.06 mg.
**Vitamin B2** 0.02 mg.
**Niacin** 5.32 mg.
**Vitamin B6** 0.1 mg.
**Vitamin B12** None.
**Folic acid** Not known.
**Pantothenic acid** 0.5 mg.
**Biotin** Not known.

Salted peanuts are very high in calories and salt.

# Peanut butter

**Portion** Thickly spread to cover one slice of bread.
**Weight** 15 g., about ½ oz.

**Food Facts**
**Energy** 93 kcal.
**Protein** 3.4 g.
**Total fat** 8.1 g.
**Saturated fat** 1.5 g.
**Polyunsaturated fat** 2 g.
**Carbohydrate** 2 g.
**Sugars** 1 g.
**Fibre** 1.1 g.

**Minerals**
**Calcium** 5.5 mg.
**Iron** 0.31 mg.
**Zinc** 0.45 mg.
**Copper** 0.1 mg.
**Sodium** 52.5 mg.
**Potassium** 105 mg.
**Magnesium** 27 mg.
**Phosphorus** 49.5 mg.

**Vitamins**
**Vitamin A** None.
**Vitamin C** None.
**Vitamin D** None.
**Vitamin E** 0.7 mg.
**Vitamin B1** 0.03 mg.
**Vitamin B2** 0.01 mg.
**Niacin** 2.98 mg.
**Vitamin B6** 0.07 mg.
**Vitamin B12** None.
**Folic acid** 7.9 µg.
**Pantothenic acid** 0.3 mg.
**Biotin** Not known.

**Peanut butter is very high in calories and should be used as sparingly as jam. An alternative to cheese.**

# Pear

**Portion** One medium sized without core.
**Weight** 150 g., about 5¼ oz.

**Food Facts**
**Energy** 61 kcal.
**Protein** 0.4 g.
**Total fat** None.
**Saturated fat** None.
**Polyunsaturated fat** None.
**Carbohydrate** 15.9 g.
**Sugars** 15.9 g.
**Fibre** 3.4 g.

**Minerals**
**Calcium** 12 mg.
**Iron** 0.3 mg.
**Zinc** 0.15 mg.
**Copper** 0.22 mg.
**Sodium** 3 mg.
**Potassium** 195 mg.
**Magnesium** 10.5 mg.
**Phosphorus** 15 mg.

**Vitamins**
**Vitamin A** 2.2 µg.
**Vitamin C** 4.5 mg.
**Vitamin D** None.
**Vitamin E** None.
**Vitamin B1** 0.04 mg.
**Vitamin B2** 0.04 mg.
**Niacin** 0.3 mg.
**Vitamin B6** 0.03 mg.
**Vitamin B12** None.
**Folic acid** 16.5 µg.
**Pantothenic acid** 0.1 mg.
**Biotin** 0.1 µg.

**Many people think pears are high in calories but they only contain a few more than an apple or orange and are also quite high in fibre.**

# Peas, frozen

**Portion** One average
tablespoon serving, boiled.
**Weight** 80 g., about 2¾ oz.

**Food Facts**
**Energy** 32 kcal.
**Protein** 4.3 g.
**Total fat** 0.3 g.
**Saturated fat** Not known.
**Polyunsaturated fat** Not known.
**Carbohydrate** 3.4 g.
**Sugars** 0.8 g.
**Fibre** 9.6 g.

**Minerals**
**Calcium** 24.8 mg.
**Iron** 1.12 mg.
**Zinc** 0.56 mg.
**Copper** 0.15 mg.
**Sodium** 1.6 mg.
**Potassium** 104 mg.
**Magnesium** 18.4 mg.
**Phosphorus** 67.2 mg.

**Vitamins**
**Vitamin A** 40 µg.
**Vitamin C** 10.4 mg.
**Vitamin D** None.
**Vitamin E** None.
**Vitamin B1** 0.19 mg.
**Vitamin B2** 0.06 mg.
**Niacin** 1.92 mg.
**Vitamin B6** 0.06 mg.
**Vitamin B12** None.
**Folic acid** 62.4 µg.
**Pantothenic acid** 0.3 mg.
**Biotin** 0.3 µg.

Adding peas to stews and
casseroles will help to increase the
fibre content.

# Peas, tinned

**Portion** One average serving
of a tablespoon.
**Weight** 85 g., about 3 oz.

**Food Facts**
**Energy** 39 kcal.
**Protein** 3.9 g.
**Total fat** 0.3 g.
**Saturated fat** Not known.
**Polyunsaturated fat** Not known.
**Carbohydrate** 5.9 g.
**Sugars** 3.1 g.
**Fibre** 5.4 g.

**Minerals**
**Calcium** 20.4 mg.
**Iron** 1.36 mg.
**Zinc** 0.59 mg.
**Copper** 0.14 mg.
**Sodium** 195 mg.
**Potassium** 110 mg.
**Magnesium** 14.4 mg.
**Phosphorus** 62 mg.

**Vitamins**
**Vitamin A** 42.5 µg.
**Vitamin C** 6.8 mg.
**Vitamin D** None.
**Vitamin E** None.
**Vitamin B1** 0.11 mg.
**Vitamin B2** 0.08 mg.
**Niacin** 2.38 mg.
**Vitamin B6** 0.05 mg.
**Vitamin B12** None.
**Folic acid** 44.2 µg.
**Pantothenic acid** 0.1 mg.
**Biotin** 0.3 µg.

Tinned peas not only have added
sugar but also contain less fibre
than frozen or fresh peas.

# Pepper, green

**Portion** Half a medium sized pepper.
**Weight** 80 g., about 3 oz.

**Food Facts**
**Energy** 12 kcal.
**Protein** 0.7 g.
**Total fat** 0.3 g.
**Saturated fat** Not known.
**Polyunsaturated fat** Not known.
**Carbohydrate** 1.8 g.
**Sugars** 1.8 g.
**Fibre** 0.7 g.

**Minerals**
**Calcium** 7.2 mg.
**Iron** 0.3 mg.
**Zinc** 0.16 mg.
**Copper** 0.06 mg.
**Sodium** 1.6 mg.
**Potassium** 168 mg.
**Magnesium** 8.8 mg.
**Phosphorus** 20 mg.

**Vitamins**
**Vitamin A** 26.8 µg.
**Vitamin C** 80 mg.
**Vitamin D** None.
**Vitamin E** 0.64 mg.
**Vitamin B1** None.
**Vitamin B2** 0.02 mg.
**Niacin** 0.72 mg.
**Vitamin B6** 0.14 mg.
**Vitamin B12** None.
**Folic acid** 8.8 µg.
**Pantothenic acid** 0.2 mg.
**Biotin** Not known.

**Red peppers are sweeter than green so contain a few more calories. Both are nutritious and rich in vitamin C.**

# Pineapple, fresh

**Portion** One large slice fresh pineapple.
**Weight** 80 g., about 3 oz.

**Food Facts**
**Energy** 36 kcal.
**Protein** 0.4 g.
**Total fat** None.
**Saturated fat** None.
**Polyunsaturated fat** None.
**Carbohydrate** 9.28 g.
**Sugars** 9.28 g.
**Fibre** 0.96 g.

**Minerals**
**Calcium** 9.6 mg.
**Iron** 0.32 mg.
**Zinc** 0.08 mg.
**Copper** 0.06 mg.
**Sodium** 1.6 mg.
**Potassium** 200 mg.
**Magnesium** 13.6 mg.
**Phosphorus** 6.4 mg.

**Vitamins**
**Vitamin A** 8 µg.
**Vitamin C** 20 mg.
**Vitamin D** None.
**Vitamin E** Not known.
**Vitamin B1** 0.06 mg.
**Vitamin B2** 0.01 mg.
**Niacin** 0.16 mg.
**Vitamin B6** 0.07 mg.
**Vitamin B12** None.
**Folic acid** 8.8 µg.
**Pantothenic acid** 0.12 mg.
**Biotin** None.

**Fresh pineapple is much lower in calories than most tinned pineapple or pineapple juice.**

# Pineapple, tinned

# Plantain

**Portion** Two pineapple rings.

**Weight** 80 g., about 3 oz.

## Food Facts
**Energy** 61 kcal.
**Protein** 0.2 g.
**Total fat** None.
**Saturated fat** None.
**Polyunsaturated fat** None.
**Carbohydrate** 16.2 g.
**Sugars** 16.2 g.
**Fibre** 0.7 g.

## Minerals
**Calcium** 10.4 mg.
**Iron** 0.32 mg.
**Zinc** 0.06 mg.
**Copper** 0.04 mg.
**Sodium** 0.8 mg.
**Potassium** 75.2 mg.
**Magnesium** 6.4 mg.
**Phosphorus** 4 mg.

## Vitamins
**Vitamin A** 5.2 µg.
**Vitamin C** 9.6 mg.
**Vitamin D** None.
**Vitamin E** Not known.
**Vitamin B1** 0.04 mg.
**Vitamin B2** 0.02 mg.
**Niacin** 0.16 mg.
**Vitamin B6** 0.06 mg.
**Vitamin B12** None.
**Folic acid** 8.8 µg.
**Pantothenic acid** 0.1 mg.
**Biotin** None.

**Tinned pineapple with added sugar contains half as much vitamin C as fresh pineapple and often twice as much sugar (look at the label).**

**Portion** One whole boiled, without skin.

**Weight** 140 g., about 5 oz.

## Food Facts
**Energy** 170 kcal.
**Protein** 1.4 g.
**Total fat** 0.1 g.
**Saturated fat** Not known.
**Polyunsaturated fat** Not known.
**Carbohydrate** 43.5 g.
**Sugars** 1.3 g.
**Fibre** 9 g.

## Minerals
**Calcium** 12.6 mg.
**Iron** 0.56 mg.
**Zinc** 0.28 mg.
**Copper** 0.14 mg.
**Sodium** 5.6 mg.
**Potassium** 4.62 mg.
**Magnesium** 47.6 mg.
**Phosphorus** 47.6 mg.

## Vitamins
**Vitamin A** 14 µg.
**Vitamin C** 4.2 mg.
**Vitamin D** None.
**Vitamin E** Not known.
**Vitamin B1** None.
**Vitamin B2** 0.01 mg.
**Niacin** 0.7 mg.
**Vitamin B6** 0.42 mg.
**Vitamin B12** None.
**Folic acid** 25.2 µg.
**Pantothenic acid** 0.4 mg.
**Biotin** Not known.

**A high fibre addition to stews and casseroles. Frying them increases the calories.**

# Plum

# Potato chips

**Portion** One eating plum without stone.
**Weight** 35 g., about 1¼ oz.

**Portion** One average fish and chip shop portion.
**Weight** 260 g., about 9¼ oz.

**Food Facts**
**Energy** 13 kcal.
**Protein** 0.2 g.
**Total fat** None.
**Saturated fat** None.
**Polyunsaturated fat** None.
**Carbohydrate** 3.4 g.
**Sugars** 3.4 g.
**Fibre** 0.7 g.

**Food Facts**
**Energy** 657 kcal.
**Protein** 9.9 g.
**Total fat** 28.3 g.
**Saturated fat** 4.6 g.
**Polyunsaturated fat** 13.9 g.
**Carbohydrate** 97 g.
**Sugars** Not known.
**Fibre** Not known.

**Minerals**
**Calcium** 3.8 mg.
**Iron** 0.14 mg.
**Zinc** None.
**Copper** 0.03 mg.
**Sodium** 0.7 mg.
**Potassium** 66.5 mg.
**Magnesium** 2.4 mg.
**Phosphorus** 5.6 mg.

**Minerals**
**Calcium** 36.4 mg.
**Iron** 2.34 mg.
**Zinc** 1.56 mg.
**Copper** 0.7 mg.
**Sodium** 31.2 mg.
**Potassium** 2,652 mg.
**Magnesium** 111 mg.
**Phosphorus** 187 mg.

**Vitamins**
**Vitamin A** 12.8 µg.
**Vitamin C** 1.05 mg.
**Vitamin D** None.
**Vitamin E** 0.24 mg.
**Vitamin B1** 0.02 mg.
**Vitamin B2** 0.01 mg.
**Niacin** 0.21 mg.
**Vitamin B6** 0.02 mg.
**Vitamin B12** None.
**Folic acid** 1 µg.
**Pantothenic acid** 0.1 mg.
**Biotin** None.

**Vitamins**
**Vitamin A** None.
**Vitamin C** 26 mg.
**Vitamin D** None.
**Vitamin E** 0.26 mg.
**Vitamin B1** 0.26 mg.
**Vitamin B2** 0.1 mg.
**Niacin** 5.4 mg.
**Vitamin B6** 0.47 mg.
**Vitamin B12** None.
**Folic acid** 26 µg.
**Pantothenic acid** 0.5 mg.
**Biotin** None.

**Plums are low in calories and so are good to eat in between meals if you are trying to lose weight.**

**Only eat chips occasionally. It is better to cook them yourself in oil that is only used a few times.**

# Potato crisps

**Portion** One small bag.

**Weight** 30 g., about 1 oz.

**Food Facts**
Energy 159 kcal.
Protein 1.9 g.
Total fat 10.8 g.
Saturated fat Not known.
Polyunsaturated fat Not known.
Carbohydrate 14.8 g.
Sugars 0.2 g.
Fibre 3.5 g.

**Minerals**
Calcium 11.1 mg.
Iron 0.63 mg.
Zinc 0.24 mg.
Copper 0.07 mg.
Sodium 165 mg.
Potassium 357 mg.
Magnesium 16.8 mg.
Phosphorus 39 mg.

**Vitamins**
Vitamin A None.
Vitamin C 5.1 mg.
Vitamin D None.
Vitamin E 1.83 mg.
Vitamin B1 0.06 mg.
Vitamin B2 0.02 mg.
Niacin 1.83 mg.
Vitamin B6 0.27 mg.
Vitamin B12 None.
Folic acid 6 µg.
Pantothenic acid Not known.
Biotin Not known.

**A raw carrot provides as much fibre and a lot less calories than a bag of crisps.**

# Potato salad

**Portion** One tablespoon, fresh or tinned.

**Weight** 100 g., about 3½ oz.

**Food Facts**
Energy 133 kcal.
Protein 1.3 g.
Total fat 8.3 g.
Saturated fat Not known.
Polyunsaturated fat Not known.
Carbohydrate 14.4 g.
Sugars 4.2 g.
Fibre 0.5 g.

**Minerals**
Calcium 12 mg.
Iron 0.4 mg.
Zinc 0.1 mg.
Copper 0.08 mg.
Sodium 254 mg.
Potassium 189 mg.
Magnesium 14 mg.
Phosphorus 42 mg.

**Vitamins**
Vitamin A Not known.
Vitamin C 4 mg.
Vitamin D Not known.
Vitamin E Not known.
Vitamin B1 0.04 mg.
Vitamin B2 0.02 mg.
Niacin 0.4 mg.
Vitamin B6 0.09 mg.
Vitamin B12 None.
Folic acid 5 µg.
Pantothenic acid 0.1 mg.
Biotin None.

**Try making a lower calorie, lower fat potato salad by mixing half mayonnaise with half plain yoghurt.**

# Potatoes, boiled

**Portion** Two medium sized, peeled potatoes.
**Weight** 200 g., about 7 oz.

**Food Facts**
**Energy** 160 kcal.
**Protein** 2.8 g.
**Total fat** 0.2 g.
**Saturated fat** Not known.
**Polyunsaturated fat** Not known.
**Carbohydrate** 39.4 g.
**Sugars** 0.8 g.
**Fibre** 2 g.

**Minerals**
**Calcium** 8 mg.
**Iron** 0.6 mg.
**Zinc** 0.4 mg.
**Copper** 0.22 mg.
**Sodium** 6 mg.
**Potassium** 600 mg.
**Magnesium** 30 mg.
**Phosphorus** 58 mg.

**Vitamins**
**Vitamin A** None.
**Vitamin C** 18 mg.
**Vitamin D** None.
**Vitamin E** 0.2 mg.
**Vitamin B1** 0.16 mg.
**Vitamin B2** 0.06 mg.
**Niacin** 2.2 mg.
**Vitamin B6** 0.36 mg.
**Vitamin B12** None.
**Folic acid** 20 µg.
**Pantothenic acid** 0.4 mg.
**Biotin** None.

**In the summer, boil new potatoes in their jackets for extra fibre.**

# Potatoes, jacket

**Portion** Two medium sized potatoes including skin.
**Weight** 260 g., about 9¼ oz.

**Food Facts**
**Energy** 221 kcal.
**Protein** 5.5 g.
**Total fat** 0.3 g.
**Saturated fat** Not known.
**Polyunsaturated fat** Not known.
**Carbohydrate** 52.8 g.
**Sugars** 1.3 g.
**Fibre** 5.2 g.

**Minerals**
**Calcium** 20.8 mg.
**Iron** 1.56 mg.
**Zinc** 0.52 mg.
**Copper** 0.39 mg.
**Sodium** 15.6 mg.
**Potassium** 1,430 mg.
**Magnesium** 62.4 mg.
**Phosphorus** 101 mg.

**Vitamins**
**Vitamin A** None.
**Vitamin C** 20.8 mg.
**Vitamin D** None.
**Vitamin E** 0.26 mg.
**Vitamin B1** 0.21 mg.
**Vitamin B2** 0.08 mg.
**Niacin** 3.9 mg.
**Vitamin B6** 0.36 mg.
**Vitamin B12** None.
**Folic acid** 20.8 µg.
**Pantothenic acid** 0.4 mg.
**Biotin** None.

**A nutritious and convenient snack as well as an addition to a main meal.**

# Potatoes, roasted

**Portion** Two medium sized, peeled and roasted in lard.
**Weight** 200 g., about 7 oz.

**Food Facts**
Energy 314 kcal.
Protein 5.6 g.
Total fat 9.6 g.
Saturated fat 4 g.
Polyunsaturated fat 0.8 g.
Carbohydrate 54.6 g.
Sugars Not known.
Fibre Not known.

**Minerals**
Calcium 20 mg.
Iron 1.4 mg.
Zinc 0.8 mg.
Copper 0.4 mg.
Sodium 18 mg.
Potassium 1,500 mg.
Magnesium 64 mg.
Phosphorus 106 mg.

**Vitamins**
Vitamin A None.
Vitamin C 20 mg.
Vitamin D None.
Vitamin E 0.2 mg.
Vitamin B1 0.2 mg.
Vitamin B2 0.08 mg.
Niacin 3.8 mg.
Vitamin B6 0.36 mg.
Vitamin B12 None.
Folic acid 14 µg.
Pantothenic acid 0.4 mg.
Biotin None.

**For a change try a jacket potato with your Sunday roast.**

# Prunes

**Portion** Six prunes without stones stewed without sugar.
**Weight** 35 g., about 1¼ oz.

**Food Facts**
Energy 28 kcal.
Protein 0.5 g.
Total fat None.
Saturated fat None.
Polyunsaturated fat None.
Carbohydrate 7.1 g.
Sugars 7.1 g.
Fibre 2.8 g.

**Minerals**
Calcium 6.6 mg.
Iron 0.49 mg.
Zinc 0.11 mg.
Copper 0.03 mg.
Sodium 2.4 mg.
Potassium 154 mg.
Magnesium 4.5 mg.
Phosphorus 14.7 mg.

**Vitamins**
Vitamin A 29.7 µg.
Vitamin C None.
Vitamin D None.
Vitamin E Not known.
Vitamin B1 0.01 mg.
Vitamin B2 0.03 mg.
Niacin 0.35 mg.
Vitamin B6 0.03 mg.
Vitamin B12 None.
Folic acid None.
Pantothenic acid 0.1 mg.
Biotin None.

**Prunes stewed without sugar are good to add to many different types of breakfast cereals.**

# Radishes

**Portion** Three medium radishes.
**Weight** 30 g., about 1 oz.

**Food Facts**
**Energy** 4 kcal.
**Protein** 0.3 g.
**Total fat** None.
**Saturated fat** None.
**Polyunsaturated fat** None.
**Carbohydrate** 0.8 g.
**Sugars** 0.8 g.
**Fibre** 0.3 g.

**Minerals**
**Calcium** 13.2 mg.
**Iron** 0.57 mg.
**Zinc** 0.03 mg.
**Copper** 0.04 mg.
**Sodium** 17.7 mg.
**Potassium** 72 mg.
**Magnesium** 3.3 mg.
**Phosphorus** 8.1 mg.

**Vitamins**
**Vitamin A** None.
**Vitamin C** 7.5 mg.
**Vitamin D** None.
**Vitamin E** None.
**Vitamin B1** 0.01 mg.
**Vitamin B2** 0.01 mg.
**Niacin** 0.12 mg.
**Vitamin B6** 0.03 mg.
**Vitamin B12** None.
**Folic acid** 7.2 µg.
**Pantothenic acid** 0.1 mg.
**Biotin** Not known.

An attractive and colourful addition to any salad.

# Raisins

**Portion** One handful of about thirty raisins.
**Weight** 15 g., about ½ oz.

**Food Facts**
**Energy** 36 kcal.
**Protein** 0.2 g.
**Total fat** None.
**Saturated fat** None.
**Polyunsaturated fat** None.
**Carbohydrate** 9.7 g.
**Sugars** 9.7 g.
**Fibre** 1 g.

**Minerals**
**Calcium** 9.1 mg.
**Iron** 0.24 mg.
**Zinc** 0.01 mg.
**Copper** 0.04 mg.
**Sodium** 7.8 mg.
**Potassium** 129 mg.
**Magnesium** 6.3 mg.
**Phosphorus** 4.9 mg.

**Vitamins**
**Vitamin A** 0.7 µg.
**Vitamin C** None.
**Vitamin D** None.
**Vitamin E** Not known.
**Vitamin B1** 0.01 mg.
**Vitamin B2** 0.01 mg.
**Niacin** 0.09 mg.
**Vitamin B6** 0.04 mg.
**Vitamin B12** None.
**Folic acid** 0.6 µg.
**Pantothenic acid** None.
**Biotin** Not known.

Like other dried fruit raisins contain a lot of natural sugar. However they are an alternative to sweets for children.

# Raspberries

**Portion** Twenty-three raspberries.

**Weight** 75 g., about 3 oz.

**Food Facts**
Energy 18 kcal.
Protein 0.7 g.
Total fat None.
Saturated fat None.
Polyunsaturated fat None.
Carbohydrate 4.2 g.
Sugars 4.2 g.
Fibre 5.5 g.

**Minerals**
Calcium 30.7 mg.
Iron 0.9 mg.
Zinc Not known.
Copper 0.16 mg.
Sodium 2.2 mg.
Potassium 165 mg.
Magnesium 16.5 mg.
Phosphorus 21.7 mg.

**Vitamins**
Vitamin A 10.1 µg.
Vitamin C 18.7 mg.
Vitamin D None.
Vitamin E 0.22 mg.
Vitamin B1 0.01 mg.
Vitamin B2 0.02 mg.
Niacin 0.37 mg.
Vitamin B6 0.04 mg.
Vitamin B12 None.
Folic acid Not known.
Pantothenic acid 0.2 mg.
Biotin 1.4 µg.

**Raspberries are high in fibre. Add them to your breakfast cereals in the summer as well as to puddings.**

# Ratatouille

**Portion** Two large tablespoons or half a tin.

**Weight** 200 g., about 7 oz.

**Food Facts**
Energy 152 kcal.
Protein 1.8 g.
Total fat 12.8 g.
Saturated fat Not known.
Polyunsaturated fat Not known.
Carbohydrate 7.8 g.
Sugars 7.4 g.
Fibre 4.2 g.

**Minerals**
Calcium 34 mg.
Iron 0.8 mg.
Zinc 0.2 mg.
Copper 0.18 mg.
Sodium 390 mg.
Potassium 536 mg.
Magnesium 28 mg.
Phosphorus 46 mg.

**Vitamins**
Vitamin A 61 µg.
Vitamin C 10 mg.
Vitamin D None.
Vitamin E 0.8 mg.
Vitamin B1 0.08 mg.
Vitamin B2 0.06 mg.
Niacin 1.8 mg.
Vitamin B6 0.22 mg.
Vitamin B12 None.
Folic acid 44 µg.
Pantothenic acid 0.4 mg.
Biotin None.

**When properly made without too much fat, this is a tasty and relatively low calorie vegetable dish.**

# Rhubarb

**Portion** One serving stewed
without sugar. Raw weight
½ lb. before trimming.
**Weight** 150 g., about 4¼ oz.

**Food Facts**
**Energy** 9 kcal.
**Protein** 0.9 g.
**Total fat** None.
**Saturated fat** None.
**Polyunsaturated fat** None.
**Carbohydrate** 1.35 g.
**Sugars** 1.35 g.
**Fibre** 3.6 g.

**Minerals**
**Calcium** 139 mg.
**Iron** 0.6 mg.
**Zinc** 0.16 mg.
**Copper** 0.18 mg.
**Sodium** 3 mg.
**Potassium** 600 mg.
**Magnesium** 19.5 mg.
**Phosphorus** 28 mg.

**Vitamins**
**Vitamin A** 13.7 µg.
**Vitamin C** 12 mg.
**Vitamin D** None.
**Vitamin E** 0.3 mg.
**Vitamin B1** None.
**Vitamin B2** 0.04 mg.
**Niacin** 0.45 mg.
**Vitamin B6** 0.03 mg.
**Vitamin B12** None.
**Folic acid** 6 µg.
**Pantothenic acid** 0.09 mg.
**Biotin** Not known.

**Rhubarb makes an excellent low
calorie high-fibre dessert. Don't just
use it in crumbles and pies, eat on
its own or with plain yoghurt.**

# Runner beans

**Portion** Two tablespoons,
cooked.
**Weight** 100 g., about 3½ oz.

**Food Facts**
**Energy** 19 kcal.
**Protein** 1.9 g.
**Total fat** 0.2 g.
**Saturated fat** Not known.
**Polyunsaturated fat** Not known.
**Carbohydrate** 2.7 g.
**Sugars** 1.3 g.
**Fibre** 3.4 g.

**Minerals**
**Calcium** 22 mg.
**Iron** 0.7 mg.
**Zinc** 0.3 mg.
**Copper** 0.05 mg.
**Sodium** 1 mg.
**Potassium** 150 mg.
**Magnesium** 17 mg.
**Phosphorus** 41 mg.

**Vitamins**
**Vitamin A** 00.5 µg.
**Vitamin C** 5 mg.
**Vitamin D** None.
**Vitamin E** 0.2 mg.
**Vitamin B1** 0.03 mg.
**Vitamin B2** 0.07 mg.
**Niacin** 0.8 mg.
**Vitamin B6** 0.04 mg.
**Vitamin B12** None.
**Folic acid** 28 µg.
**Pantothenic acid** None.
**Biotin** 0.5 µg.

**Runner beans, like many
vegetables, are very low in calories.**

# Spinach

# Spring greens

**Portion** One average serving of a heaped tablespoon.
**Weight** 100 g., about 3½ oz.

**Food Facts**
**Energy** 30 kcal.
**Protein** 5.1 g.
**Total fat** 0.5 g.
**Saturated fat** Not known.
**Polyunsaturated fat** Not known.
**Carbohydrate** 1.4 g.
**Sugars** 1.2 g.
**Fibre** 6.3 g.

**Minerals**
**Calcium** 600 mg.
**Iron** 4 mg.
**Zinc** 0.4 mg.
**Copper** 0.26 mg.
**Sodium** 120 mg.
**Potassium** 490 mg.
**Magnesium** 59 mg.
**Phosphorus** 93 mg.

**Vitamins**
**Vitamin A** 1,000 µg.
**Vitamin C** 25 mg.
**Vitamin D** None.
**Vitamin E** 2 mg.
**Vitamin B1** 0.07 mg.
**Vitamin B2** 0.15 mg.
**Niacin** 1.8 mg.
**Vitamin B6** 0.18 mg.
**Vitamin B12** None.
**Folic acid** 140 µg.
**Pantothenic acid** 0.2 mg.
**Biotin** 0.1 µg.

This vegetable is very rich in vitamins and minerals and can be added to many main course dishes.

**Portion** Half a large bunch or a small one of about four leaves.
**Weight** 40 g., about 1½ oz.

**Food Facts**
**Energy** 4 kcal.
**Protein** 0.7 g.
**Total fat** None.
**Saturated fat** None.
**Polyunsaturated fat** None.
**Carbohydrate** 0.4 g.
**Sugars** 0.4 g.
**Fibre** 1.5 g.

**Minerals**
**Calcium** 34.4 mg.
**Iron** 0.5 mg.
**Zinc** 0.16 mg.
**Copper** 0.03 mg.
**Sodium** 4 mg.
**Potassium** 48 mg.
**Magnesium** 3.6 mg.
**Phosphorus** 12.4 mg.

**Vitamins**
**Vitamin A** 266 µg.
**Vitamin C** 12 mg.
**Vitamin D** None.
**Vitamin E** 0.44 mg.
**Vitamin B1** 0.02 mg.
**Vitamin B2** 0.08 mg.
**Niacin** 0.32 mg.
**Vitamin B6** 0.06 mg.
**Vitamin B12** None.
**Folic acid** 44 µg.
**Pantothenic acid** 0.1 mg.
**Biotin** 0.2 µg.

Do not add any sodium bicarbonate to the cooking water. Greens will keep their colour by quick cooking in a small amount of water.

# Strawberries

**Portion** Ten strawberries.

**Weight** 120 g., about 4 oz.

**Food Facts**
**Energy** 31 kcal.
**Protein** 0.7 g.
**Total fat** None.
**Saturated fat** None.
**Polyunsaturated fat** None.
**Carbohydrate** 7.4 g.
**Sugars** 7.4 g.
**Fibre** 2.6 g.

**Minerals**
**Calcium** 26.4 mg.
**Iron** 0.84 mg.
**Zinc** 0.12 mg.
**Copper** 0.16 mg.
**Sodium** 2.4 mg.
**Potassium** 192 mg.
**Magnesium** 14.4 mg.
**Phosphorus** 27.6 mg.

**Vitamins**
**Vitamin A** 6 µg
**Vitamin C** 72 mg.
**Vitamin D** None.
**Vitamin E** 0.24 mg.
**Vitamin B1** 0.02 mg.
**Vitamin B2** 0.04 mg.
**Niacin** 0.6 mg.
**Vitamin B6** 0.07 mg.
**Vitamin B12** None.
**Folic acid** 24 µg.
**Pantothenic acid** 0.4 mg.
**Biotin** 1.3 µg.

Strawberries are low in calories as well as containing a lot of vitamin C. They taste just as good without sugar or cream.

# Sultanas

**Portion** One handful of about thirty sultanas.

**Weight** 15 g., about ½ oz.

**Food Facts**
**Energy** 37 kcal.
**Protein** 0.3 g.
**Total fat** None.
**Saturated fat** None.
**Polyunsaturated fat** None.
**Carbohydrate** 9.7 g.
**Sugars** 9.7 g.
**Fibre** 1.05 g.

**Minerals**
**Calcium** 7.8 mg.
**Iron** 0.27 mg.
**Zinc** 0.01 mg.
**Copper** 0.05 mg.
**Sodium** 7.9 mg.
**Potassium** 129 mg.
**Magnesium** 5.2 mg.
**Phosphorus** 14.2 mg.

**Vitamins**
**Vitamin A** 0.7 µg.
**Vitamin C** None.
**Vitamin D** None.
**Vitamin E** 0.1 mg.
**Vitamin B1** 0.01 mg.
**Vitamin B2** 0.01 mg.
**Niacin** 0.09 mg.
**Vitamin B6** 0.04 mg.
**Vitamin B12** None.
**Folic acid** 0.6 µg.
**Pantothenic acid** None.
**Biotin** Not known.

Adding a few sultanas to stewed fruit will make it more interesting. Give them to children instead of sweets.

# Swede

**Portion** 1½ tablespoons mashed. About ⅛ medium sized swede.
**Weight** 100 g., about 3½ oz.

**Food Facts**
Energy 18 kcal.
Protein 0.9 g.
Total fat None.
Saturated fat None.
Polyunsaturated fat None.
Carbohydrate 3.8 g.
Sugars 3.7 g.
Fibre 2.8 g.

**Minerals**
Calcium 42 mg.
Iron 0.3 mg.
Zinc Not known.
Copper 0.04 mg.
Sodium 14 mg.
Potassium 100 mg.
Magnesium 7 mg.
Phosphorus 18 mg.

**Vitamins**
Vitamin A None.
Vitamin C 17 mg.
Vitamin D None.
Vitamin E None.
Vitamin B1 0.04 mg.
Vitamin B2 0.03 mg.
Niacin 0.8 mg.
Vitamin B6 0.12 mg.
Vitamin B12 None.
Folic acid 21 µg.
Pantothenic acid 0.07 mg.
Biotin None.

If you normally mash swede, do not add butter but you can use plenty of black pepper.

# Sweet potato

**Portion** The size of two large eggs.
**Weight** 130 g., about 4½ oz.

**Food Facts**
Energy 110 kcal.
Protein 1.4 g.
Total fat 0.8 g.
Saturated fat Not known.
Polyunsaturated fat Not known.
Carbohydrate 26 g.
Sugars 11.8 g.
Fibre 3 g.

**Minerals**
Calcium 27.3 mg.
Iron 0.78 mg.
Zinc Not known.
Copper 0.19 mg.
Sodium 23.4 mg.
Potassium 390 mg.
Magnesium 15.6 mg.
Phosphorus 57.2 mg.

**Vitamins**
Vitamin A 866 µg.
Vitamin C 19.5 mg.
Vitamin D None.
Vitamin E 5.2 mg.
Vitamin B1 0.1 mg.
Vitamin B2 0.05 mg.
Niacin 1.17 mg.
Vitamin B6 0.17 mg.
Vitamin B12 None.
Folic acid 32.5 µg.
Pantothenic acid 0.9 mg.
Biotin Not known.

Use instead of ordinary potatoes baked in their jackets. An acquired taste becoming more popular in the UK.

# Sweetcorn

**Portion** One heaped tablespoon, tinned.
**Weight** 100 g., about 3½ oz.

**Food Facts**
Energy 76 kcal.
Protein 2.9 g.
Total fat 0.5 g.
Saturated fat Not known.
Polyunsaturated fat Not known.
Carbohydrate 16.1 g.
Sugars 8.9 g.
Fibre 5.7 g.

**Minerals**
Calcium 3 mg.
Iron 0.6 mg.
Zinc 0.6 mg.
Copper 0.05 mg.
Sodium 310 mg.
Potassium 200 mg.
Magnesium 23 mg.
Phosphorus 67 mg.

**Vitamins**
Vitamin A 210 µg.
Vitamin C 5 mg.
Vitamin D None.
Vitamin E 0.5 mg.
Vitamin B1 0.05 mg.
Vitamin B2 0.08 mg.
Niacin 1.5 mg.
Vitamin B6 0.16 mg.
Vitamin B12 None.
Folic acid 32 µg.
Pantothenic acid 0.2 mg.
Biotin Not known.

**Use small amounts of sweetcorn to add colour to salads. Avoid eating a lot of it if you are trying to lose weight.**

# Tangerine

**Portion** One medium-sized, peeled.
**Weight** 70 g., about 2½ oz.

**Food Facts**
Energy 23 kcal.
Protein 0.6 g.
Total fat None.
Saturated fat None.
Polyunsaturated fat None.
Carbohydrate 5.6 g.
Sugars 5.6 g.
Fibre 1.3 g.

**Minerals**
Calcium 29.4 mg.
Iron 0.21 mg.
Zinc 0.07 mg.
Copper 0.06 mg.
Sodium 1.4 mg.
Potassium 112 mg.
Magnesium 7.7 mg.
Phosphorus 11.9 mg.

**Vitamins**
Vitamin A 11.5 µg.
Vitamin C 21 mg.
Vitamin D None.
Vitamin E Not known.
Vitamin B1 0.05 mg.
Vitamin B2 0.01 mg.
Niacin 0.21 mg.
Vitamin B6 0.05 mg.
Vitamin B12 None.
Folic acid 14.7 µg.
Pantothenic acid 0.1 mg.
Biotin Not known.

**Tangerines make a welcome change from oranges but contain less vitamin C.**

# Tinned fruit salad

**Portion** One bowlful.

**Weight** 130 g., about 4½ oz.

**Food Facts**
**Energy** 123 kcal.
**Protein** 0.4 g.
**Total fat** None.
**Saturated fat** None.
**Polyunsaturated fat** None.
**Carbohydrate** 32.5 g.
**Sugars** 32.5 g.
**Fibre** 1.4 g.

**Minerals**
**Calcium** 10.4 mg.
**Iron** 1.3 mg.
**Zinc** Not known.
**Copper** 0.04 mg.
**Sodium** 2.6 mg.
**Potassium** 156 mg.
**Magnesium** 10.4 mg.
**Phosphorus** 13 mg.

**Vitamins**
**Vitamin A** 65 µg.
**Vitamin C** 3.9 mg.
**Vitamin D** None.
**Vitamin E** Not known.
**Vitamin B1** 0.03 mg.
**Vitamin B2** 0.01 mg.
**Niacin** 0.39 mg.
**Vitamin B6** 0.01 mg.
**Vitamin B12** None.
**Folic acid** 5.2 µg.
**Pantothenic acid** 0.1 mg.
**Biotin** 0.1 µg.

**Tinned fruit salad contains twice the calories and half the fibre of fresh fruit salad. Buy tins without added sugar.**

# Tofu, soya bean curd

**Portion** One steamed cube 2 in. × 2 in. × 1 in.

**Weight** 140 g., about 5 oz.

**Food Facts**
**Energy** 98 kcal.
**Protein** 10.3 g.
**Total fat** 5.8 g.
**Saturated fat** Not known.
**Polyunsaturated fat** Not known.
**Carbohydrate** 0.84 g.
**Sugars** Not known.
**Fibre** 0.42 g.

**Minerals**
**Calcium** 709 mg.
**Iron** 1.6 mg.
**Zinc** 0.98 mg.
**Copper** 2.3 mg.
**Sodium** 5.6 mg.
**Potassium** 88 mg.
**Magnesium** 32 mg.
**Phosphorus** Not known.

**Vitamins**
**Vitamin A** None.
**Vitamin C** None.
**Vitamin D** None.
**Vitamin E** Not known.
**Vitamin B1** 0.08 mg.
**Vitamin B2** 0.02 mg.
**Niacin** 0.14 mg.
**Vitamin B6** Not known.
**Vitamin B12** None.
**Folic acid** Not known.
**Pantothenic acid** Not known.
**Biotin** Not known.

**Add tofu to vegetable casseroles or stir-fried dishes to increase the protein content.**

# Tomato, raw

**Portion** One medium-sized tomato.
**Weight** 75 g., about 2¾oz.

**Food Facts**
**Energy** 10 kcal.
**Protein** 0.7 g.
**Total fat** None.
**Saturated fat** None.
**Polyunsaturated fat** None.
**Carbohydrate** 2.1 g.
**Sugars** 2.1 g.
**Fibre** 1.1 g.

**Minerals**
**Calcium** 9.7 mg.
**Iron** 0.3 mg.
**Zinc** 0.15 mg.
**Copper** 0.07 mg.
**Sodium** 2.2 mg.
**Potassium** 217 mg.
**Magnesium** 8.2 mg.
**Phosphorus** 15.7 mg.

**Vitamins**
**Vitamin A** 75 µg.
**Vitamin C** 15 mg.
**Vitamin D** None.
**Vitamin E** 0.9 mg.
**Vitamin B1** 0.04 mg.
**Vitamin B2** 0.03 mg.
**Niacin** 0.6 mg.
**Vitamin B6** 0.08 mg.
**Vitamin B12** None.
**Folic acid** 21 µg.
**Pantothenic acid** 0.2 mg.
**Biotin** 1.1 µg.

**Fresh tomatoes make a tasty snack or sandwich filling all year round.**

# Tomato, fried

**Portion** One medium-sized tomato fried in butter.
**Weight** 69 g., about 2½ oz.

**Food Facts**
**Energy** 46 kcal.
**Protein** 0.69 g.
**Total fat** 4 g.
**Saturated fat** 1.9 g.
**Polyunsaturated fat** 0.08 g.
**Carbohydrate** 2.2 g.
**Sugars** 2.2 g.
**Fibre** Not known.

**Minerals**
**Calcium** 10.3 mg.
**Iron** 0.34 mg.
**Zinc** 0.13 mg.
**Copper** 0.07 mg.
**Sodium** 2.0 mg.
**Potassium** 233 mg.
**Magnesium** 8.8 mg.
**Phosphorus** 17.2 mg.

**Vitamins**
**Vitamin A** None.
**Vitamin C** 6.9 mg.
**Vitamin D** None.
**Vitamin E** Not known.
**Vitamin B1** Not known.
**Vitamin B2** Not known.
**Niacin** 0.06 mg.
**Vitamin B6** Not known.
**Vitamin B12** None.
**Folic acid** Not known.
**Pantothenic acid** Not known.
**Biotin** Not known.

**Try grilling or baking tomatoes instead of frying to reduce your fat intake.**

# Tomatoes, tinned

**Portion** Half a medium-sized tin.
**Weight** 200 g., about 7 oz.

**Food Facts**
**Energy** 24 kcal.
**Protein** 2.2 g.
**Total fat** None.
**Saturated fat** None.
**Polyunsaturated fat** None.
**Carbohydrate** 4 g.
**Sugars** 4 g.
**Fibre** 1.8 g.

**Minerals**
**Calcium** 18 mg.
**Iron** 1.8 mg.
**Zinc** 0.6 mg.
**Copper** 0.22 mg.
**Sodium** 58 mg.
**Potassium** 540 mg.
**Magnesium** 22 mg.
**Phosphorus** 44 mg.

**Vitamins**
**Vitamin A** 167 µg.
**Vitamin C** 36 mg.
**Vitamin D** None.
**Vitamin E** 2.4 mg.
**Vitamin B1** 0.12 mg.
**Vitamin B2** 0.06 mg.
**Niacin** 1.6 mg.
**Vitamin B6** 0.22 mg.
**Vitamin B12** None.
**Folic acid** 50 µg.
**Pantothenic acid** 0.4 mg.
**Biotin** 3 µg.

Tinned tomatoes make an excellent base for many dishes. A tomato sauce is a good substitute for a milk-based sauce.

# Tomato puree

**Portion** One tablespoon.

**Weight** 15 g., about ½ oz.

**Food Facts**
**Energy** 10 kcal.
**Protein** 0.9 g.
**Total fat** None.
**Saturated fat** None.
**Polyunsaturated fat** None.
**Carbohydrate** 1.7 g.
**Sugars** 1.7 g.
**Fibre** Not known.

**Minerals**
**Calcium** 7.6 mg.
**Iron** 0.76 mg.
**Zinc** 0.25 mg.
**Copper** 0.09 mg.
**Sodium** 3 mg.
**Potassium** 231 mg.
**Magnesium** 9.9 mg.
**Phosphorus** 19.5 mg.

**Vitamins**
**Vitamin A** 71.5 µg.
**Vitamin C** 15 mg.
**Vitamin D** None.
**Vitamin E** 1.03 mg.
**Vitamin B1** 0.05 mg.
**Vitamin B2** 0.03 mg.
**Niacin** 0.72 mg.
**Vitamin B6** 0.09 mg.
**Vitamin B12** None.
**Folic acid** 21 µg.
**Pantothenic acid** 0.2 mg.
**Biotin** 1.2 µg.

Add tomato puree to soups and stews. It will thicken them without increasing the calorie value.

# Turnip

## Vegetable curry

**Portion** One turnip the size of a tennis ball, boiled.
**Weight** 100 g., about 3½ oz.

**Portion** One serving, about two to three tablespoons.
**Weight** 200 g., about 7 oz.

**Food Facts**
**Energy** 14 kcal.
**Protein** 0.7 g.
**Total fat** 0.3 g.
**Saturated fat** Not known.
**Polyunsaturated fat** Not known.
**Carbohydrate** 2.3 g.
**Sugars** 2.3 g.
**Fibre** 2.2 g.

**Food Facts**
**Energy** 362 kcal.
**Protein** 3.6 g.
**Total fat** 30.4 g.
**Saturated fat** Not known.
**Polyunsaturated fat** Not known.
**Carbohydrate** 20 g.
**Sugars** Not known.
**Fibre** Not known.

**Minerals**
**Calcium** 55 mg.
**Iron** 0.4 mg.
**Zinc** Not known.
**Copper** 0.04 mg.
**Sodium** 28 mg.
**Potassium** 160 mg.
**Magnesium** 7 mg.
**Phosphorus** 19 mg.

**Minerals**
**Calcium** 78 mg.
**Iron** 1.6 mg.
**Zinc** 0.6 mg.
**Copper** 0.24 mg.
**Sodium** 896 mg.
**Potassium** 832 mg.
**Magnesium** 42 mg.
**Phosphorus** Not known.

**Vitamins**
**Vitamin A** None.
**Vitamin C** 17 mg.
**Vitamin D** None.
**Vitamin E** None.
**Vitamin B1** 0.03 mg.
**Vitamin B2** 0.04 mg.
**Niacin** 0.6 mg.
**Vitamin B6** 0.06 mg.
**Vitamin B12** None.
**Folic acid** 10 µg.
**Pantothenic acid** 0.1 mg.
**Biotin** None.

**Vitamins**
**Vitamin A** 1,426 µg.
**Vitamin C** 24 mg.
**Vitamin D** 0.2 µg.
**Vitamin E** Not known.
**Vitamin B1** 0.14 mg.
**Vitamin B2** 0.1 mg.
**Niacin** 2.2 mg.
**Vitamin B6** Not known.
**Vitamin B12** None.
**Folic acid** 30 µg.
**Pantothenic acid** Not known.
**Biotin** Not known.

**Try turnips as a change from parsnips. They only take a few minutes to cook and contain fewer calories.**

**Vegetable curry is best made at home using as little oil as possible. Curry spices have no calorie value.**

# Walnuts

# Watercress

**Portion** Six walnut halves.

**Weight** 20 g., about ⅔ oz.

**Food Facts**
**Energy** 105 kcal.
**Protein** 2.1 g.
**Total fat** 10.3 g.
**Saturated fat** 1.1 g.
**Polyunsaturated fat** 7.3 g.
**Carbohydrate** 1 g.
**Sugars** 0.6 g.
**Fibre** 1 g.

**Minerals**
**Calcium** 12 mg.
**Iron** 0.48 mg.
**Zinc** 0.6 mg.
**Copper** 0.06 mg.
**Sodium** 0.6 mg.
**Potassium** 138 mg.
**Magnesium** 26 mg.
**Phosphorus** 102 mg.

**Vitamins**
**Vitamin A** None.
**Vitamin C** None.
**Vitamin D** None.
**Vitamin E** 0.16 mg.
**Vitamin B1** 0.06 mg.
**Vitamin B2** 0.02 mg.
**Niacin** 0.2 mg.
**Vitamin B6** 0.15 mg.
**Vitamin B12** None.
**Folic acid** 13.2 µg.
**Pantothenic acid** 0.18 mg.
**Biotin** 0.4 µg.

**70% of the fat contained in walnuts is polyunsaturated fat. In other nuts the amount is usually 30% or less.**

**Portion** One quarter of an average bunch.

**Weight** 20 g., about ⅔ oz.

**Food Facts**
**Energy** 2 kcal.
**Protein** 0.6 g.
**Total fat** None.
**Saturated fat** None.
**Polyunsaturated fat** None.
**Carbohydrate** 0.1 g.
**Sugars** 0.1 g.
**Fibre** 0.7 g.

**Minerals**
**Calcium** 44 mg.
**Iron** 0.32 mg.
**Zinc** 0.04 mg.
**Copper** 0.03 mg.
**Sodium** 12 mg.
**Potassium** 62 mg.
**Magnesium** 3.4 mg.
**Phosphorus** 10.4 mg.

**Vitamins**
**Vitamin A** 100 µg.
**Vitamin C** 12 mg.
**Vitamin D** None.
**Vitamin E** 0.2 mg.
**Vitamin B1** 0.02 mg.
**Vitamin B2** 0.02 mg.
**Niacin** 0.22 mg.
**Vitamin B6** 0.03 mg.
**Vitamin B12** None.
**Folic acid** Not known.
**Pantothenic acid** None.
**Biotin** 0.1 µg.

**Watercress adds a lot of flavour and colour to soups and salads. It also makes a good sandwich filling.**

# Watermelon

**Portion** One slice without pips or skin.
**Weight** 180 g., about 6½ oz.

**Food Facts**
Energy 37 kcal.
Protein 0.7 g.
Total fat None.
Saturated fat None.
Polyunsaturated fat None.
Carbohydrate 9.5 g.
Sugars 9.5 g.
Fibre 1.6 g.

**Minerals**
Calcium 9 mg.
Iron 0.54 mg.
Zinc 0.18 mg.
Copper 0.05 mg.
Sodium 7.2 mg.
Potassium 216 mg.
Magnesium 19.8 mg.
Phosphorus 14.4 mg.

**Vitamins**
Vitamin A 6.3 µg.
Vitamin C 9 mg.
Vitamin D None.
Vitamin E 0.18 mg.
Vitamin B1 0.04 mg.
Vitamin B2 0.04 mg.
Niacin 0.54 mg.
Vitamin B6 0.13 mg.
Vitamin B12 None.
Folic acid 5.4 µg.
Pantothenic acid 2.8 mg.
Biotin Not known.

**Watermelon tastes very sweet but one large slice contains less calories than most other fruits. Try it instead of other melons for a change.**

# Yam

**Portion** The size of a medium potato, boiled.
**Weight** 130 g., about 4½ oz.

**Food Facts**
Energy 154 kcal.
Protein 2.1 g.
Total fat 0.1 g.
Saturated fat Not known.
Polyunsaturated fat Not known.
Carbohydrate 38 g.
Sugars 0.3 g.
Fibre 5.1 g.

**Minerals**
Calcium 11.7 mg.
Iron 0.39 mg.
Zinc 0.52 mg.
Copper 0.19 mg.
Sodium 22.1 mg.
Potassium 390 mg.
Magnesium 18.2 mg.
Phosphorus 42.9 mg.

**Vitamins**
Vitamin A 2.6 µg.
Vitamin C 2.6 mg.
Vitamin D None.
Vitamin E Not known.
Vitamin B1 0.06 mg.
Vitamin B2 0.01 mg.
Niacin 1.04 mg.
Vitamin B6 Not known.
Vitamin B12 None.
Folic acid 7.8 µg.
Pantothenic acid 0.6 mg.
Biotin Not known.

**Yams should be eaten and cooked like potatoes but contain more calories.**

# 8

# Everyday foods

Bread, cereals, biscuits, cakes, drinks, sweets, spreads, soups and all those other foods you and your family eat everyday are given in this chapter. Watch out for the tips at the bottom of each food. Remember that shop bought food is often more salty than when you make it yourself.

# All-Bran

**Portion** One small bowlful or four tablespoons.
**Weight** 40 g., about 1⅓ oz.

## Food Facts
**Energy** 100 kcal.
**Protein** 6 g.
**Total fat** 0.88 g.
**Saturated fat** Not known.
**Polyunsaturated fat** Not known.
**Carbohydrate** 18 g.
**Sugars** 6.1 g.
**Fibre** 11.5 g.

## Minerals
**Calcium** 27.9 mg.
**Iron** 4.8 mg.
**Zinc** 3.36 mg.
**Copper** 0.48 mg.
**Sodium** 588 mg.
**Potassium** 355 mg.
**Magnesium** 148 mg.
**Phosphorus** 149 mg.

## Vitamins
**Vitamin A** None.
**Vitamin C** None.
**Vitamin D** 1.12 µg.
**Vitamin E** 0.8 mg.
**Vitamin B1** 0.4 mg.
**Vitamin B2** 0.6 mg.
**Niacin** 6.4 mg.
**Vitamin B6** 0.72 mg.
**Vitamin B12** 0.68 µg.
**Folic acid** 100 µg.
**Pantothenic acid** Not known.
**Biotin** Not known.

All-Bran is high in fibre and other nutrients. If you cannot eat it on its own, mix a small amount with another breakfast cereal.

# Apple juice

**Portion** One wine glass.

**Weight** 140 g., about 5 oz.

## Food Facts
**Energy** 51 kcal.
**Protein** None.
**Total fat** None.
**Saturated fat** None.
**Polyunsaturated fat** None.
**Carbohydrate** 13.8 g.
**Sugars** 13.8 g.
**Fibre** None.

## Minerals
**Calcium** 9.8 mg.
**Iron** 0.14 mg.
**Zinc** None.
**Copper** None.
**Sodium** 2.8 mg.
**Potassium** 154 mg.
**Magnesium** 7 mg.
**Phosphorus** 8.4 mg.

## Vitamins
**Vitamin A** None.
**Vitamin C** None.
**Vitamin D** None.
**Vitamin E** None.
**Vitamin B1** 0.01 mg.
**Vitamin B2** 0.01 mg.
**Niacin** 0.14 mg.
**Vitamin B6** None.
**Vitamin B12** None.
**Folic acid** 1.26 µg.
**Pantothenic acid** None.
**Biotin** None.

Apple juice contains far fewer vitamins than other fruit juices but some brands have vitamin C added.

# Beef extract (Bovril)

**Portion** To make up one mug.

**Weight** 12 g., about ½ oz.

**Food Facts**
Energy 20 kcal.
Protein 4.9 g.
Total fat 0.01 g.
Saturated fat Not known.
Polyunsaturated fat Not known.
Carbohydrate 0.3 g.
Sugars None.
Fibre None.

**Minerals**
Calcium 3 mg.
Iron 0.76 mg.
Zinc 0.22 mg.
Copper 0.18 mg.
Sodium 537 mg.
Potassium 142 mg.
Magnesium 0.6 mg.
Phosphorus 39.9 mg.

**Vitamins**
Vitamin A None.
Vitamin C None.
Vitamin D None.
Vitamin E Not known.
Vitamin B1 0.19 mg.
Vitamin B2 0.81 mg.
Niacin 4.5 mg.
Vitamin B6 0.06 mg.
Vitamin B12 0.33 mg.
Folic acid 50.4 µg.
Pantothenic acid Not known.
Biotin Not known.

**Beef extract makes a good warming, low-calorie winter drink, particularly useful for people watching their weight.**

# Beer

**Portion** One pint of draught bitter.

**Weight** 560 g., about 20 oz.

**Food Facts**
Energy 179 kcal.
Protein 1.7 g.
Total fat None.
Saturated fat None.
Polyunsaturated fat None.
Carbohydrate 12.9 g.
Sugars 12.9 g.
Fibre None.

**Minerals**
Calcium 61 mg.
Iron 0.06 mg.
Zinc Not known.
Copper 0.45 mg.
Sodium 67 mg.
Potassium 212 mg.
Magnesium 50.4 mg.
Phosphorus 72.8 mg.

**Vitamins**
Vitamin A None.
Vitamin C None.
Vitamin D None.
Vitamin E Not known.
Vitamin B1 None.
Vitamin B2 0.22 mg.
Niacin 3.36 mg.
Vitamin B6 0.13 mg.
Vitamin B12 0.95 µg.
Folic acid 49.3 µg.
Pantothenic acid 0.6 mg.
Biotin 2.8 µg.

**One pint of beer contains slightly more alcohol than two pub measures of spirits.**

# Biscuits, chocolate

**Portion** Two half-coated chocolate digestives.
**Weight** 30 g., about 1 oz.

## Food Facts
**Energy** 146 kcal.
**Protein** 2 g.
**Total fat** 7.2 g.
**Saturated fat** 3.6 g.
**Polyunsaturated fat** 0.46 g.
**Carbohydrate** 20 g.
**Sugars** 8.6 g.
**Fibre** 1 g.

## Minerals
**Calcium** 252 mg.
**Iron** 0.62 mg.
**Zinc** 0.3 mg.
**Copper** 0.08 mg.
**Sodium** 134 mg.
**Potassium** 62 mg.
**Magnesium** 12.2 mg.
**Phosphorus** 39 mg.

## Vitamins
**Vitamin A** None.
**Vitamin C** None.
**Vitamin D** None.
**Vitamin E** 0.3 mg.
**Vitamin B1** 0.02 mg.
**Vitamin B2** 0.04 mg.
**Niacin** 0.8 mg.
**Vitamin B6** 0.02 mg.
**Vitamin B12** None.
**Folic acid** Not known.
**Pantothenic acid** Not known.
**Biotin** Not known.

There is very little difference between digestive and chocolate biscuits. Both are very high in calories.

# Biscuits, cream sandwich

**Portion** Two biscuits.

**Weight** 24 g., about 1 oz.

## Food Facts
**Energy** 123 kcal.
**Protein** 1.2 g.
**Total fat** 6.2 g.
**Saturated fat** 3.45 g.
**Polyunsaturated fat** 0.42 g.
**Carbohydrate** 16.6 g.
**Sugars** 7.2 g.
**Fibre** 0.3 g.

## Minerals
**Calcium** 24 mg.
**Iron** 0.38 mg.
**Zinc** 0.12 mg.
**Copper** 0.02 mg.
**Sodium** 52.8 mg.
**Potassium** 28.8 mg.
**Magnesium** 3.1 mg.
**Phosphorus** 19.7 mg.

## Vitamins
**Vitamin A** None.
**Vitamin C** None.
**Vitamin D** None.
**Vitamin E** 0.82 mg.
**Vitamin B1** 0.03 mg.
**Vitamin B2** 0.03 mg.
**Niacin** 0.5 mg.
**Vitamin B6** 0.01 mg.
**Vitamin B12** None.
**Folic acid** 1.7 µg.
**Pantothenic acid** Not known.
**Biotin** Not known.

Keep all biscuits to a minimum if you want to eat a healthy diet. Some are artifically coloured.

# Biscuits, digestive

**Portion** Two biscuits.

**Weight** 30 g., about 1 oz.

**Food Facts**
**Energy** 141 kcal.
**Protein** 2.9 g.
**Total fat** 6.1 g.
**Saturated fat** Not known.
**Polyunsaturated fat** Not known.
**Carbohydrate** 19.8 g.
**Sugars** 4.9 g.
**Fibre** 1.6 g.

**Minerals**
**Calcium** 33 mg.
**Iron** 0.6 mg.
**Zinc** 0.18 mg.
**Copper** 0.07 mg.
**Sodium** 132 mg.
**Potassium** 48 mg.
**Magnesium** 9.6 mg.
**Phosphorus** 39 mg.

**Vitamins**
**Vitamin A** None.
**Vitamin C** None.
**Vitamin D** None.
**Vitamin E** Not known.
**Vitamin B1** 0.04 mg.
**Vitamin B2** 0.02 mg.
**Niacin** 1.05 mg.
**Vitamin B6** 0.02 mg.
**Vitamin B12** None.
**Folic acid** 3 µg.
**Pantothenic acid** Not known.
**Biotin** Not known.

**Digestive biscuits contain four times the fibre of plain biscuits but also twice as many calories and fat.**

# Biscuits, plain

**Portion** Two biscuits
eg rich tea or lincoln.

**Weight** 16 g., about ½ oz.

**Food Facts**
**Energy** 73 kcal.
**Protein** 1.1 g.
**Total fat** 2.7 g.
**Saturated fat** 1.26 g.
**Polyunsaturated fat** 0.27 g.
**Carbohydrate** 12 g.
**Sugars** 3.6 g.
**Fibre** 0.4 g.

**Minerals**
**Calcium** 19.2 mg.
**Iron** 0.34 mg.
**Zinc** 0.1 mg.
**Copper** 0.01 mg.
**Sodium** 65.6 mg.
**Potassium** 22.4 mg.
**Magnesium** 2.7 mg.
**Phosphorus** 13.4 mg.

**Vitamins**
**Vitamin A** None.
**Vitamin C** None.
**Vitamin D** None.
**Vitamin E** 0.22 mg.
**Vitamin B1** 0.02 mg.
**Vitamin B2** 0.01 mg.
**Niacin** 0.46 mg.
**Vitamin B6** 0.01 mg.
**Vitamin B12** None.
**Folic acid** 1.6 µg.
**Pantothenic acid** Not known.
**Biotin** Not known.

**Home made biscuits may be much higher in calories. Compare plain biscuits with others like chocolate or digestive elsewhere in this book.**

# Blackcurrant drink    Bran

**Portion** Concentrate needed to make one large glass with water.
**Weight** 30 g., about 1 oz.

**Food Facts**
Energy 68 kcal.
Protein None.
Total fat None.
Saturated fat None.
Polyunsaturated fat None.
Carbohydrate 18.3 g.
Sugars 18.3 g.
Fibre None.

**Minerals**
Calcium 2.7 mg.
Iron 0.15 mg.
Zinc Not known.
Copper 0.01 mg.
Sodium 6 mg.
Potassium 25.8 mg.
Magnesium 1.5 mg.
Phosphorus 3 mg.

**Vitamins**
Vitamin A None.
Vitamin C 63 mg.
Vitamin D None.
Vitamin E Not known.
Vitamin B1 Not known.
Vitamin B2 Not known.
Niacin None.
Vitamin B6 Not known.
Vitamin B12 None.
Folic acid Not known.
Pantothenic acid Not known.
Biotin Not known.

**Most blackcurrant cordials contain a lot of sugar and are therefore not suitable for babies. Buy fruit juices made especially for babies.**

**Portion** One tablespoon.

**Weight** 21 g., about ¾ oz.

**Food Facts**
Energy 43 kcal.
Protein 3.0 g.
Total fat 1.2 g.
Saturated fat 0.19 g.
Polyunsaturated fat 0.6 g.
Carbohydrate 5.6 g.
Sugars 0.8 g.
Fibre 9.2 g.

**Minerals**
Calcium 23.1 mg.
Iron 2.7 mg.
Zinc 3.4 mg.
Copper 0.28 mg.
Sodium 5.9 mg.
Potassium 243 mg.
Magnesium 109 mg.
Phosphorus 252 mg.

**Vitamins**
Vitamin A None.
Vitamin C None.
Vitamin D None.
Vitamin E 0.34 mg.
Vitamin B1 0.19 mg.
Vitamin B2 0.08 mg.
Niacin 6.85 mg.
Vitamin B6 0.29 mg.
Vitamin B12 None.
Folic acid 54 µg.
Pantothenic acid 0.5 mg.
Biotin 2.9 µg.

**Taking bran is not a good way to increase your fibre intake. However if you do take it remember to drink plenty of fluids.**

# Bread, granary

# Bread, white

**Portion** One medium slice
from a large loaf.
**Weight** 40 g., about 1⅓ oz.

**Portion** One medium slice
from a large loaf.
**Weight** 40 g., about 1⅓ oz.

**Food Facts**
**Energy** 94 kcal.
**Protein** 3.6 g.
**Total fat** 1.08 g.
**Saturated fat** Not known.
**Polyunsaturated fat** Not known.
**Carbohydrate** 18.5 g.
**Sugars** 0.88 g.
**Fibre** 2.92 g.

**Food Facts**
**Energy** 93 kcal.
**Protein** 3.1 g.
**Total fat** 0.7 g.
**Saturated fat** 0.16 g.
**Polyunsaturated fat** 0.26 g.
**Carbohydrate** 19.9 g.
**Sugars** 0.7 g.
**Fibre** 1.1 g.

**Minerals**
**Calcium** 30.8 mg.
**Iron** 1.08 mg.
**Zinc** 0.6 mg.
**Copper** 0.07 mg.
**Sodium** 230 mg.
**Potassium** 76 mg.
**Magnesium** 23.6 mg.
**Phosphorus** 70 mg.

**Minerals**
**Calcium** 40 mg.
**Iron** 0.68 mg.
**Zinc** 0.32 mg.
**Copper** 0.06 mg.
**Sodium** 216 mg.
**Potassium** 40 mg.
**Magnesium** 10.4 mg.
**Phosphorus** 38.8 mg.

**Vitamins**
**Vitamin A** Not known.
**Vitamin C** Not known.
**Vitamin D** Not known.
**Vitamin E** Not known.
**Vitamin B1** 0.12 mg.
**Vitamin B2** 0.04 mg.
**Niacin** 1.2 mg.
**Vitamin B6** 0.06 mg.
**Vitamin B12** Not known.
**Folic acid** 36 µg.
**Pantothenic acid** Not known.
**Biotin** Not known.

**Vitamins**
**Vitamin A** None.
**Vitamin C** None.
**Vitamin D** None.
**Vitamin E** None.
**Vitamin B1** 0.07 mg.
**Vitamin B2** 0.01 mg.
**Niacin** 1.2 mg.
**Vitamin B6** 0.02 mg.
**Vitamin B12** None.
**Folic acid** 10.8 µg.
**Pantothenic acid** 0.1 mg.
**Biotin** 0.4 µg.

**Granary bread contains nearly as
much fibre as wholemeal bread, and
is a suitable alternative. It does
however contain more calories.**

**White bread contains less than half
as much fibre as wholemeal bread
and is higher in calories.**

# Bread, wholemeal

## Bread roll

**Portion** One medium slice from a large loaf.
**Weight** 40 g., about 1⅓ oz.

**Portion** One white bread roll.

**Weight** 50 g., about 1¾ oz.

### Food Facts
**Energy** 86 kcal.
**Protein** 3.5 g.
**Total fat** 1.1 g.
**Saturated fat** 0.21 g.
**Polyunsaturated fat** 0.46 g.
**Carbohydrate** 16.7 g.
**Sugars** 0.8 g.
**Fibre** 3.4 g.

### Food Facts
**Energy** 152 kcal.
**Protein** 4.9 g.
**Total fat** 3.6 g.
**Saturated fat** 0.88 g.
**Polyunsaturated fat** 1.42 g.
**Carbohydrate** 26.8 g.
**Sugars** 0.9 g.
**Fibre** 1.4 g.

### Minerals
**Calcium** 9.2 mg.
**Iron** 1 mg.
**Zinc** 0.8 mg.
**Copper** 0.11 mg.
**Sodium** 216 mg.
**Potassium** 88 mg.
**Magnesium** 37.2 mg.
**Phosphorus** 92 mg.

### Minerals
**Calcium** 60 mg.
**Iron** 0.9 mg.
**Zinc** 0.45 mg.
**Copper** 0.08 mg.
**Sodium** 315 mg.
**Potassium** 55 mg.
**Magnesium** 14 mg.
**Phosphorus** 50 mg.

### Vitamins
**Vitamin A** None.
**Vitamin C** None.
**Vitamin D** None.
**Vitamin E** 0.08 mg.
**Vitamin B1** 0.1 mg.
**Vitamin B2** 0.02 mg.
**Niacin** 2.24 mg.
**Vitamin B6** 0.06 mg.
**Vitamin B12** None.
**Folic acid** 15.6 µg.
**Pantothenic acid** 0.2 mg.
**Biotin** 2.4 µg.

### Vitamins
**Vitamin A** None.
**Vitamin C** None.
**Vitamin D** None.
**Vitamin E** None.
**Vitamin B1** 0.12 mg.
**Vitamin B2** 0.04 mg.
**Niacin** 1.7 mg.
**Vitamin B6** 0.03 mg.
**Vitamin B12** None.
**Folic acid** 13.5 µg.
**Pantothenic acid** 0.1 mg.
**Biotin** 0.5 µg.

**If you want to eat more fibre, buy wholemeal or granary bread. 'Brown' bread usually has the same amount of fibre as white bread.**

**A filled bread roll will have a similar calorie value to a sandwich which contains the same filling.**

# Bread and butter pudding

**Portion** One bowlful.

**Weight** 120 g., about 4¼ oz.

**Food Facts**
Energy 190 kcal.
Protein 7.3 g.
Total fat 9.4 g.
Saturated fat 4.86 g.
Polyunsaturated fat 0.52 g.
Carbohydrate 20.6 g.
Sugars 14.4 g.
Fibre 0.7 g.

**Minerals**
Calcium 156 mg.
Iron 0.84 mg.
Zinc 0.84 mg.
Copper 0.1 mg.
Sodium 180 mg.
Potassium 240 mg.
Magnesium 21.6 mg.
Phosphorus 168 mg.

**Vitamins**
Vitamin A 120 µg.
Vitamin C None.
Vitamin D 0.64 µg.
Vitamin E 0.48 mg.
Vitamin B1 0.06 mg.
Vitamin B2 0.24 mg.
Niacin 2.16 mg.
Vitamin B6 0.06 mg.
Vitamin B12 None.
Folic acid 7.2 µg.
Pantothenic acid 0.6 mg.
Biotin 8.4 µg.

**Make your bread and butter pudding with wholemeal bread and add less sugar and more dried fruit.**

# Brown sauce

**Portion** One teaspoon.

**Weight** 5 g., about ⅕ oz.

**Food Facts**
Energy 4 kcal.
Protein 0.1 g.
Total fat None.
Saturated fat None.
Polyunsaturated fat None.
Carbohydrate 1.3 g.
Sugars 1.2 g.
Fibre Not known.

**Minerals**
Calcium 2.1 mg.
Iron 0.15 mg.
Zinc Not known.
Copper 0.02 mg.
Sodium 49 mg.
Potassium 19.5 mg.
Magnesium 1.4 mg.
Phosphorus 1.8 mg.

**Vitamins**
Vitamin A None.
Vitamin C Not known.
Vitamin D None.
Vitamin E Not known.
Vitamin B1 Not known.
Vitamin B2 Not known.
Niacin 0.01 mg.
Vitamin B6 Not known.
Vitamin B12 None.
Folic acid None.
Pantothenic acid Not known.
Biotin Not known.

**It is surprising how much sugar sauces and ketchups contain. A tablespoonful of brown sauce contains a teaspoonful of sugar.**

# Chapatti

**Portion** One chapatti made without fat.

**Weight** 60 g., about 2 oz.

**Food Facts**
Energy 121 kcal.
Protein 4.4 g.
Total fat 0.6 g.
Saturated fat 0.07 g.
Polyunsaturated fat 0.27 g.
Carbohydrate 26.2 g.
Sugars 1 g.
Fibre 2.0 g.

**Minerals**
Calcium 36 mg.
Iron 1.26 mg.
Zinc 0.6 mg.
Copper 0.12 mg.
Sodium 72 mg.
Potassium 90 mg.
Magnesium 22.2 mg.
Phosphorus 72 mg.

**Vitamins**
Vitamin A None.
Vitamin C None.
Vitamin D None.
Vitamin E None.
Vitamin B1 0.14 mg.
Vitamin B2 0.02 mg.
Niacin 1.8 mg.
Vitamin B6 0.11 mg.
Vitamin B12 None.
Folic acid 8.4 µg.
Pantothenic acid 0.2 mg.
Biotin 1.2 µg.

**Chappattis are quite high in fibre because they are usually made with wholemeal flour. They are often low in fat unlike papadums.**

# Cheesecake

**Portion** One slice.

**Weight** 82 g., about 3 oz.

**Food Facts**
Energy 345 kcal.
Protein 3.4 g.
Total fat 28.6 g.
Saturated fat 15.3 g.
Polyunsaturated fat 1.7 g.
Carbohydrate 19.7 g.
Sugars 11.4 g.
Fibre 0.7 g.

**Minerals**
Calcium 54 mg.
Iron 0.57 mg.
Zinc 0.41 mg.
Copper 0.08 mg.
Sodium 213 mg.
Potassium 98 mg.
Magnesium 9 mg.
Phosphorus 71 mg.

**Vitamins**
Vitamin A 244 µg.
Vitamin C 1.64 mg.
Vitamin D 0.77 µg.
Vitamin E Not known.
Vitamin B1 0.04 mg.
Vitamin B2 0.08 mg.
Niacin 1.07 mg.
Vitamin B6 0.02 mg.
Vitamin B12 None.
Folic acid 2.5 µg.
Pantothenic acid Not known.
Biotin Not known.

**Always use cottage or curd cheese to make cheesecake and top with fresh fruit or fruit tinned in natural juice.**

# Cheese sauce

**Portion** A quarter of a pint or five tablespoons
**Weight** 140 g., about 5 oz.

**Food Facts**
Energy 277 kcal.
Protein 11.6 g.
Total fat 20.4 g.
Saturated fat 10.5 g.
Polyunsaturated fat 1.49 g.
Carbohydrate 12.6 g.
Sugars 5.9 g.
Fibre 0.3 g.

**Minerals**
Calcium 364 mg.
Iron 0.42 mg.
Zinc 1.54 mg.
Copper 0.04 mg.
Sodium 630 mg.
Potassium 210 mg.
Magnesium 25.2 mg.
Phosphorus 266 mg.

**Vitamins**
Vitamin A 207 µg.
Vitamin C None.
Vitamin D 0.78 µg.
Vitamin E 0.84 mg.
Vitamin B1 0.07 mg.
Vitamin B2 0.32 mg.
Niacin 2.94 mg.
Vitamin B6 0.07 mg.
Vitamin B12 None.
Folic acid 7 µg.
Pantothenic acid 0.4 mg.
Biotin 2.8 µg.

**When making cheese sauce, use a small amount of a very strong cheese, rather than a lot of a very mild cheese.**

# Chicken soup

**Portion** One small tin of ready-to-serve cream of chicken soup.
**Weight** 290 g., about 10¼ oz.

**Food Facts**
Energy 168 kcal.
Protein 4.9 g.
Total fat 11 g.
Saturated fat Not known.
Polyunsaturated fat Not known.
Carbohydrate 13 g.
Sugars 3.2 g.
Fibre Not known.

**Minerals**
Calcium 78 mg.
Iron 1.16 mg.
Zinc 0.87 mg.
Copper 0.06 mg.
Sodium 1334 mg.
Potassium 118 mg.
Magnesium 14.5 mg.
Phosphorus 78.3 mg.

**Vitamins**
Vitamin A None.
Vitamin C None.
Vitamin D None.
Vitamin E Not known.
Vitamin B1 0.03 mg.
Vitamin B2 0.09 mg.
Niacin 1.45 mg.
Vitamin B6 0.03 mg.
Vitamin B12 None.
Folic acid Not known.
Pantothenic acid Not known.
Biotin Not known.

**Cream of chicken soup contains more calories and fat than most other soups. Chicken broth is a good substitute with less calories.**

# Chocolate bar with nuts

**Portion** One small Topic bar.

**Weight** 50 g., about 2 oz.

**Food Facts**
**Energy** 248 kcal.
**Protein** 3.9 g.
**Total fat** 12.9 g.
**Saturated fat** 5.7 g.
**Polyunsaturated fat** Not known.
**Carbohydrate** 29.9 g.
**Sugars** 27.6 g.
**Fibre** 1.9 g.

**Minerals**
**Calcium** 75 mg.
**Iron** 1.2 mg.
**Zinc** 0.07 mg.
**Copper** 0.24 mg.
**Sodium** 36 mg.
**Potassium** 175 mg.
**Magnesium** 38 mg.
**Phosphorus** 93 mg.

**Vitamins**
**Vitamin A** 5.6 µg.
**Vitamin C** 0.5 mg.
**Vitamin D** None.
**Vitamin E** 5.6 mg.
**Vitamin B1** Not known.
**Vitamin B2** 0.1 mg.
**Niacin** Not known.
**Vitamin B6** 0.04 mg.
**Vitamin B12** 0.1 µg.
**Folic acid** 4.8 µg.
**Pantothenic acid** Not known.
**Biotin** 0.5 µg.

**Although nuts are quite high in protein, they also contain a lot of fat and will make a high calorie snack even higher.**

# Chocolate bar, milk

**Portion** One medium bar.

**Weight** 100 g., about 3½ oz.

**Food Facts**
**Energy** 529 kcal.
**Protein** 8.4 g.
**Total fat** 30.3 g.
**Saturated fat** 17.67 g.
**Polyunsaturated fat** 1.06 g.
**Carbohydrate** 59.4 g.
**Sugars** 56.5 g.
**Fibre** Not known.

**Minerals**
**Calcium** 220 mg.
**Iron** 1.6 mg.
**Zinc** 0.2 mg.
**Copper** 0.3 mg.
**Sodium** 120 mg.
**Potassium** 420 mg.
**Magnesium** 55 mg.
**Phosphorus** 240 mg.

**Vitamins**
**Vitamin A** 6.5 µg.
**Vitamin C** None.
**Vitamin D** None.
**Vitamin E** 0.5 mg.
**Vitamin B1** 0.1 mg.
**Vitamin B2** 0.23 mg.
**Niacin** 1.6 mg.
**Vitamin B6** 0.02 mg.
**Vitamin B12** None.
**Folic acid** 10 µg.
**Pantothenic acid** 0.6 mg.
**Biotin** 3 µg.

**Milk chocolate is nearly two-thirds sugar and one third fat.**

# Chocolate bar, plain

**Portion** One medium bar

**Weight** 100 g., about 3½ oz.

**Food Facts**
**Energy** 525 kcal.
**Protein** 4.7 g.
**Total fat** 29.2 g.
**Saturated fat** 17.39 g.
**Polyunsaturated fat** 0.92 g.
**Carbohydrate** 64.8 g.
**Sugars** 59.5 g.
**Fibre** Not known.

**Minerals**
**Calcium** 38 mg.
**Iron** 2.4 mg.
**Zinc** 0.2 mg.
**Copper** 0.7 mg.
**Sodium** 11 mg.
**Potassium** 300 mg.
**Magnesium** 100 mg.
**Phosphorus** 140 mg.

**Vitamins**
**Vitamin A** 6.5 µg.
**Vitamin C** None.
**Vitamin D** None.
**Vitamin E** 0.5 mg.
**Vitamin B1** 0.07 mg.
**Vitamin B2** 0.08 mg.
**Niacin** 1.2 mg.
**Vitamin B6** 0.02 mg.
**Vitamin B12** None.
**Folic acid** 10 µg.
**Pantothenic acid** 0.6 mg.
**Biotin** 3 µg.

**Plain chocolate is just as high in calories as milk chocolate and actually contains more sugar.**

# Chocolate cake

**Portion** One slice.

**Weight** 37 g., about 1⅓ oz.

**Food Facts**
**Energy** 185 kcal.
**Protein** 2.1 g.
**Total fat** 11.4 g.
**Saturated fat** Not known.
**Polyunsaturated fat** Not known.
**Carbohydrate** 19.6 g.
**Sugars** 13.1 g.
**Fibre** Not known.

**Minerals**
**Calcium** 49.2 mg.
**Iron** 0.59 mg.
**Zinc** 0.33 mg.
**Copper** 0.11 mg.
**Sodium** 160 mg.
**Potassium** 54.8 mg.
**Magnesium** 13.7 mg.
**Phosphorus** 63.6 mg.

**Vitamins**
**Vitamin A** 110 µg.
**Vitamin C** None.
**Vitamin D** 1.12 µg.
**Vitamin E** 1.11 mg.
**Vitamin B1** 0.03 mg.
**Vitamin B2** 0.03 mg.
**Niacin** 0.18 mg.
**Vitamin B6** 0.01 mg.
**Vitamin B12** None.
**Folic acid** 2.2 µg.
**Pantothenic acid** 0.1 mg.
**Biotin** 2.2 µg.

**Instead of filling sandwich cakes with cream or butter icing, use a low sugar jam and plain yoghurt.**

# Chocolate drink

**Portion** One teaspoon of powder (not including milk)
**Weight** 5 g., about ⅕ oz.

## Food Facts
**Energy** 18 kcal.
**Protein** 0.3 g.
**Total fat** 0.3 g.
**Saturated fat** 0.17 g.
**Polyunsaturated fat** None.
**Carbohydrate** 3.9 g.
**Sugars** 3.7 g.
**Fibre** Not known.

## Minerals
**Calcium** 1.6 mg.
**Iron** 0.12 mg.
**Zinc** 0.09 mg.
**Copper** 0.05 mg.
**Sodium** 12.5 mg.
**Potassium** 20.5 mg.
**Magnesium** 7.5 mg.
**Phosphorus** 9.5 mg.

## Vitamins
**Vitamin A** None.
**Vitamin C** None.
**Vitamin D** None.
**Vitamin E** None.
**Vitamin B1** None.
**Vitamin B2** None.
**Niacin** 0.1 mg.
**Vitamin B6** None.
**Vitamin B12** None.
**Folic acid** 0.5 µg.
**Pantothenic acid** Not known.
**Biotin** Not known.

Although it contains a lot more sugar, drinking chocolate is not much higher in calories than cocoa because it contains less fat.

# Chocolates, boxed

**Portion** One average chocolate.
**Weight** 10 g., about ⅓ oz.

## Food Facts
**Energy** 46 kcal.
**Protein** 0.4 g.
**Total fat** 1.9 g.
**Saturated fat** Not known.
**Polyunsaturated fat** Not known.
**Carbohydrate** 7.3 g.
**Sugars** 6.6 g.
**Fibre** Not known.

## Minerals
**Calcium** 9.2 mg.
**Iron** 0.18 mg.
**Zinc** Not known.
**Copper** 0.04 mg.
**Sodium** 6 mg.
**Potassium** 24 mg.
**Magnesium** 5.1 mg.
**Phosphorus** 12 mg.

## Vitamins
**Vitamin A** 0.6 µg.
**Vitamin C** None.
**Vitamin D** None.
**Vitamin E** Not known.
**Vitamin B1** 0.01 mg.
**Vitamin B2** 0.01 mg.
**Niacin** 0.10 mg.
**Vitamin B6** None.
**Vitamin B12** None.
**Folic acid** 1 µg.
**Pantothenic acid** 0.1 mg.
**Biotin** 0.3 µg.

Individual chocolates contain different amounts. A bouquet of flowers or a plant will give as much pleasure without the calories.

# Chutney

**Portion** One teaspoon.

**Weight** 10 g., about ⅓ oz.

**Food Facts**
Energy 15 kcal.
Protein 0.1 g.
Total fat None.
Saturated fat None.
Polyunsaturated fat None.
Carbohydrate 4 g.
Sugars 3.9 g.
Fibre 0.2 g.

**Minerals**
Calcium 3 mg.
Iron 0.11 mg.
Zinc 0.02 mg.
Copper 0.01 mg.
Sodium 13 mg.
Potassium 31 mg.
Magnesium 2 mg.
Phosphorus 3.9 mg.

**Vitamins**
Vitamin A 6 µg.
Vitamin C 0.8 mg.
Vitamin D None.
Vitamin E 0.08 mg.
Vitamin B1 None.
Vitamin B2 None.
Niacin 0.06 mg.
Vitamin B6 0.01 mg.
Vitamin B12 None.
Folic acid 1.1 µg.
Pantothenic acid None.
Biotin 0.1 µg.

Chutneys usually contain a lot more sugar than pickle and can add quite a few calories to a sandwich or salad.

# Cider

**Portion** One pint of dry cider.

**Weight** 560 g., about 20 oz.

**Food Facts**
Energy 201 kcal.
Protein None.
Total fat None.
Saturated fat None.
Polyunsaturated fat None.
Carbohydrate 14.6 g.
Sugars 14.6 g.
Fibre None.

**Minerals**
Calcium 44.8 mg.
Iron 2.74 mg.
Zinc Not known.
Copper 0.22 mg.
Sodium 39.2 mg.
Potassium 403 mg.
Magnesium 16.8 mg.
Phosphorus 16.8 mg.

**Vitamins**
Vitamin A None.
Vitamin C None.
Vitamin D None.
Vitamin E Not known.
Vitamin B1 None.
Vitamin B2 None.
Niacin 0.06 mg.
Vitamin B6 0.03 mg.
Vitamin B12 None.
Folic acid Not known.
Pantothenic acid 0.2 mg.
Biotin 3.4 µg.

Even dry cider contains a lot of sugar, almost twice as much as there is in lager.

# Coca Cola

**Portion** One can.

**Weight** 330 ml. volume.

**Food Facts**
**Energy** 128 kcal.
**Protein** None.
**Total fat** None.
**Saturated fat** None.
**Polyunsaturated fat** None.
**Carbohydrate** 34.6 g.
**Sugars** 34.6 g.
**Fibre** None.

**Minerals**
**Calcium** 13.2 mg.
**Iron** None.
**Zinc** None.
**Copper** 0.1 mg.
**Sodium** 26.4 mg.
**Potassium** 3.3 mg.
**Magnesium** 3.3 mg.
**Phosphorus** 49.5 mg.

**Vitamins**
**Vitamin A** None.
**Vitamin C** None.
**Vitamin D** None.
**Vitamin E** None.
**Vitamin B1** None.
**Vitamin B2** None.
**Niacin** None.
**Vitamin B6** None.
**Vitamin B12** None.
**Folic acid** None.
**Pantothenic acid** None.
**Biotin** None.

Like some other fizzy drinks, cola drinks contain the equivalent of seven teaspoons of sugar in every can.

# Cocoa

**Portion** One teaspoon of powder.

**Weight** 5 g., about ⅕ oz.

**Food Facts**
**Energy** 15 kcal.
**Protein** 0.9 g.
**Total fat** 1.1 g.
**Saturated fat** 0.63 g.
**Polyunsaturated fat** 0.03 g.
**Carbohydrate** 0.6 g.
**Sugars** None.
**Fibre** Not known.

**Minerals**
**Calcium** 6.5 mg.
**Iron** 0.52 mg.
**Zinc** 0.34 mg.
**Copper** 0.19 mg.
**Sodium** 47 mg.
**Potassium** 75 mg.
**Magnesium** 26 mg.
**Phosphorus** 33 mg.

**Vitamins**
**Vitamin A** 0.3 µg.
**Vitamin C** None.
**Vitamin D** None.
**Vitamin E** 0.02 mg.
**Vitamin B1** 0.01 mg.
**Vitamin B2** None.
**Niacin** 0.36 mg.
**Vitamin B6** None.
**Vitamin B12** None.
**Folic acid** 1.9 µg.
**Pantothenic acid** Not known.
**Biotin** Not known.

Although cocoa does not contain sugar, you may find you need to add a lot in order for it to taste sweet enough.

# Coffee

**Portion** One teaspoon of instant coffee.
**Weight** 2.5 g., about ¹/₁₀ oz.

**Food Facts**
**Energy** 2.5 kcal.
**Protein** 0.4 g.
**Total fat** None.
**Saturated fat** None.
**Polyunsaturated fat** None.
**Carbohydrate** 0.3 g.
**Sugars** 0.2 g.
**Fibre** Not known.

**Minerals**
**Calcium** 4 mg.
**Iron** 0.11 mg.
**Zinc** 0.01 mg.
**Copper** None.
**Sodium** 1 mg.
**Potassium** 100 mg.
**Magnesium** 9.75 mg.
**Phosphorus** 8.75 mg.

**Vitamins**
**Vitamin A** None.
**Vitamin C** None.
**Vitamin D** None.
**Vitamin E** Not known.
**Vitamin B1** None.
**Vitamin B2** None.
**Niacin** 0.62 mg.
**Vitamin B6** None.
**Vitamin B12** None.
**Folic acid** None.
**Pantothenic acid** None.
**Biotin** None.

**Coffee has very few nutrients, but does contain caffeine. Some experts say drink less, particularly those with heart conditions.**

# Kellogg's Corn Flakes

**Portion** One bowlful.

**Weight** 30 g., about 1 oz.

**Food Facts**
**Energy** 105 kcal.
**Protein** 2.4 g.
**Total fat** 0.09 g.
**Saturated fat** Not known.
**Polyunsaturated fat** Not known.
**Carbohydrate** 25.3 g.
**Sugars** 2.2 g.
**Fibre** 0.42 g.

**Minerals**
**Calcium** 4.4 mg.
**Iron** 2.01 mg.
**Zinc** 0.09 mg.
**Copper** 0.01 mg.
**Sodium** 330 mg.
**Potassium** 31 mg.
**Magnesium** 4.2 mg.
**Phosphorus** 13.3 mg.

**Vitamins**
**Vitamin A** None.
**Vitamin C** None.
**Vitamin D** 0.84 µg.
**Vitamin E** 0.12 mg.
**Vitamin B1** 0.3 mg.
**Vitamin B2** 0.45 mg.
**Niacin** 4.8 mg.
**Vitamin B6** 0.54 mg.
**Vitamin B12** 0.51 µg.
**Folic acid** 75 µg.
**Pantothenic acid** Not known.
**Biotin** Not known.

**Avoid cereals which are sugar coated.**

# Cream crackers

**Portion** Two cream crackers.

**Weight** 14 g., about ½ oz.

**Food Facts**
**Energy** 61 kcal.
**Protein** 1.3 g.
**Total fat** 2.3 g.
**Saturated fat** Not known.
**Polyunsaturated fat** Not known.
**Carbohydrate** 9.6 g.
**Sugars** None.
**Fibre** 0.4 g.

**Minerals**
**Calcium** 15.4 mg.
**Iron** 0.24 mg.
**Zinc** 0.08 mg.
**Copper** Not known.
**Sodium** 85.4 mg.
**Potassium** 16.8 mg.
**Magnesium** 3.5 mg.
**Phosphorus** 15.4 mg.

**Vitamins**
**Vitamin A** None.
**Vitamin C** None.
**Vitamin D** None.
**Vitamin E** Not known.
**Vitamin B1** 0.02 mg.
**Vitamin B2** 0.01 mg.
**Niacin** 0.48 mg.
**Vitamin B6** 0.01 mg.
**Vitamin B12** None.
**Folic acid** 2.1 µg.
**Pantothenic acid** Not known.
**Biotin** Not known.

**Cream crackers are not very much lower in calories than sweet biscuits. They are not as calorie free as many people think.**

# Crispbread

**Portion** Three crispbread.

**Weight** 25 g., about 1 oz.

**Food Facts**
**Energy** 80 kcal.
**Protein** 2.3 g.
**Total fat** 0.5 g.
**Saturated fat** 0.07 g.
**Polyunsaturated fat** 0.24 g.
**Carbohydrate** 17.6 g.
**Sugars** 0.8 g.
**Fibre** 2.9 g.

**Minerals**
**Calcium** 12.5 mg.
**Iron** 0.92 mg.
**Zinc** 0.77 mg.
**Copper** 0.09 mg.
**Sodium** 55 mg.
**Potassium** 125 mg.
**Magnesium** 25 mg.
**Phosphorus** 77.5 mg.

**Vitamins**
**Vitamin A** None.
**Vitamin C** None.
**Vitamin D** None.
**Vitamin E** 0.12 mg.
**Vitamin B1** 0.07 mg.
**Vitamin B2** 0.03 mg.
**Niacin** 0.72 mg.
**Vitamin B6** 0.07 mg.
**Vitamin B12** None.
**Folic acid** 10.0 µg.
**Pantothenic acid** 0.3 mg.
**Biotin** 1.7 µg.

**If you are on a calorie-controlled diet, remember that crispbreads contain some calories.**

# Crumpet

**Portion** One crumpet.

**Weight** 55 g., about 2 oz.

**Food Facts**
Energy 107 kcal.
Protein 3.9 g.
Total fat 0.4 g.
Saturated fat Not known.
Polyunsaturated fat Not known.
Carbohydrate 23.6 g.
Sugars 0.5 g.
Fibre 1.2 g.

**Minerals**
Calcium 62 mg.
Iron 0.82 mg.
Zinc 0.38 mg.
Copper 0.12 mg.
Sodium 325 mg.
Potassium 59.4 mg.
Magnesium 15.4 mg.
Phosphorus 66 mg.

**Vitamins**
Vitamin A None.
Vitamin C None.
Vitamin D None.
Vitamin E None.
Vitamin B1 0.11 mg.
Vitamin B2 0.05 mg.
Niacin 1.65 mg.
Vitamin B6 0.06 mg.
Vitamin B12 None.
Folic acid 23.6 µg.
Pantothenic acid 0.2 mg.
Biotin 2.2 µg.

**Crumpets are quite high in calories and will absorb a lot of butter or margarine to increase the calories still further.**

# Custard

**Portion** One ladleful.

**Weight** 130 g., about 4½ oz.

**Food Facts**
Energy 153 kcal.
Protein 4.9 g.
Total fat 5.7 g.
Saturated fat 3.4 g.
Polyunsaturated fat 0.15 g.
Carbohydrate 21.8 g.
Sugars 14.9 g.
Fibre None.

**Minerals**
Calcium 182 mg.
Iron 0.13 mg.
Zinc 0.52 mg.
Copper 0.04 mg.
Sodium 98 mg.
Potassium 221 mg.
Magnesium 18.2 mg.
Phosphorus 143 mg.

**Vitamins**
Vitamin A 56 µg.
Vitamin C None.
Vitamin D 0.04 µg.
Vitamin E 0.13 mg.
Vitamin B1 0.06 mg.
Vitamin B2 0.27 mg.
Niacin 1.3 mg.
Vitamin B6 0.06 mg.
Vitamin B12 None.
Folic acid 6.5 µg.
Pantothenic acid 0.5 mg.
Biotin 2.6 µg.

**Try to add less sugar when making custard. A dash of vanilla essence and a sprinkling of cinnamon will add extra flavour.**

# Danish pastry

**Portion** One Danish pastry.

**Weight** 70 g., about 2½ oz.

**Food Facts**
Energy 294 kcal.
Protein 5.6 g.
Total fat 17.9 g.
Saturated fat Not known.
Polyunsaturated fat Not known.
Carbohydrate 29.5 g.
Sugars 6 g.
Fibre 1.3 g.

**Minerals**
Calcium 67 mg.
Iron 1.19 mg.
Zinc 0.56 mg.
Copper 0.16 mg.
Sodium 373 mg.
Potassium 98 mg.
Magnesium 18.2 mg.
Phosphorus 91 mg.

**Vitamins**
Vitamin A 176 µg.
Vitamin C None.
Vitamin D 1.77 µg.
Vitamin E 1.75 mg.
Vitamin B1 0.1 mg.
Vitamin B2 0.12 mg.
Niacin 2.24 mg.
Vitamin B6 0.06 mg.
Vitamin B12 None.
Folic acid 32.2 µg.
Pantothenic acid 0.3 mg.
Biotin 4.9 µg.

Like other pastry, Danish pastry is high in fat. Eat only occasionally as a treat.

# Doughnut

**Portion** One doughnut with jam.

**Weight** 75 g., about 2⅔ oz.

**Food Facts**
Energy 261 kcal.
Protein 4.5 g.
Total fat 11.8 g.
Saturated fat Not known.
Polyunsaturated fat Not known.
Carbohydrate 36.6 g.
Sugars 11.2 g.
Fibre 1.1 g.

**Minerals**
Calcium 52 mg.
Iron 1.42 mg.
Zinc 0.37 mg.
Copper 0.08 mg.
Sodium 45 mg.
Potassium 82 mg.
Magnesium 12 mg.
Phosphorus 41 mg.

**Vitamins**
Vitamin A None.
Vitamin C None.
Vitamin D None.
Vitamin E Not known.
Vitamin B1 Not known.
Vitamin B2 Not known.
Niacin 0.9 mg.
Vitamin B6 0.04 mg.
Vitamin B12 None.
Folic acid 5.2 µ g
Pantothenic acid 0.4 mg.
Biotin 6 µg.

Most doughnuts are deep fat fried and contain quite a lot of calories and fat.

# Flour, white

**Portion** One tablespoon.

**Weight** 15 g., about ½ oz.

**Food Facts**
**Energy** 52 kcal.
**Protein** 1.5 g.
**Total fat** 0.2 g.
**Saturated fat** 0.02 g.
**Polyunsaturated fat** 0.07 g.
**Carbohydrate** 12 g.
**Sugars** 0.3 g.
**Fibre** 0.5 g.

**Minerals**
**Calcium** 22.5 mg.
**Iron** 0.36 mg.
**Zinc** 0.1 mg.
**Copper** 0.03 mg.
**Sodium** 0.3 mg.
**Potassium** 21 mg.
**Magnesium** 3 mg.
**Phosphorus** 16.5 mg.

**Vitamins**
**Vitamin A** None.
**Vitamin C** None.
**Vitamin D** None.
**Vitamin E** None.
**Vitamin B1** 0.05 mg.
**Vitamin B2** None.
**Niacin** 0.6 mg.
**Vitamin B6** 0.02 mg.
**Vitamin B12** None.
**Folic acid** 3.3 µg.
**Pantothenic acid** None.
**Biotin** 0.1 µg.

Try to avoid using fat and flour to thicken sauces and gravies. Simmer over a low heat to reduce them and they will gradually thicken.

# Flour, wholemeal

**Portion** One tablespoon.

**Weight** 15 g., about ½ oz.

**Food Facts**
**Energy** 47 kcal.
**Protein** 2 g.
**Total fat** 0.3 g.
**Saturated fat** 0.04 g.
**Polyunsaturated fat** 0.13 g.
**Carbohydrate** 9.9 g.
**Sugars** 0.3 g.
**Fibre** 1.4 g.

**Minerals**
**Calcium** 5.2 mg.
**Iron** 0.6 mg.
**Zinc** 0.45 mg.
**Copper** 0.06 mg.
**Sodium** 0.4 mg.
**Potassium** 54 mg.
**Magnesium** 21 mg.
**Phosphorus** 51 mg.

**Vitamins**
**Vitamin A** None.
**Vitamin C** None.
**Vitamin D** None.
**Vitamin E** 0.15 mg.
**Vitamin B1** 0.07 mg.
**Vitamin B2** 0.01 mg.
**Niacin** 1.21 mg.
**Vitamin B6** 0.07 mg.
**Vitamin B12** None.
**Folic acid** 8.5 µg.
**Pantothenic acid** 0.1 mg.
**Biotin** 1 µg.

Try replacing half the white flour in your recipes with wholemeal. Once you get used to it you can gradually increase the proportion.

# Fruit cake

**Portion** One slice.

**Weight** 56 g., about 2 oz.

**Food Facts**
Energy 198 kcal.
Protein 2.9 g.
Total fat 7.2 g.
Saturated fat 3.2 g.
Polyunsaturated fat 0.63 g.
Carbohydrate 32.4 g.
Sugars 24.1 g.
Fibre 1.6 g.

**Minerals**
Calcium 33.6 mg.
Iron 0.95 mg.
Zinc 0.28 mg.
Copper 0.14 mg.
Sodium 140 mg.
Potassium 218.4 mg.
Magnesium 14 mg.
Phosphorus 61.6 mg.

**Vitamins**
Vitamin A 72.8 µg.
Vitamin C None.
Vitamin D 0.64 µg.
Vitamin E Not known.
Vitamin B1 0.04 mg.
Vitamin B2 0.04 mg.
Niacin 0.90 mg.
Vitamin B6 0.07 mg.
Vitamin B12 None.
Folic acid 2.2 µg.
Pantothenic acid 0.1 mg.
Biotin 2.2 µg.

Fruit cake generally contains more fibre than other cakes. This does not compensate for its high sugar content.

# Fruit crumble

**Portion** One bowlful.

**Weight** 130 g., about 4½ oz.

**Food Facts**
Energy 270 kcal.
Protein 2.3 g.
Total fat 9 g.
Saturated fat 3.23 g.
Polyunsaturated fat 1.45 g.
Carbohydrate 48 g.
Sugars 30.9 g.
Fibre 3.2 g.

**Minerals**
Calcium 36 mg.
Iron 0.78 mg.
Zinc 0.26 mg.
Copper 0.12 mg.
Sodium 88 mg.
Potassium 130 mg.
Magnesium 6.5 mg.
Phosphorus 39 mg.

**Vitamins**
Vitamin A 90.2 µg.
Vitamin C 7.8 mg.
Vitamin D 0.86 µg.
Vitamin E 1.04 mg.
Vitamin B1 0.09 mg.
Vitamin B2 0.03 mg.
Niacin 0.91 mg.
Vitamin B6 0.05 mg.
Vitamin B12 None.
Folic acid 5.2 µg.
Pantothenic acid 0.1 mg.
Biotin None.

Do not add any sugar to the fruit, but a small amount of fruit juice. Make the topping using wholemeal flour adding oats and nuts for extra fibre.

# Fruit gums

**Portion** Five fruit gums.

**Weight** 10 g., about ⅓ oz.

**Food Facts**
**Energy** 17 kcal.
**Protein** 0.1 g.
**Total fat** None.
**Saturated fat** None.
**Polyunsaturated fat** None.
**Carbohydrate** 4.5 g.
**Sugars** 4.3 g.
**Fibre** Not known.

**Minerals**
**Calcium** 36 mg.
**Iron** 0.42 mg.
**Zinc** Not known.
**Copper** 0.14 mg.
**Sodium** 6.4 mg.
**Potassium** 36 mg.
**Magnesium** 11 mg.
**Phosphorus** 0.4 mg.

**Vitamins**
**Vitamin A** None.
**Vitamin C** None.
**Vitamin D** None.
**Vitamin E** None.
**Vitamin B1** None.
**Vitamin B2** None.
**Niacin** None.
**Vitamin B6** None.
**Vitamin B12** None.
**Folic acid** None.
**Pantothenic acid** None.
**Biotin** None.

**These type of sweets are lower in calories than many other kinds, but are still half sugar and contain additives.**

# Fruit pastilles

**Portion** Three fruit pastilles (one packet weighs 40 g.)

**Weight** 10 g., about ⅓ oz.

**Food Facts**
**Energy** 25 kcal.
**Protein** 0.5 g.
**Total fat** None.
**Saturated fat** None.
**Polyunsaturated fat** None.
**Carbohydrate** 6.2 g.
**Sugars** 6.2 g.
**Fibre** Not known.

**Minerals**
**Calcium** 4 mg.
**Iron** 0.14 mg.
**Zinc** Not known.
**Copper** 0.03 mg.
**Sodium** 7.7 mg.
**Potassium** 4 mg.
**Magnesium** 1.2 mg.
**Phosphorus** None.

**Vitamins**
**Vitamin A** None.
**Vitamin C** None.
**Vitamin D** None.
**Vitamin E** None.
**Vitamin B1** None.
**Vitamin B2** None.
**Niacin** None.
**Vitamin B6** None.
**Vitamin B12** None.
**Folic acid** None.
**Pantothenic acid** None.
**Biotin** None.

**If children eat sweets all day, they often do not eat proper meals. Allow them sweets after they have eaten their meal.**

# Fruit pie

**Portion** One sixth of large pie, pastry top and bottom.
**Weight** 70 g., about 2½ oz.

## Food Facts
**Energy** 258 kcal.
**Protein** 3 g.
**Total fat** 10.8 g.
**Saturated fat** 4.13 g.
**Polyunsaturated fat** 1.35 g.
**Carbohydrate** 39.7 g.
**Sugars** 21.6 g.
**Fibre** 1.8 g.

## Minerals
**Calcium** 35 mg.
**Iron** 0.84 mg.
**Zinc** 0.35 mg.
**Copper** 0.07 mg.
**Sodium** 147 mg.
**Potassium** 84 mg.
**Magnesium** 8.4 mg.
**Phosphorus** 44 mg.

## Vitamins
**Vitamin A** None.
**Vitamin C** None.
**Vitamin D** None.
**Vitamin E** Not known.
**Vitamin B1** 0.03 mg.
**Vitamin B2** 0.01 mg.
**Niacin** 0.91 mg.
**Vitamin B6** 0.02 mg.
**Vitamin B12** None.
**Folic acid** 2.8 µg.
**Pantothenic acid** 0.1 mg.
**Biotin** None.

**Fruit pies taste as good with just a pastry top. Make your pastry using half wholemeal and half white flour.**

# Gateau

**Portion** One slice with fruit and cream.
**Weight** 75 g., about 2¾ oz.

## Food Facts
**Energy** 244 kcal.
**Protein** 4.3 g.
**Total fat** 117 g.
**Saturated fat** Not known.
**Polyunsaturated fat** Not known.
**Carbohydrate** 32.5 g.
**Sugars** 24.7 g.
**Fibre** 0.4 g.

## Minerals
**Calcium** 44.2 mg.
**Iron** 0.75 mg.
**Zinc** 0.45 mg.
**Copper** 0.08 mg.
**Sodium** 39.7 mg.
**Potassium** 71.2 mg.
**Magnesium** 6 mg.
**Phosphorus** 66.7 mg.

## Vitamins
**Vitamin A** 37.1 µg.
**Vitamin C** None.
**Vitamin D** 0.37 µg.
**Vitamin E** 0.52 mg.
**Vitamin B1** 0.04 mg.
**Vitamin B2** 0.11 mg.
**Niacin** 0.22 mg.
**Vitamin B6** 0.04 mg.
**Vitamin B12** 0.75 µg.
**Folic acid** 4.5 µg.
**Pantothenic acid** 0.4 mg.
**Biotin** 6 µg.

**Go for gateaux with lots of fresh fruit on or in them. Use sugar-free tinned fruit if you are making your own.**

# Gin, whisky, vodka, brandy.

**Portion** One pub measure at 70% proof.
**Weight** 25 g., about 1 oz.

## Food Facts
**Energy** 55 kcal.
**Protein** None.
**Total fat** None.
**Saturated fat** None.
**Polyunsaturated fat** None.
**Carbohydrate** None.
**Sugars** None.
**Fibre** None.

## Minerals
**Calcium** None.
**Iron** None.
**Zinc** None.
**Copper** None.
**Sodium** None.
**Potassium** None.
**Magnesium** None.
**Phosphorus** None.

## Vitamins
**Vitamin A** None.
**Vitamin C** None.
**Vitamin D** None.
**Vitamin E** None.
**Vitamin B1** None.
**Vitamin B2** None.
**Niacin** None.
**Vitamin B6** None.
**Vitamin B12** None.
**Folic acid** None.
**Pantothenic acid** None.
**Biotin** None.

Although spirits may seem low in calories, the mixer drinks you add such as tonic water will add quite a few.

# Ginger ale

**Portion** One small bottle.

**Weight** 113 g., about 4 oz.

## Food Facts
**Energy** 23 kcal.
**Protein** None.
**Total fat** None.
**Saturated fat** None.
**Polyunsaturated fat** None.
**Carbohydrate** 6.3 g.
**Sugars** 6.3 g.
**Fibre** None.

## Minerals
**Calcium** 5.6 mg.
**Iron** None.
**Zinc** Not known.
**Copper** 0.01 mg.
**Sodium** 7.9 mg.
**Potassium** 1.1 mg.
**Magnesium** None.
**Phosphorus** None.

## Vitamins
**Vitamin A** None.
**Vitamin C** None.
**Vitamin D** None.
**Vitamin E** None.
**Vitamin B1** None.
**Vitamin B2** None.
**Niacin** None.
**Vitamin B6** None.
**Vitamin B12** None.
**Folic acid** None.
**Pantothenic acid** None.
**Biotin** None.

Ginger ale is normally used as a mixer with whisky. However many people find it settles the stomach if they are feeling sick.

# Golden syrup

**Portion** One tablespoon.

**Weight** 20 g., about ¾ oz.

**Food Facts**
**Energy** 59 kcal.
**Protein** 0.1 g.
**Total fat** None.
**Saturated fat** None.
**Polyunsaturated fat** None.
**Carbohydrate** 15.8 g.
**Sugars** 15.8 g.
**Fibre** None.

**Minerals**
**Calcium** 5.2 mg.
**Iron** 0.3 mg.
**Zinc** Not known.
**Copper** 0.02 mg.
**Sodium** 54 mg.
**Potassium** 48 mg.
**Magnesium** 2 mg.
**Phosphorus** 4 mg.

**Vitamins**
**Vitamin A** None.
**Vitamin C** None.
**Vitamin D** None.
**Vitamin E** None.
**Vitamin B1** None.
**Vitamin B2** None.
**Niacin** None.
**Vitamin B6** None.
**Vitamin B12** None.
**Folic acid** None.
**Pantothenic acid** None.
**Biotin** None.

**Golden syrup contains no vitamins and few minerals. Treat it as sugar which it is and use sparingly.**

# Grapefruit juice, unsweetened

**Portion** One wine glass

**Weight** 140 g., about 5 oz.

**Food Facts**
**Energy** 43 kcal.
**Protein** 0.4 g.
**Total fat** None.
**Saturated fat** None.
**Polyunsaturated fat** None.
**Carbohydrate** 11.1 g.
**Sugars** 11.1 g.
**Fibre** Not known.

**Minerals**
**Calcium** 12.6 mg.
**Iron** 0.42 mg.
**Zinc** 0.56 mg.
**Copper** 0.04 mg.
**Sodium** 4.2 mg.
**Potassium** 154 mg.
**Magnesium** 11.2 mg.
**Phosphorus** 16.8 mg.

**Vitamins**
**Vitamin A** None.
**Vitamin C** 39.2 mg.
**Vitamin D** None.
**Vitamin E** None.
**Vitamin B1** 0.06 mg.
**Vitamin B2** 0.01 mg.
**Niacin** 0.42 mg.
**Vitamin B6** 0.01 mg.
**Vitamin B12** None.
**Folic acid** 8.4 μg
**Pantothenic acid** 0.2 mg.
**Biotin** 1.4 μg.

**Grapefruit juice is not as calorie free as many people think. One glass contains almost as many calories as unsweetened orange juice.**

# Gravy

# Honey

**Portion** Four tablespoons with
meat juices, fat, flour and stock.
**Weight** 80 g., about 2¾ oz.

**Portion** One tablespoon.

**Weight** 20 g., about ¾ oz.

**Food Facts**
Energy 87 kcal.
Protein 1.5 g.
Total fat 7.5 g.
Saturated fat Not known.
Polyunsaturated fat Not known.
Carbohydrate 3.6 g.
Sugars Not known.
Fibre None.

**Food Facts**
Energy 57 kcal.
Protein 0.1 g.
Total fat None.
Saturated fat None.
Polyunsaturated fat None.
Carbohydrate 15.3 g.
Sugars 15.3 g.
Fibre Not known.

**Minerals**
Calcium Not known.
Iron Not known.
Zinc Not known.
Copper Not known.
Sodium Not known.
Potassium Not known.
Magnesium Not known.
Phosphorus Not known.

**Minerals**
Calcium 1 mg.
Iron 0.08 mg.
Zinc Not known.
Copper 0.01 mg.
Sodium 2.2 mg.
Potassium 10.2 mg.
Magnesium 0.4 mg.
Phosphorus 3.4 mg.

**Vitamins**
Vitamin A Not known.
Vitamin C Not known.
Vitamin D Not known.
Vitamin E Not known.
Vitamin B1 Not known.
Vitamin B2 Not known.
Niacin Not known.
Vitamin B6 Not known.
Vitamin B12 Not known.
Folic acid Not known.
Pantothenic acid Not known.
Biotin Not known.

**Vitamins**
Vitamin A None.
Vitamin C None.
Vitamin D None.
Vitamin E Not known.
Vitamin B1 None.
Vitamin B2 0.01 mg.
Niacin 0.04 mg.
Vitamin B6 Not known.
Vitamin B12 None.
Folic acid Not known.
Pantothenic acid Not known.
Biotin Not known.

**Make home-made gravy without fat
from the meat. Thicken juices by
simmering or add tomato puree or
a little cornflour.**

**Honey can be used as a sweetening
agent instead of sugar, but apart
from its pleasant taste it is hardly
nutritionally better for you.**

# Ice cream

**Portion** One ice cream scoop of vanilla.
**Weight** 56 g., about 2 oz.

## Food Facts
**Energy** 93 kcal.
**Protein** 2.1 g.
**Total fat** 3.7 g.
**Saturated fat** 2.4 g.
**Polyunsaturated fat** 0.08 g.
**Carbohydrate** 13.9 g.
**Sugars** 12.7 g.
**Fibre** None.

## Minerals
**Calcium** 78 mg.
**Iron** 0.11 mg.
**Zinc** 0.22 mg.
**Copper** 0.02 mg.
**Sodium** 44.8 mg.
**Potassium** 100 mg.
**Magnesium** 7.3 mg.
**Phosphorus** 56 mg.

## Vitamins
**Vitamin A** 7.0 µg.
**Vitamin C** None.
**Vitamin D** None.
**Vitamin E** 0.22 mg.
**Vitamin B1** 0.02 mg.
**Vitamin B2** 0.1 mg.
**Niacin** 0.56 mg.
**Vitamin B6** 0.01 mg.
**Vitamin B12** None.
**Folic acid** 1.1 µg.
**Pantothenic acid** Not known.
**Biotin** Not known.

Ice cream that contains "non-milk fat" is not usually any lower in calories than dairy ice cream.

# Iced bun

**Portion** One iced bun.

**Weight** 95 g., about 3⅓ oz.

## Food Facts
**Energy** 344 kcal.
**Protein** 7.2 g.
**Total fat** 13.1 g.
**Saturated fat** Not known.
**Polyunsaturated fat** Not known.
**Carbohydrate** 52.5 g.
**Sugars** 20.8 g.
**Fibre** 2.3 g.

## Minerals
**Calcium** 104 mg.
**Iron** 1.6 mg.
**Zinc** 0.6 mg.
**Copper** 0.2 mg.
**Sodium** 313 mg.
**Potassium** 205 mg.
**Magnesium** 26.6 mg.
**Phosphorus** 114 mg.

## Vitamins
**Vitamin A** 127 µg.
**Vitamin C** None.
**Vitamin D** 1.28 µg.
**Vitamin E** 1.33 mg.
**Vitamin B1** 0.13 mg.
**Vitamin B2** 0.13 mg.
**Niacin** 1.2 mg.
**Vitamin B6** 0.11 mg.
**Vitamin B12** None.
**Folic acid** 30 µg.
**Pantothenic acid** 0.3 mg.
**Biotin** 4.75 µg.

Iced buns are high in calories, even though they do not always taste very sweet. Keep them for special tea-time treats.

# Instant pudding

**Portion** A quarter of sachet made with ¼ pint milk.
**Weight** 160 g., about 5¾ oz.

**Food Facts**
**Energy** 172 kcal.
**Protein** 4.9 g.
**Total fat** 7.6 g.
**Saturated fat** Not known.
**Polyunsaturated fat** Not known.
**Carbohydrate** 22.4 g.
**Sugars** 17.1 g.
**Fibre** 0.32 g.

**Minerals**
**Calcium** 144 mg.
**Iron** 0.16 mg.
**Zinc** 0.64 mg.
**Copper** 0.06 mg.
**Sodium** 360 mg.
**Potassium** 208 mg.
**Magnesium** 16 mg.
**Phosphorus** 296 mg.

**Vitamins**
**Vitamin A** 74 µg.
**Vitamin C** 2.08 mg.
**Vitamin D** 0.03 µg.
**Vitamin E** Not known.
**Vitamin B1** 0.06 mg.
**Vitamin B2** 0.22 mg.
**Niacin** 1.28 mg.
**Vitamin B6** 0.16 mg.
**Vitamin B12** 0.64 µg.
**Folic acid** 8 µg.
**Pantothenic acid** Not known.
**Biotin** Not known.

**Instant puddings are useful but home-made fruit fools are much healthier if made with sugar free tinned fruit and skimmed milk.**

# Jam

**Portion** Two teaspoons – enough to spread on one slice of bread.
**Weight** 20 g., about ¾ oz.

**Food Facts**
**Energy** 52 kcal.
**Protein** 0.1 g.
**Total fat** None.
**Saturated fat** None.
**Polyunsaturated fat** None.
**Carbohydrate** 13.8 g.
**Sugars** 13.8 g.
**Fibre** 0.2 g.

**Minerals**
**Calcium** 4.8 mg.
**Iron** 0.3 mg.
**Zinc** Not known.
**Copper** 0.05 mg.
**Sodium** 3.2 mg.
**Potassium** 22 mg.
**Magnesium** 2 mg.
**Phosphorus** 3.6 mg.

**Vitamins**
**Vitamin A** None.
**Vitamin C** 2 mg.
**Vitamin D** None.
**Vitamin E** None.
**Vitamin B1** None.
**Vitamin B2** None.
**Niacin** None.
**Vitamin B6** None.
**Vitamin B12** None.
**Folic acid** None.
**Pantothenic acid** None.
**Biotin** None.

**Many jams are now made with much less sugar, which are better for you, but will not keep as long and may need to be refrigerated.**

# Jelly

**Portion** One serving, the size of an individual mousse.
**Weight** 100 g., about 3½ oz.

**Food Facts**
**Energy** 59 kcal.
**Protein** 1.4 g.
**Total fat** None.
**Saturated fat** None.
**Polyunsaturated fat** None.
**Carbohydrate** 14.2 g.
**Sugars** 14.2 g.
**Fibre** None.

**Minerals**
**Calcium** 7 mg.
**Iron** 0.4 mg.
**Zinc** None.
**Copper** 0.04 mg.
**Sodium** 6 mg.
**Potassium** 6 mg.
**Magnesium** 1 mg.
**Phosphorus** 2 mg.

**Vitamins**
**Vitamin A** None.
**Vitamin C** None.
**Vitamin D** None.
**Vitamin E** None.
**Vitamin B1** None.
**Vitamin B2** None.
**Niacin** None.
**Vitamin B6** None.
**Vitamin B12** None.
**Folic acid** None.
**Pantothenic acid** None.
**Biotin** None.

Jelly contains no vitamins or fibre and often has artificial colouring added. Eat fresh or tinned fruit instead as a dessert.

# Jelly sweets

**Portion** Three jelly sweets

**Weight** 15 g., about ½ oz.

**Food Facts**
**Energy** 37 kcal.
**Protein** 0.8 g.
**Total fat** None.
**Saturated fat** None.
**Polyunsaturated fat** None.
**Carbohydrate** 9.3 g.
**Sugars** 9.3 g.
**Fibre** Not known.

**Minerals**
**Calcium** 6 mg.
**Iron** 0.21 mg.
**Zinc** Not known.
**Copper** 0.05 mg.
**Sodium** 11.5 mg.
**Potassium** 6 mg.
**Magnesium** 1.8 mg.
**Phosphorus** None.

**Vitamins**
**Vitamin A** None.
**Vitamin C** None.
**Vitamin D** None.
**Vitamin E** None.
**Vitamin B1** None.
**Vitamin B2** None.
**Niacin** None.
**Vitamin B6** None.
**Vitamin B12** None.
**Folic acid** None.
**Pantothenic acid** None.
**Biotin** None.

The best time for children to eat a sweet is after a meal. Eating sweets frequently contributes to tooth decay.

# Lager

# Lemon curd

**Portion** One pint of lager

**Weight** 560 g., about 20 oz.

**Food Facts**
**Energy** 162 kcal.
**Protein** 1.1 g.
**Total fat** None.
**Saturated fat** None.
**Polyunsaturated fat** None.
**Carbohydrate** 8.4 g.
**Sugars** 8.4 g.
**Fibre** None.

**Minerals**
**Calcium** 22.4 mg.
**Iron** None.
**Zinc** Not known.
**Copper** None.
**Sodium** 22.4 mg.
**Potassium** 190 mg.
**Magnesium** 33.6 mg.
**Phosphorus** 67.2 mg.

**Vitamins**
**Vitamin A** None.
**Vitamin C** None.
**Vitamin D** None.
**Vitamin E** Not known.
**Vitamin B1** None.
**Vitamin B2** 0.11 mg.
**Niacin** 3.02 mg.
**Vitamin B6** 0.12 mg.
**Vitamin B12** 0.78 µg.
**Folic acid** 24.1 µg.
**Pantothenic acid** 0.6 mg.
**Biotin** 2.8 µg.

Diluting your lager or beer with
lemonade will mean it contains less
alcohol but still just as many
calories.

**Portion** Two teaspoons – enough
to spread on one slice of bread.

**Weight** 20 g., about ¾ oz.

**Food Facts**
**Energy** 56 kcal.
**Protein** 0.1 g.
**Total fat** 1 g.
**Saturated fat** Not known.
**Polyunsaturated fat** Not known.
**Carbohydrate** 12.5 g.
**Sugars** 8.1 g.
**Fibre** None.

**Minerals**
**Calcium** 1.8 mg.
**Iron** 0.1 mg.
**Zinc** 0.26 mg.
**Copper** 0.01 mg.
**Sodium** 13 mg.
**Potassium** 2.2 mg.
**Magnesium** 0.4 mg.
**Phosphorus** 3 mg.

**Vitamins**
**Vitamin A** 2 µg.
**Vitamin C** None.
**Vitamin D** 0.02 µg.
**Vitamin E** Not known.
**Vitamin B1** None.
**Vitamin B2** None.
**Niacin** 0.02 mg.
**Vitamin B6** None.
**Vitamin B12** None.
**Folic acid** None.
**Pantothenic acid** None.
**Biotin** 0.2 µg.

These figures are for commercially-
made lemon curd. The home-made
variety will often be much higher in
calories and fat.

# Lemonade

**Portion** One large glass.

**Weight** 220 g., about 7¾ oz.

## Food Facts
**Energy** 46 kcal.
**Protein** None.
**Total fat** None.
**Saturated fat** None.
**Polyunsaturated fat** None.
**Carbohydrate** 12.3 g.
**Sugars** 12.3 g.
**Fibre** None.

## Minerals
**Calcium** 11 mg.
**Iron** None.
**Zinc** Not known.
**Copper** 0.02 mg.
**Sodium** 15.4 mg.
**Potassium** 2.2 mg.
**Magnesium** None.
**Phosphorus** None.

## Vitamins
**Vitamin A** None.
**Vitamin C** None.
**Vitamin D** None.
**Vitamin E** None.
**Vitamin B1** None.
**Vitamin B2** None.
**Niacin** None.
**Vitamin B6** None.
**Vitamin B12** None.
**Folic acid** None.
**Pantothenic acid** None.
**Biotin** None.

Contains less sugar and calories
than most fizzy drinks. Buy the low
calorie version if you are watching
your weight.

# Liquor

**Portion** One liquor glass of
cherry brandy.

**Weight** 15 g., about ½ oz.

## Food Facts
**Energy** 38 kcal.
**Protein** None.
**Total fat** None.
**Saturated fat** None.
**Polyunsaturated fat** None.
**Carbohydrate** 4.9 g.
**Sugars** 4.9 g.
**Fibre** None.

## Minerals
**Calcium** Not known.
**Iron** Not known.
**Zinc** Not known.
**Copper** Not known.
**Sodium** Not known.
**Potassium** Not known.
**Magnesium** Not known.
**Phosphorus** Not known.

## Vitamins
**Vitamin A** None.
**Vitamin C** None.
**Vitamin D** None.
**Vitamin E** None.
**Vitamin B1** None.
**Vitamin B2** None.
**Niacin** None.
**Vitamin B6** None.
**Vitamin B12** None.
**Folic acid** None.
**Pantothenic acid** Not known.
**Biotin** Not known.

Liquors which contain cream have a
much higher calorie value. These
figures represent a very small glass
of liquor.

# Liquorice sweets

# Malt loaf

**Portion** Six liquorice sweets

**Weight** 30 g., about 1 oz.

**Food Facts**
**Energy** 93 kcal.
**Protein** 1.2 g.
**Total fat** 0.7 g.
**Saturated fat** Not known.
**Polyunsaturated fat** Not known.
**Carbohydrate** 22.2 g.
**Sugars** 20.2 g.
**Fibre** Not known.

**Minerals**
**Calcium** 18.9 mg.
**Iron** 2.43 mg.
**Zinc** Not known.
**Copper** 0.12 mg.
**Sodium** 22.5 mg.
**Potassium** 66 mg.
**Magnesium** 11.4 mg.
**Phosphorus** 8.7 mg.

**Vitamins**
**Vitamin A** None.
**Vitamin C** None.
**Vitamin D** None.
**Vitamin E** None.
**Vitamin B1** None.
**Vitamin B2** None.
**Niacin** 0.21 mg.
**Vitamin B6** None.
**Vitamin B12** None.
**Folic acid** None.
**Pantothenic acid** None.
**Biotin** None.

**Liquorice sweets are surprisingly
high in calories as they still contain
quite a lot of sugar even if they don't
taste very sweet.**

**Portion** One slice, equivalent
to 1/8 of a loaf.

**Weight** 28 g., about 1 oz.

**Food Facts**
**Energy** 69 kcal.
**Protein** 2.3 g.
**Total fat** 0.9 g.
**Saturated fat** Not known.
**Polyunsaturated fat** Not known.
**Carbohydrate** 13.8 g.
**Sugars** 5.2 g.
**Fibre** 1.4 g.

**Minerals**
**Calcium** 26.3 mg.
**Iron** 1.01 mg.
**Zinc** 0.22 mg.
**Copper** 0.02 mg.
**Sodium** 78.4 mg.
**Potassium** 106 mg.
**Magnesium** 21.8 mg.
**Phosphorus** 70 mg.

**Vitamins**
**Vitamin A** None.
**Vitamin C** None.
**Vitamin D** None.
**Vitamin E** Not known.
**Vitamin B1** Not known.
**Vitamin B2** Not known.
**Niacin** 0.48 mg.
**Vitamin B6** Not known.
**Vitamin B12** None.
**Folic acid** Not known.
**Pantothenic acid** Not known.
**Biotin** Not known.

**Buy the wholemeal version and if
you have butter on it, spread it
thinly.**

# Malted milk drink

**Portion** Two teaspoons of powder.
**Weight** 10 g., about ⅓ oz.

**Food Facts**
Energy 39 kcal.
Protein 1.4 g.
Total fat 0.7 g.
Saturated fat Not known.
Polyunsaturated fat Not known.
Carbohydrate 7.3 g.
Sugars 4.9 g.
Fibre Not known.

**Minerals**
Calcium 23 mg.
Iron 0.18 mg.
Zinc Not known.
Copper 0.08 mg.
Sodium 35 mg.
Potassium 75 mg.
Magnesium 4.6 mg.
Phosphorus 30 mg.

**Vitamins**
Vitamin A 46.5
Vitamin C Not known.
Vitamin D 0.15 µg.
Vitamin E Not known.
Vitamin B1 0.08 mg.
Vitamin B2 Not known.
Niacin 1.41 mg.
Vitamin B6 Not known.
Vitamin B12 Not known.
Folic acid Not known.
Pantothenic acid Not known.
Biotin Not known.

Malted milk drinks are supposed to help you sleep at night, but taking plenty of exercise will also accomplish this.

# Marmalade

**Portion** Two teaspoons – enough to spread on one slice of bread.
**Weight** 20 g., about ¾ oz.

**Food Facts**
Energy 52 kcal.
Protein None.
Total fat None.
Saturated fat None.
Polyunsaturated fat None.
Carbohydrate 13.9 g.
Sugars 13.9 g.
Fibre 0.1 g.

**Minerals**
Calcium 7 mg.
Iron 0.12 mg.
Zinc Not known.
Copper 0.02 mg.
Sodium 3.6 mg.
Potassium 8.8 mg.
Magnesium 0.8 mg.
Phosphorus 2.6 mg.

**Vitamins**
Vitamin A 1.7 µg.
Vitamin C 2 mg.
Vitamin D None.
Vitamin E None.
Vitamin B1 None.
Vitamin B2 None.
Niacin None.
Vitamin B6 None.
Vitamin B12 None.
Folic acid 1 µg.
Pantothenic acid None.
Biotin None.

Thick-cut marmalade contains more fibre than jelly marmalade. Look out for the reduced sugar versions.

# Mars bar

**Portion** One normal sized Mars bar.
**Weight** 65 g., about 2 oz.

**Food Facts**
**Energy** 295 kcal.
**Protein** 3.8 g.
**Total fat** 11.5 g.
**Saturated fat** 7.6 g.
**Polyunsaturated fat** Not known.
**Carbohydrate** 45.2 g.
**Sugars** 42.7 g.
**Fibre** 1.17 g.

**Minerals**
**Calcium** 110.5 mg.
**Iron** 1.04 mg.
**Zinc** 0.03 mg.
**Copper** 0.21 mg.
**Sodium** 104 mg.
**Potassium** 201 mg.
**Magnesium** 20 mg.
**Phosphorus** 93 mg.

**Vitamins**
**Vitamin A** 19.5 µg.
**Vitamin C** 1.2 mg.
**Vitamin D** None.
**Vitamin E** 1.5 mg.
**Vitamin B1** 0.03 mg.
**Vitamin B2** 0.23 mg.
**Niacin** 0.78 mg.
**Vitamin B6** 0.04 mg.
**Vitamin B12** 0.2 µg.
**Folic acid** 3.7 µg.
**Pantothenic acid** None.
**Biotin** 2.4 µg.

**Chocolate bars provide energy but so do many other foods in a much more healthy form.**

# Marzipan

**Portion** The amount on a small slice of Christmas cake.
**Weight** 60 g., about 2¼ oz.

**Food Facts**
**Energy** 265 kcal.
**Protein** 5.2 g.
**Total fat** 14.9 g.
**Saturated fat** 1.18 g.
**Polyunsaturated fat** 2.8 g.
**Carbohydrate** 29.5 g.
**Sugars** 29.5 g.
**Fibre** 3.8 g.

**Minerals**
**Calcium** 72 mg.
**Iron** 1.2 mg.
**Zinc** 0.9 mg.
**Copper** 0.05 mg.
**Sodium** 7.8 mg.
**Potassium** 240 mg.
**Magnesium** 72 mg.
**Phosphorus** 132 mg.

**Vitamins**
**Vitamin A** 6 µg.
**Vitamin C** 1.2 mg.
**Vitamin D** 0.08 µg.
**Vitamin E** 5.46 mg.
**Vitamin B1** 0.07 mg.
**Vitamin B2** 0.27 mg.
**Niacin** 1.44 mg.
**Vitamin B6** 0.04 mg.
**Vitamin B12** None.
**Folic acid** 27.0 µg.
**Pantothenic acid** 0.2 mg.
**Biotin** 1.2 µg.

**Marzipan adds a lot of calories to cakes, so it is just as well most people only eat it on Christmas cake.**

# Mayonnaise

**Portion** One tablespoon.

**Weight** 15 g., about ½ oz.

**Food Facts**
**Energy** 107 kcal.
**Protein** 0.3 g.
**Total fat** 11.8 g.
**Saturated fat** Not known.
**Polyunsaturated fat** Not known.
**Carbohydrate** None.
**Sugars** None.
**Fibre** None.

**Minerals**
**Calcium** 2.4 mg.
**Iron** 0.1 mg.
**Zinc** 0.06 mg.
**Copper** None.
**Sodium** 54 mg.
**Potassium** 3.6 mg.
**Magnesium** 1 mg.
**Phosphorus** 8.8 mg.

**Vitamins**
**Vitamin A** 12 µg.
**Vitamin C** None.
**Vitamin D** 0.15 µg.
**Vitamin E** 0.73 mg.
**Vitamin B1** 0.01 mg.
**Vitamin B2** 0.02 mg.
**Niacin** 0.15 mg.
**Vitamin B6** 0.01 mg.
**Vitamin B12** 0.15 µg.
**Folic acid** 2.1 µg.
**Pantothenic acid** 0.1 mg.
**Biotin** 1.8 µg.

**To reduce the fat content of mayonnaise use half the quantity and make it up with low fat plain yoghurt.**

# Mince pie

**Portion** One individual.

**Weight** 56 g., about 2 oz.

**Food Facts**
**Energy** 243 kcal.
**Protein** 2.4 g.
**Total fat** 11.6 g.
**Saturated fat** 4.3 g.
**Polyunsaturated fat** 1.9 g.
**Carbohydrate** 34.6 g.
**Sugars** 16.8 g.
**Fibre** 1.6 g.

**Minerals**
**Calcium** 42 mg.
**Iron** 0.95 mg.
**Zinc** 0.22 mg.
**Copper** 0.1 mg.
**Sodium** 190 mg.
**Potassium** 84 mg.
**Magnesium** 7.8 mg.
**Phosphorus** 30.8 mg.

**Vitamins**
**Vitamin A** 51 µg.
**Vitamin C** None.
**Vitamin D** 0.45 µg.
**Vitamin E** 0.46 mg.
**Vitamin B1** 0.06 mg.
**Vitamin B2** 0.01 mg.
**Niacin** 0.95 mg.
**Vitamin B6** 0.04 mg.
**Vitamin B12** None.
**Folic acid** 2.8 µg.
**Pantothenic acid** 0.1 mg.
**Biotin** 0.6 µg.

**The high calorie value of mince pies makes it easy to see why so many people put weight on over Christmas.**

# Mincemeat

**Portion** One tablespoon.

**Weight** 30 g., about 1 oz.

**Food Facts**
**Energy** 70 kcal.
**Protein** 0.2 g.
**Total fat** 1.3 g.
**Saturated fat** Not known.
**Polyunsaturated fat** Not known.
**Carbohydrate** 18.6 g.
**Sugars** 18.6 g.
**Fibre** 1 g.

**Minerals**
**Calcium** 9 mg.
**Iron** 0.45 mg.
**Zinc** 0.06 mg.
**Copper** 0.06 mg.
**Sodium** 42 mg.
**Potassium** 57 mg.
**Magnesium** 3 mg.
**Phosphorus** 5.1 mg.

**Vitamins**
**Vitamin A** 3 µg.
**Vitamin C** None.
**Vitamin D** None.
**Vitamin E** Not known.
**Vitamin B1** 0.01 mg.
**Vitamin B2** 0.01 mg.
**Niacin** 0.09 mg.
**Vitamin B6** 0.03 mg.
**Vitamin B12** None.
**Folic acid** None.
**Pantothenic acid** None.
**Biotin** None.

If you like mince pie, make a large one with a thin pastry case on the bottom and lattice-work pastry on the top.

# Minestrone Soup

**Portion** Half a sachet of dried soup made with half a pint of water.

**Weight** 300 g., about 10¾ oz.

**Food Facts**
**Energy** 69 kcal.
**Protein** 2.4 g.
**Total fat** 2.1 g.
**Saturated fat** Not known.
**Polyunsaturated fat** Not known.
**Carbohydrate** 11.1 g.
**Sugars** 3.6 g.
**Fibre** 1.5 g.

**Minerals**
**Calcium** 27 mg.
**Iron** 0.6 mg.
**Zinc** 0.3 mg.
**Copper** 0.06 mg.
**Sodium** 1290 mg.
**Potassium** 186 mg.
**Magnesium** 21 mg.
**Phosphorus** 36 mg.

**Vitamins**
**Vitamin A** None.
**Vitamin C** None.
**Vitamin D** None.
**Vitamin E** Not known.
**Vitamin B1** 0.06 mg.
**Vitamin B2** 0.03 mg.
**Niacin** 0.9 mg.
**Vitamin B6** Not known.
**Vitamin B12** None.
**Folic acid** Not known.
**Pantothenic acid** Not known.
**Biotin** Not known.

Minestrone and other clear soups often contain less than half the calories of thick or cream soups.

# Mints

**Portion** Five hard mints.

**Weight** 10 g., about ⅓ oz.

## Food Facts
**Energy** 39 kcal.
**Protein** None.
**Total fat** 0.1 g.
**Saturated fat** Not known.
**Polyunsaturated fat** Not known.
**Carbohydrate** 10 g.
**Sugars** 10 g.
**Fibre** None.

## Minerals
**Calcium** 0.7 mg.
**Iron** 0.02 mg.
**Zinc** Not known.
**Copper** None.
**Sodium** 0.9 mg.
**Potassium** None.
**Magnesium** 0.3 mg.
**Phosphorus** None.

## Vitamins
**Vitamin A** None.
**Vitamin C** None.
**Vitamin D** None.
**Vitamin E** None.
**Vitamin B1** None.
**Vitamin B2** None.
**Niacin** None.
**Vitamin B6** None.
**Vitamin B12** None.
**Folic acid** None.
**Pantothenic acid** None.
**Biotin** None.

**Mints are just as high in calories as other sweets. It is easy to eat more of them because they are not as sweet.**

# Mousse

**Portion** One individual fruit mousse.

**Weight** 105 g., about 3¾ oz.

## Food Facts
**Energy** 163 kcal.
**Protein** 3.4 g.
**Total fat** 7.3 g.
**Saturated fat** Not known.
**Polyunsaturated fat** Not known.
**Carbohydrate** 22.3 g.
**Sugars** Not known.
**Fibre** Not known.

## Minerals
**Calcium** 97.6 mg.
**Iron** 0.21 mg.
**Zinc** 0.31 mg.
**Copper** Not known.
**Sodium** 59.8 mg.
**Potassium** Not known.
**Magnesium** Not known.
**Phosphorus** Not known.

## Vitamins
**Vitamin A** Not known.
**Vitamin C** Not known.
**Vitamin D** Not known.
**Vitamin E** Not known.
**Vitamin B1** 0.03 mg.
**Vitamin B2** 0.18 mg.
**Niacin** 0.94 mg.
**Vitamin B6** 0.04 mg.
**Vitamin B12** Not known.
**Folic acid** 3.15 µg.
**Pantothenic acid** Not known.
**Biotin** Not known.

**Fruit or plain yoghurt is usually a more nutritious dessert for children, especially ones without colourings or a lot of sugar.**

# Muesli

# Mustard

**Portion** One small bowlful.
About five tablespoons.
**Weight** 60 g., about 2¼ oz.

**Portion** One teaspoon.

**Weight** 5 g., about ⅕ oz.

**Food Facts**
**Energy** 220 kcal.
**Protein** 7.7 g.
**Total fat** 4.5 g.
**Saturated fat** 0.79 g.
**Polyunsaturated fat** 1.8 g.
**Carbohydrate** 39.7 g.
**Sugars** 15.7 g.
**Fibre** 4.4 g.

**Food Facts**
**Energy** 8.8 kcal.
**Protein** 0.3 g.
**Total fat** 0.4 g.
**Saturated fat** Not known.
**Polyunsaturated fat** Not known.
**Carbohydrate** 0.8 g.
**Sugars** Not known.
**Fibre** None.

**Minerals**
**Calcium** 120 mg.
**Iron** 2.76 mg.
**Zinc** 1.32 mg.
**Copper** 0.25 mg.
**Sodium** 108 mg.
**Potassium** 360 mg.
**Magnesium** 60 mg.
**Phosphorus** 228 mg.

**Minerals**
**Calcium**
**Iron** Not known.
**Zinc** Not known.
**Copper** Not known.
**Sodium** 20 mg.
**Potassium** 10 mg.
**Magnesium** Not known.
**Phosphorus** Not known.

**Vitamins**
**Vitamin A** None.
**Vitamin C** None.
**Vitamin D** None.
**Vitamin E** 1.92 mg.
**Vitamin B1** 0.2 mg.
**Vitamin B2** 0.16 mg.
**Niacin** 3.42 mg.
**Vitamin B6** 0.08 mg.
**Vitamin B12** None.
**Folic acid** 28.8 µg.
**Pantothenic acid** Not known.
**Biotin** Not known.

**Vitamins**
**Vitamin A** Not known.
**Vitamin C** Not known.
**Vitamin D** Not known.
**Vitamin E** Not known.
**Vitamin B1** Not known.
**Vitamin B2** Not known.
**Niacin** Not known.
**Vitamin B6** Not known.
**Vitamin B12** Not known.
**Folic acid** Not known.
**Pantothenic acid** Not known.
**Biotin** Not known.

**Muesli may contain a reasonable amount of fibre and minerals, but it is often high in sugars, both natural and added.**

**Mustard is a useful flavouring. Only one gram will spice up meat and fish dishes.**

# Orange juice, unsweetened

**Portion** One wine glass.

**Weight** 140 g., about 5 oz.

**Food Facts**
Energy 46 kcal.
Protein 0.6 g.
Total fat None.
Saturated fat None.
Polyunsaturated fat None.
Carbohydrate 11.9 g.
Sugars 11.9 g.
Fibre None.

**Minerals**
Calcium 12.6 mg.
Iron 0.7 mg.
Zinc 0.42 mg.
Copper 0.04 mg.
Sodium 5.6 mg.
Potassium 182 mg.
Magnesium 12.6 mg.
Phosphorus 21 mg.

**Vitamins**
Vitamin A 11.9 µg.
Vitamin C 49 mg.
Vitamin D None.
Vitamin E None.
Vitamin B1 0.1 mg.
Vitamin B2 0.03 mg.
Niacin 0.42 mg.
Vitamin B6 0.06 mg.
Vitamin B12 None.
Folic acid 9.8 µg.
Pantothenic acid 0.2 mg.
Biotin 1.4 µg.

Orange juice has a similar calorie
value to grapefruit juice. However,
orange juice sold in pubs and cafes
often has added sugar.

# Orange squash

**Portion** Concentrate to make
one large glass with water.

**Weight** 30 g., about 1 oz.

**Food Facts**
Energy 32 kcal.
Protein None.
Total fat None.
Saturated fat None.
Polyunsaturated fat None.
Carbohydrate 8.5 g.
Sugars 8.5 g.
Fibre None.

**Minerals**
Calcium 2.4 mg.
Iron 0.03 mg.
Zinc Not known.
Copper None.
Sodium 6.3 mg.
Potassium 5.1 mg.
Magnesium 0.9 mg.
Phosphorus 0.6 mg.

**Vitamins**
Vitamin A None.
Vitamin C None.
Vitamin D None.
Vitamin E None.
Vitamin B1 None.
Vitamin B2 None.
Niacin None.
Vitamin B6 None.
Vitamin B12 None.
Folic acid None.
Pantothenic acid None.
Biotin None.

Fruit squash often contains very
little fruit juice and many additives.
Drink natural fruit juice with
sparkling mineral water.

# Oxtail Soup

**Portion** One small tin of ready to serve oxtail soup.
**Weight** 300 g., about 10½ oz.

**Food Facts**
Energy 132 kcal.
Protein 7.2 g.
Total fat 5.1 g.
Saturated fat Not known.
Polyunsaturated fat Not known.
Carbohydrate 15.3 g.
Sugars 2.7 g.
Fibre Not known.

**Minerals**
Calcium 120 mg.
Iron 3 mg.
Zinc 1.2 mg.
Copper 0.12 mg.
Sodium 1320 mg.
Potassium 279 mg.
Magnesium 18 mg.
Phosphorus 111 mg.

**Vitamins**
Vitamin A None.
Vitamin C None.
Vitamin D None.
Vitamin E Not known.
Vitamin B1 0.06 mg.
Vitamin B2 0.09 mg.
Niacin 3.6 mg.
Vitamin B6 0.09 mg.
Vitamin B12 None.
Folic acid Not known.
Pantothenic acid Not known.
Biotin Not known.

**When having soup as a main course, oxtail is a good one to choose. Unlike other soups it contains good amounts of protein and iron.**

# Pancake

**Portion** One pancake without added sugar.
**Weight** 60 g., about 2 oz.

**Food Facts**
Energy 184 kcal.
Protein 3.7 g.
Total fat 9.8 g.
Saturated fat 4.2 g.
Polyunsaturated fat 0.87 g.
Carbohydrate 21.7 g.
Sugars 10 g.
Fibre 0.5 g.

**Minerals**
Calcium 72 mg.
Iron 0.54 mg.
Zinc 0.36 mg.
Copper 0.04 mg.
Sodium 30 mg.
Potassium 84 mg.
Magnesium 8.4 mg.
Phosphorus 72 mg.

**Vitamins**
Vitamin A 24.9 µg.
Vitamin C None.
Vitamin D 0.14 µg.
Vitamin E 0.18 mg.
Vitamin B1 0.08 mg.
Vitamin B2 0.11 mg.
Niacin 1.2 mg.
Vitamin B6 0.05 mg.
Vitamin B12 None.
Folic acid 3.6 µg.
Pantothenic acid 0.3 mg.
Biotin 3 µg.

**You can make savoury pancakes as well as sweet ones. Beans or vegetables make good low fat fillings.**

# Pasta, boiled

**Portion** One plateful, eg spaghetti, macaroni.
**Weight** 190 g., about 6¾ oz.

**Food Facts**
Energy 222 kcal.
Protein 8.2 g.
Total fat 1.1 g.
Saturated fat 0.07 g.
Polyunsaturated fat 0.22 g.
Carbohydrate 47 g.
Sugars None.
Fibre 1.9 g.

**Minerals**
Calcium 15.2 mg.
Iron 0.95 mg.
Zinc 0.57 mg.
Copper 0.04 mg.
Sodium 15.2 mg.
Potassium 127 mg.
Magnesium 34 mg.
Phosphorus 89 mg.

**Vitamins**
Vitamin A None.
Vitamin C None.
Vitamin D None.
Vitamin E None.
Vitamin B1 0.02 mg.
Vitamin B2 0.02 mg.
Niacin 2.28 mg.
Vitamin B6 0.02 mg.
Vitamin B12 None.
Folic acid 3.8 µg.
Pantothenic acid None.
Biotin None.

There are many wholewheat types of pasta now available. They take slightly longer to cook, but will not stick together as much.

# Piccalilli

**Portion** One tablespoon.

**Weight** 30 g., about 1 oz.

**Food Facts**
Energy 9 kcal.
Protein 0.3 g.
Total fat 0.2 g.
Saturated fat Not known.
Polyunsaturated fat Not known.
Carbohydrate 1.8 g.
Sugars 0.8 g.
Fibre 0.6 g.

**Minerals**
Calcium 7.2 mg.
Iron 0.27 mg.
Zinc 0.06 mg.
Copper 0.03 mg.
Sodium 360 mg.
Potassium 16.5 mg.
Magnesium 3 mg.
Phosphorus 6.9 mg.

**Vitamins**
Vitamin A None.
Vitamin C None.
Vitamin D None.
Vitamin E Not known.
Vitamin B1 0.05 mg.
Vitamin B2 None.
Niacin 0.12 mg.
Vitamin B6 Not known.
Vitamin B12 None.
Folic acid Not known.
Pantothenic acid Not known.
Biotin None.

Piccalilli adds texture and taste to salads, without greatly increasing their calorie value.

# Pickle

# Pineapple juice

**Portion** One teaspoon.

**Portion** One wine glass.

**Weight** 10 g., about ⅓ oz.

**Weight** 140 g., about 5 oz.

**Food Facts**
**Energy** 13 kcal.
**Protein** 0.1 g.
**Total fat** None.
**Saturated fat** None.
**Polyunsaturated fat** None.
**Carbohydrate** 3.4 g.
**Sugars** 3.3 g.
**Fibre** 0.2 g.

**Food Facts**
**Energy** 74 kcal.
**Protein** 0.6 g.
**Total fat** 0.1 g.
**Saturated fat** Not known.
**Polyunsaturated fat** Not known.
**Carbohydrate** 18.8 g.
**Sugars** 18.8 g.
**Fibre** Not known.

**Minerals**
**Calcium** 1.9 mg.
**Iron** 0.2 mg.
**Zinc** 0.14 mg.
**Copper** 0.01 mg.
**Sodium** 170 mg.
**Potassium** 11 mg.
**Magnesium** 1 mg.
**Phosphorus** 1.1 mg.

**Minerals**
**Calcium** 16.8 mg.
**Iron** 0.98 mg.
**Zinc** Not known.
**Copper** 0.13 mg.
**Sodium** 1.4 mg.
**Potassium** 196 mg.
**Magnesium** 16.8 mg.
**Phosphorus** 14 mg.

**Vitamins**
**Vitamin A** None.
**Vitamin C** Not known.
**Vitamin D** None.
**Vitamin E** Not known.
**Vitamin B1** None.
**Vitamin B2** None.
**Niacin** 0.03 mg.
**Vitamin B6** Not known.
**Vitamin B12** None.
**Folic acid** Not known.
**Pantothenic acid** Not known.
**Biotin** Not known.

**Vitamins**
**Vitamin A** 9.1 µg.
**Vitamin C** 11.2 mg.
**Vitamin D** None.
**Vitamin E** Not known.
**Vitamin B1** 0.07 mg.
**Vitamin B2** 0.03 mg.
**Niacin** 0.42 mg.
**Vitamin B6** 0.14 mg.
**Vitamin B12** None.
**Folic acid** Not known.
**Pantothenic acid** 0.1 mg.
**Biotin** Not known.

**A small amount of pickle adds taste to sandwiches but a lot also adds extra calories.**

**Pineapple juice contains a lot of natural sugar, and is not as high in vitamin C as some other fruit juices.**

# Pitta bread

**Portion** One pitta bread.

**Weight** 74 g., about 2½ oz.

**Food Facts**
**Energy** 196 kcal.
**Protein** 6.8 g.
**Total fat** 0.8 g.
**Saturated fat** Not known.
**Polyunsaturated fat** Not known.
**Carbohydrate** 42.8 g.
**Sugars** Not known.
**Fibre** 3.1 g.

**Minerals**
**Calcium** 67 mg.
**Iron** 1.25 mg.
**Zinc** 0.4 mg.
**Copper** 0.15 mg.
**Sodium** 384 mg.
**Potassium** 77.7 mg.
**Magnesium** 17.7 mg.
**Phosphorus** Not known.

**Vitamins**
**Vitamin A** Not known.
**Vitamin C** None.
**Vitamin D** Not known.
**Vitamin E** Not known.
**Vitamin B1** 0.17 mg.
**Vitamin B2** 0.03 mg.
**Niacin** 1.03 mg.
**Vitamin B6** Not known.
**Vitamin B12** Not known.
**Folic acid** 15.5 µg.
**Pantothenic acid** Not known.
**Biotin** Not known.

These figures are for white pitta bread. It is now also available in a wholemeal version, which will contain more fibre.

# Porridge

**Portion** One bowlful without milk or sugar.

**Weight** 260 g., about 9¼ oz. (uncooked 50 g.)

**Food Facts**
**Energy** 114 kcal.
**Protein** 3.6 g.
**Total fat** 2.3 g.
**Saturated fat** 0.36 g.
**Polyunsaturated fat** 0.93 g.
**Carbohydrate** 21.3 g.
**Sugars** None.
**Fibre** 2.1 g.

**Minerals**
**Calcium** 15.6 mg.
**Iron** 1.3 mg.
**Zinc** 0.78 mg.
**Copper** 0.08 mg.
**Sodium** 1508 mg.
**Potassium** 109 mg.
**Magnesium** 33.8 mg.
**Phosphorus** 111 mg.

**Vitamins**
**Vitamin A** None.
**Vitamin C** None.
**Vitamin D** None.
**Vitamin E** None.
**Vitamin B1** 0.13 mg.
**Vitamin B2** 0.03 mg.
**Niacin** 1.04 mg.
**Vitamin B6** 0.03 mg.
**Vitamin B12** None.
**Folic acid** 15.6 µg.
**Pantothenic acid** 0.3 mg.
**Biotin** 5.2 µg.

Porridge has a similar calorie content to other breakfast cereals before milk and sugar are added.

# Port

**Portion** One wine glass.

**Weight** 140 g., about 5 oz.

**Food Facts**
**Energy** 219 kcal.
**Protein** 0.1 g.
**Total fat** None.
**Saturated fat** None.
**Polyunsaturated fat** None.
**Carbohydrate** 16.8 g.
**Sugars** 16.8 g.
**Fibre** None.

**Minerals**
**Calcium** 5.6 mg.
**Iron** 0.56 mg.
**Zinc** Not known.
**Copper** 0.14 mg.
**Sodium** 5.6 mg.
**Potassium** 135 mg.
**Magnesium** 15.4 mg.
**Phosphorus** 16.8 mg.

**Vitamins**
**Vitamin A** None.
**Vitamin C** None.
**Vitamin D** None.
**Vitamin E** None.
**Vitamin B1** None.
**Vitamin B2** 0.01 mg.
**Niacin** 0.08 mg.
**Vitamin B6** 0.01 mg.
**Vitamin B12** None.
**Folic acid** 0.1 µg.
**Pantothenic acid** Not known.
**Biotin** Not known.

Because port is a fortified wine, one glass contains twice as many calories and a lot more sugar than ordinary red wine.

# Ravioli in tomato sauce

**Portion** Half a large tin.

**Weight** 215 g., about 7¾ oz.

**Food Facts**
**Energy** 150 kcal.
**Protein** 6.4 g.
**Total fat** 4.7 g.
**Saturated fat** Not known.
**Polyunsaturated fat** Not known.
**Carbohydrate** 22.1 g.
**Sugars** Not known.
**Fibre** Not known.

**Minerals**
**Calcium** 516 mg.
**Iron** 1.72 mg.
**Zinc** 0.86 mg.
**Copper** Not known.
**Sodium** 1053 mg.
**Potassium** Not known.
**Magnesium** Not known.
**Phosphorus** Not known.

**Vitamins**
**Vitamin A** Not known.
**Vitamin C** Not known.
**Vitamin D** Not known.
**Vitamin E** 0.21 mg.
**Vitamin B1** 0.1 mg.
**Vitamin B2** 0.08 mg.
**Niacin** 3.22 mg.
**Vitamin B6** 0.21 mg.
**Vitamin B12** Not known.
**Folic acid** 6.45 µg.
**Pantothenic acid** Not known.
**Biotin** Not known.

It is becoming more common to find wholewheat tinned pasta products. They may look unfamiliar but taste much better.

# Red wine

**Portion** One wine glass of medium red wine.
**Weight** 140 g., about 5 oz.

## Food Facts
**Energy** 95 kcal.
**Protein** 0.3 g.
**Total fat** None.
**Saturated fat** None.
**Polyunsaturated fat** None.
**Carbohydrate** 0.4 g.
**Sugars** 0.4 g.
**Fibre** None.

## Minerals
**Calcium** 9.8 mg.
**Iron** 1.26 mg.
**Zinc** Not known.
**Copper** 0.17 mg.
**Sodium** 14 mg.
**Potassium** 182 mg.
**Magnesium** 15.4 mg.
**Phosphorus** 19.6 mg.

## Vitamins
**Vitamin A** None.
**Vitamin C** None.
**Vitamin D** None.
**Vitamin E** Not known.
**Vitamin B1** None.
**Vitamin B2** 0.03 mg.
**Niacin** 0.13 mg.
**Vitamin B6** 0.02 mg.
**Vitamin B12** None.
**Folic acid** 0.3 µg.
**Pantothenic acid** 0.1 mg.
**Biotin** Not known.

**If you want a long low-calorie drink that is a little sweet, dilute red wine with low calorie lemonade and add orange segments and sprig of mint.**

# Rice, brown, boiled

**Portion** Four tablespoons (uncooked: half a mug; 100 g.)
**Weight** 200 g., about 7 oz.

## Food Facts
**Energy** 238 kcal.
**Protein** 4.4 g.
**Total fat** 1.8 g.
**Saturated fat** Not known.
**Polyunsaturated fat** Not known.
**Carbohydrate** 54.2 g.
**Sugars** Not known.
**Fibre** Not known.

## Minerals
**Calcium** 6 mg.
**Iron** 0.94 mg.
**Zinc** 1.2 mg.
**Copper** Not known.
**Sodium** 2 mg.
**Potassium** Not known.
**Magnesium** Not known.
**Phosphorus** Not known.

## Vitamins
**Vitamin A** Not known.
**Vitamin C** Not known.
**Vitamin D** Not known.
**Vitamin E** Not known.
**Vitamin B1** 0.3 mg.
**Vitamin B2** 0.04 mg.
**Niacin** 4.2 mg.
**Vitamin B6** 0.4 mg.
**Vitamin B12** Not known.
**Folic acid** 32 µg.
**Pantothenic acid** Not known.
**Biotin** Not known.

**Although brown rice takes longer to cook, it is more filling, tastier and less sticky than white rice. New varieties may cook more quickly.**

# Rice, white, boiled

# Rice Krispies

**Portion** Four tablespoons (uncooked: half cup; 100 g.)
**Weight** 200 g., about 7 oz.

**Portion** One bowlful.

**Weight** 30 g., about 1 oz.

**Food Facts**
**Energy** 246 kcal.
**Protein** 4.4 g.
**Total fat** 0.6 g.
**Saturated fat** 0.12 g.
**Polyunsaturated fat** 0.22 g.
**Carbohydrate** 59 g.
**Sugars** None.
**Fibre** 1.6 g.

**Food Facts**
**Energy** 105 kcal.
**Protein** 1.8 g.
**Total fat** 0.12 g.
**Saturated fat** Not known.
**Polyunsaturated fat** Not known.
**Carbohydrate** 25.8 g.
**Sugars** 2.7 g.
**Fibre** 0.27 g.

**Minerals**
**Calcium** 2 mg.
**Iron** 0.4 mg.
**Zinc** 0.8 mg.
**Copper** 0.04 mg.
**Sodium** 4 mg.
**Potassium** 76 mg.
**Magnesium** 8 mg.
**Phosphorus** 68 mg.

**Minerals**
**Calcium** 6.09 mg.
**Iron** 2.01 mg.
**Zinc** 0.33 mg.
**Copper** 0.04 mg.
**Sodium** 381 mg.
**Potassium** 46 mg.
**Magnesium** 15 mg.
**Phosphorus** 40 mg.

**Vitamins**
**Vitamin A** None.
**Vitamin C** None.
**Vitamin D** None.
**Vitamin E** 0.2 mg.
**Vitamin B1** 0.02 mg.
**Vitamin B2** 0.02 mg.
**Niacin** 1.6 mg.
**Vitamin B6** 0.1 mg.
**Vitamin B12** None.
**Folic acid** 12 µg.
**Pantothenic acid** 0.4 mg.
**Biotin** 2 µg.

**Vitamins**
**Vitamin A** None.
**Vitamin C** None.
**Vitamin D** 0.84 µg.
**Vitamin E** 0.18 mg.
**Vitamin B1** 0.3 mg.
**Vitamin B2** 0.45 mg.
**Niacin** 4.8 mg.
**Vitamin B6** 0.54 mg.
**Vitamin B12** 0.51 µg.
**Folic acid** 75 µg.
**Pantothenic acid** Not known.
**Biotin** Not known.

Rinsing boiled rice to get rid of the starch, will not lower its calorie value. Brown rice tastes better and contains more fibre.

Try mixing a low fibre breakfast cereal with All-Bran or another high fibre cereal.

# Rice pudding

**Portion** One ladleful.
(one tin contains 434 g.)
**Weight** 150 g., about 5¼ oz.

**Food Facts**
**Energy** 136 kcal.
**Protein** 5.1 g.
**Total fat** 3.7 g.
**Saturated fat** 3.7 g.
**Polyunsaturated fat** 0.18 g.
**Carbohydrate** 22 g.
**Sugars** 13.3 g.
**Fibre** 0.6 g.

**Minerals**
**Calcium** 139 mg.
**Iron** 0.3 mg.
**Zinc** 0.6 mg.
**Copper** 0.04 mg.
**Sodium** 75 mg.
**Potassium** 210 mg.
**Magnesium** 16.5 mg.
**Phosphorus** 120 mg.

**Vitamins**
**Vitamin A** 75 µg.
**Vitamin C** None.
**Vitamin D** 0.03 µg.
**Vitamin E** 0.15 mg.
**Vitamin B1** 0.04 mg.
**Vitamin B2** 0.21 mg.
**Niacin** 1.35 mg.
**Vitamin B6** 0.03 mg.
**Vitamin B12** None.
**Folic acid** 6 µg.
**Pantothenic acid** 0.4 mg.
**Biotin** 3 µg.

**You can make milk puddings as
successfully with skimmed or semi-
skimmed milk, as you can with full-
cream milk.**

# Salad cream

**Portion** One tablespoon.

**Weight** 15 g., about ½ oz.

**Food Facts**
**Energy** 46 kcal.
**Protein** 0.3 g.
**Total fat** 4.1 g.
**Saturated fat** Not known.
**Polyunsaturated fat** Not known.
**Carbohydrate** 2.3 g.
**Sugars** 2 g.
**Fibre** Not known.

**Minerals**
**Calcium** 5.1 mg.
**Iron** 0.12 mg.
**Zinc** Not known.
**Copper** 0.01 mg.
**Sodium** 126 mg.
**Potassium** 12 mg.
**Magnesium** 3.1 mg.
**Phosphorus** 13.5 mg.

**Vitamins**
**Vitamin A** Not known.
**Vitamin C** None.
**Vitamin D** Not known.
**Vitamin E** Not known.
**Vitamin B1** Not known.
**Vitamin B2** Not known.
**Niacin** 0.06 mg.
**Vitamin B6** Not known.
**Vitamin B12** Not known.
**Folic acid** Not known.
**Pantothenic acid** Not known.
**Biotin** Not known.

**Make unusual tasty salads using
beans, raw carrot, nuts,
beansprouts and other vegetables
without adding salad cream.**

# Scone

**Portion** One scone.

**Weight** 55 g., about 2 oz.

**Food Facts**
Energy 204 kcal.
Protein 4.1 g.
Total fat 8 g.
Saturated fat 3.06 g.
Polyunsaturated fat 1.23 g.
Carbohydrate 30.7 g.
Sugars 3.4 g.
Fibre 1.2 g.

**Minerals**
Calcium 341 mg.
Iron 0.82 mg.
Zinc 0.33 mg.
Copper 0.07 mg.
Sodium 440 mg.
Potassium 77 mg.
Magnesium 10.4 mg.
Phosphorus 258 mg.

**Vitamins**
Vitamin A 83 µg.
Vitamin C None.
Vitamin D 0.68 µg.
Vitamin E 0.71 mg.
Vitamin B1 None.
Vitamin B2 0.04 mg.
Niacin 1.48 mg.
Vitamin B6 0.04 mg.
Vitamin B12 None.
Folic acid 4.4 µg.
Pantothenic acid 0.1 mg.
Biotin 1.1 µg.

**Have wholemeal scones for a change. If you have jam with them, leave out the butter and the cream.**

# Sherry

**Portion** One schooner full of medium sherry.

**Weight** 70 g., about 2½ oz.

**Food Facts**
Energy 82 kcal.
Protein 0.1 g.
Total fat None.
Saturated fat None.
Polyunsaturated fat None.
Carbohydrate 2.5 g.
Sugars 2.5 g.
Fibre None.

**Minerals**
Calcium 6.3 mg.
Iron 0.37 mg.
Zinc 0.19 mg.
Copper 0.07 mg.
Sodium 4.2 mg.
Potassium 62.3 mg.
Magnesium 5.6 mg.
Phosphorus 4.9 mg.

**Vitamins**
Vitamin A None.
Vitamin C None.
Vitamin D None.
Vitamin E None.
Vitamin B1 None.
Vitamin B2 0.01 mg.
Niacin 0.06 mg.
Vitamin B6 0.01 mg.
Vitamin B12 None.
Folic acid 0.1 µg.
Pantothenic acid Not known.
Biotin Not known.

**Sherry contains twice the calories of white wine, but because it is a fortified wine, it is generally drunk in smaller amounts.**

# Shortbread

**Portion** Two shortbread fingers.
**Weight** 20 g., about ⅔ oz.

**Food Facts**
**Energy** 100 kcal.
**Protein** 1.2 g.
**Total fat** 5.2 g.
**Saturated fat** 3 g.
**Polyunsaturated fat** 0.2 g.
**Carbohydrate** 13.1 g.
**Sugars** 3.4 g.
**Fibre** 0.4 g.

**Minerals**
**Calcium** 19.4 mg.
**Iron** 0.3 mg.
**Zinc** 0.1 mg.
**Copper** 0.02 mg.
**Sodium** 54 mg.
**Potassium** 18 mg.
**Magnesium** 2.6 mg.
**Phosphorus** 15 mg.

**Vitamins**
**Vitamin A** 50 µg.
**Vitamin C** None.
**Vitamin D** 0.05 µg.
**Vitamin E** 0.12 mg.
**Vitamin B1** 0.03 mg.
**Vitamin B2** None.
**Niacin** 0.48 mg.
**Vitamin B6** 0.01 mg.
**Vitamin B12** None.
**Folic acid** 1.4 µg.
**Pantothenic acid** Not known.
**Biotin** Not known.

**If you are trying to lose weight, the only biscuits you should keep in the house are thin crispbreads.**

# Shredded Wheat

**Portion** Two shredded wheat.

**Weight** 45 g., about 1½ oz.

**Food Facts**
**Energy** 145 kcal.
**Protein** 4.8 g.
**Total fat** 1.3 g.
**Saturated fat** Not known.
**Polyunsaturated fat** Not known.
**Carbohydrate** 30.6 g.
**Sugars** 0.2 g.
**Fibre** 5.5 g.

**Minerals**
**Calcium** 17 mg.
**Iron** 1.89 mg.
**Zinc** 1.03 mg.
**Copper** 0.18 mg.
**Sodium** 3.6 mg.
**Potassium** 148 mg.
**Magnesium** 58 mg.
**Phosphorus** 153 mg.

**Vitamins**
**Vitamin A** None.
**Vitamin C** None.
**Vitamin D** None.
**Vitamin E** 0.45 mg.
**Vitamin B1** 0.12 mg.
**Vitamin B2** 0.02 mg.
**Niacin** 2.97 mg.
**Vitamin B6** 0.11 mg.
**Vitamin B12** None.
**Folic acid** 13 µg.
**Pantothenic acid** Not known.
**Biotin** Not known.

**Not only is Shredded Wheat very high in fibre but it also contains no added sugar or salt.**

# Soy sauce

**Portion** One tablespoon dark
soy sauce.
**Weight** 20 g., about ⅓ oz.

**Food Facts**
**Energy** 17.2 kcal.
**Protein** 1.1 g.
**Total fat** 0.12 g.
**Saturated fat** Not known.
**Polyunsaturated fat** Not known.
**Carbohydrate** 2.9 g.
**Sugars** Not known.
**Fibre** Not known.

**Minerals**
**Calcium** 17 mg.
**Iron** 0.88 mg.
**Zinc** Not known.
**Copper** Not known.
**Sodium** Not known.
**Potassium** 54 mg.
**Magnesium** Not known.
**Phosphorus** Not known.

**Vitamins**
**Vitamin A** None.
**Vitamin C** None.
**Vitamin D** None.
**Vitamin E** Not known.
**Vitamin B1** 0.04 mg.
**Vitamin B2** Not known.
**Niacin** 0.24 mg.
**Vitamin B6** Not known.
**Vitamin B12** None.
**Folic acid** Not known.
**Pantothenic acid** Not known.
**Biotin** Not known.

Although there are no figures for the
sodium content of soy sauce, it
contains a lot, so use sparingly in
stir-fried dishes.

# Spaghetti in tomato sauce

**Portion** Half a large tin.

**Weight** 220 g., about 7¾ oz.

**Food Facts**
**Energy** 129 kcal.
**Protein** 3.7 g.
**Total fat** 1.5 g.
**Saturated fat** Not known.
**Polyunsaturated fat** Not known.
**Carbohydrate** 26.8 g.
**Sugars** 7.5 g.
**Fibre** 2 g.

**Minerals**
**Calcium** 46 mg.
**Iron** 0.88 mg.
**Zinc** 0.66 mg.
**Copper** 0.29 mg.
**Sodium** 1100 mg.
**Potassium** 286 mg.
**Magnesium** 24.2 mg.
**Phosphorus** 66 mg.

**Vitamins**
**Vitamin A** None.
**Vitamin C** None.
**Vitamin D** None.
**Vitamin E** Not known.
**Vitamin B1** 0.02 mg.
**Vitamin B2** 0.02 mg.
**Niacin** 1.54 mg.
**Vitamin B6** 0.02 mg.
**Vitamin B12** None.
**Folic acid** 4.4 µg.
**Pantothenic acid** None.
**Biotin** None.

This is quite a low fat food. You can
increase its low protein value by
adding some grated cheese.

# Sponge pudding

# Stock cube

**Portion** One square of sponge without fruit or custard.
**Weight** 50 g., about 1¾ oz.

**Portion** One stock cube.

**Weight** 10 g., about ⅓ oz.

## Food Facts
**Energy** 172 kcal.
**Protein** 2.9 g.
**Total fat** 8.2 g.
**Saturated fat** 2.94 g.
**Polyunsaturated fat** 1.25 g.
**Carbohydrate** 23 g.
**Sugars** 9.4 g.
**Fibre** 0.6 g.

## Food Facts
**Energy** 22 kcal.
**Protein** 3.8 g.
**Total fat** 0.3 g.
**Saturated fat** Not known.
**Polyunsaturated fat** Not known.
**Carbohydrate** 1.2 g.
**Sugars** Not known.
**Fibre** None.

## Minerals
**Calcium** 105 mg.
**Iron** 0.6 mg.
**Zinc** 0.25 mg.
**Copper** 0.04 mg.
**Sodium** 155 mg.
**Potassium** 44 mg.
**Magnesium** 5.5 mg.
**Phosphorus** 95 mg.

## Minerals
**Calcium** 18 mg.
**Iron** 2.45 mg.
**Zinc** Not known.
**Copper** 0.07 mg.
**Sodium** 1030 mg.
**Potassium** 73 mg.
**Magnesium** 5.9 mg.
**Phosphorus** 36 mg.

## Vitamins
**Vitamin A** 90 µg.
**Vitamin C** None.
**Vitamin D** 0.82 µg.
**Vitamin E** 0.8 mg.
**Vitamin B1** None.
**Vitamin B2** 0.04 mg.
**Niacin** 1.05 mg.
**Vitamin B6** 0.02 mg.
**Vitamin B12** None.
**Folic acid** 3.5 µg.
**Pantothenic acid** 0.1 mg.
**Biotin** 2.5 µg.

## Vitamins
**Vitamin A** None.
**Vitamin C** None.
**Vitamin D** None.
**Vitamin E** Not known.
**Vitamin B1** Not known.
**Vitamin B2** Not known.
**Niacin** Not known.
**Vitamin B6** Not known.
**Vitamin B12** Not known.
**Folic acid** Not known.
**Pantothenic acid** Not known.
**Biotin** Not known.

**Most puddings contain substantial amounts of fat and sugar and very little fibre.**

**If you want to cut down on your salt, remember that stock cubes contain about 2½ grams of salt so use sparingly.**

# Stout

**Portion** One pint of stout.

**Weight** 560 g., about 20 oz.

**Food Facts**
Energy 207 kcal.
Protein 1.7 g.
Total fat None.
Saturated fat None.
Polyunsaturated fat None.
Carbohydrate 23.5 g.
Sugars 23.5 g.
Fibre None.

**Minerals**
Calcium 44.8 mg.
Iron 0.28 mg.
Zinc Not known.
Copper 0.45 mg.
Sodium 128 mg.
Potassium 252 mg.
Magnesium 44.8 mg.
Phosphorus 95.2 mg.

**Vitamins**
Vitamin A None.
Vitamin C None.
Vitamin D None.
Vitamin E Not known.
Vitamin B1 None.
Vitamin B2 0.17 mg.
Niacin 2.41 mg.
Vitamin B6 0.08 mg.
Vitamin B12 0.62 µg.
Folic acid 24.6 µg.
Pantothenic acid 0.6 mg.
Biotin 2.8 µg.

**Stout is no better for you than ordinary beer. It contains twice as much sugar and smaller amounts of B vitamins.**

# Sugar, demerara

**Portion** One teaspoon.

**Weight** 5 g., about 1/5 oz.

**Food Facts**
Energy 19 kcal.
Protein None.
Total fat None.
Saturated fat None.
Polyunsaturated fat None.
Carbohydrate 5 g.
Sugars 5 g.
Fibre None.

**Minerals**
Calcium 2.6 mg.
Iron 0.04 mg.
Zinc Not known.
Copper None.
Sodium 0.3 mg.
Potassium 4.4 mg.
Magnesium 0.7 mg.
Phosphorus 1 mg.

**Vitamins**
Vitamin A None.
Vitamin C None.
Vitamin D None.
Vitamin E None.
Vitamin B1 None.
Vitamin B2 None.
Niacin None.
Vitamin B6 None.
Vitamin B12 None.
Folic acid None.
Pantothenic acid None.
Biotin None.

**Demerara sugar may be white sugar which has been coloured brown. Real demerara sugar contains very small amount of minerals.**

# Sugar, Muscavado

**Portion** One teaspoon.

**Weight** 5 g., about ⅕ oz.

**Food Facts**
**Energy** 19.4 kcal.
**Protein** 0.01 g.
**Total fat** None.
**Saturated fat** None.
**Polyunsaturated fat** None.
**Carbohydrate** 4.8 g.
**Sugars** 4.8 g.
**Fibre** None.

**Minerals**
**Calcium** 1.5 mg.
**Iron** 0.1 mg.
**Zinc** Not known.
**Copper** Not known.
**Sodium** Not known.
**Potassium** Not known.
**Magnesium** Not known.
**Phosphorus** Not known.

**Vitamins**
**Vitamin A** Not known.
**Vitamin C** None.
**Vitamin D** Not known.
**Vitamin E** Not known.
**Vitamin B1** None.
**Vitamin B2** None.
**Niacin** 0.01 mg.
**Vitamin B6** Not known.
**Vitamin B12** Not known.
**Folic acid** Not known.
**Pantothenic acid** Not known.
**Biotin** Not known.

**Adds a pleasant flavour to desserts when used in place of white sugar. Its highly distinctive taste will mean you will need to use less of it.**

# Sugar, white

**Portion** One teaspoon.

**Weight** 5 g., about ⅕ oz.

**Food Facts**
**Energy** 19 kcal.
**Protein** None.
**Total fat** None.
**Saturated fat** None.
**Polyunsaturated fat** None.
**Carbohydrate** 5 g.
**Sugars** 5 g.
**Fibre** None.

**Minerals**
**Calcium** 0.1 mg.
**Iron** None.
**Zinc** None.
**Copper** None.
**Sodium** None.
**Potassium** 0.1 mg.
**Magnesium** None.
**Phosphorus** None.

**Vitamins**
**Vitamin A** None.
**Vitamin C** None.
**Vitamin D** None.
**Vitamin E** None.
**Vitamin B1** None.
**Vitamin B2** None.
**Niacin** None.
**Vitamin B6** None.
**Vitamin B12** None.
**Folic acid** None.
**Pantothenic acid** None.
**Biotin** None.

**If you take sugar in tea and coffee, you will be surprised how many calories it adds to your diet during one day.**

# Sugar Puffs

**Portion** One bowlful.

**Weight** 30 g., about 1 oz.

**Food Facts**
Energy 111 kcal.
Protein 1.8 g.
Total fat 0.4 g.
Saturated fat 0.03 g.
Polyunsaturated fat 0.1 g.
Carbohydrate 26.4 g.
Sugars 15.3 g.
Fibre 2.1 g.

**Minerals**
Calcium 4.2 mg.
Iron 0.63 mg.
Zinc 0.45 mg.
Copper 0.07 mg.
Sodium 2.7 mg.
Potassium 48 mg.
Magnesium 16.5 mg.
Phosphorus 42 mg.

**Vitamins**
Vitamin A None.
Vitamin C None.
Vitamin D None.
Vitamin E 0.06 mg.
Vitamin B1 None.
Vitamin B2 0.01 mg.
Niacin 0.75 mg.
Vitamin B6 0.01 mg.
Vitamin B12 None.
Folic acid 3.6 µg.
Pantothenic acid Not known.
Biotin Not known.

**Despite their high sugar content, Sugar Puffs do not appear to be very high in calories because they contain a lot of air.**

# Sweets

**Portion** One boiled sweet.

**Weight** 5 g., about ¹/₁₀ oz.

**Food Facts**
Energy 16 kcal.
Protein None.
Total fat None.
Saturated fat None.
Polyunsaturated fat None.
Carbohydrate 4.4 g.
Sugars 4.3 g.
Fibre None.

**Minerals**
Calcium 0.2 mg.
Iron 0.02 mg.
Zinc Not known.
Copper None.
Sodium 1.3 mg.
Potassium 0.4 mg.
Magnesium 0.1 mg.
Phosphorus 0.6 mg.

**Vitamins**
Vitamin A None.
Vitamin C None.
Vitamin D None.
Vitamin E None.
Vitamin B1 None.
Vitamin B2 None.
Niacin None.
Vitamin B6 None.
Vitamin B12 None.
Folic acid None.
Pantothenic acid None.
Biotin None.

**Sweets contain mostly sugar and colourings. They have very little nutritional value compared to nuts or dried fruit.**

# Swiss roll

**Portion** One slice, equivalent of ⅙ of a swiss roll.
**Weight** 30 g., about 1 oz.

**Food Facts**
Energy 90 kcal.
Protein 1.3 g.
Total fat 1.5 g.
Saturated fat 0.56 g.
Polyunsaturated fat 0.23 g.
Carbohydrate 19.3 g.
Sugars 14.3 g.
Fibre 0.4 g.

**Minerals**
Calcium 13.2 mg.
Iron 0.48 mg.
Zinc 0.15 mg.
Copper 0.06 mg.
Sodium 126 mg.
Potassium 42 mg.
Magnesium 4.2 mg.
Phosphorus 66 mg.

**Vitamins**
Vitamin A 24 µg.
Vitamin C None.
Vitamin D 0.3 µg.
Vitamin E Not known.
Vitamin B1 0.01 mg.
Vitamin B2 0.02 mg.
Niacin 0.39 mg.
Vitamin B6 0.02 mg.
Vitamin B12 None.
Folic acid 2.1 µg.
Pantothenic acid 0.1 mg.
Biotin 2.4 µg.

Swiss rolls which contain chocolate or cream are higher in calories than jam filled ones. Only eat occasionally.

# Tea

**Portion** One mug made with one tea bag, no milk.
**Weight** 250 g., about 9 oz.

**Food Facts**
Energy 2 kcal.
Protein 0.2 g.
Total fat None.
Saturated fat None.
Polyunsaturated fat None.
Carbohydrate None.
Sugars None.
Fibre None.

**Minerals**
Calcium None.
Iron None.
Zinc None.
Copper None.
Sodium None.
Potassium 42.5 mg.
Magnesium 2.5 mg.
Phosphorus 2.5 mg.

**Vitamins**
Vitamin A None.
Vitamin C None.
Vitamin D None.
Vitamin E Not known.
Vitamin B1 None.
Vitamin B2 0.02 mg.
Niacin 0.25 mg.
Vitamin B6 None.
Vitamin B12 None.
Folic acid None.
Pantothenic acid None.
Biotin None.

Tea contains very few calories until you add milk and sugar. Tea with milk and two sugar contains about 60 calories.

# Toffee apple

**Portion** One toffee apple.

**Weight** 130 g., about 4½ oz.

**Food Facts**
**Energy** 144 kcal.
**Protein** 0.3 g.
**Total fat** None.
**Saturated fat** None.
**Polyunsaturated fat** None.
**Carbohydrate** 38.1 g.
**Sugars** 37.9 g.
**Fibre** 2 g.

**Minerals**
**Calcium** 4.5 mg.
**Iron** 0.15 mg.
**Zinc** 1.1 mg.
**Copper** 0.07 mg.
**Sodium** 7.5 mg.
**Potassium** 5.4 mg.
**Magnesium** 3.6 mg.
**Phosphorus** 11.6 mg.

**Vitamins**
**Vitamin A** 5 µg.
**Vitamin C** 3 mg.
**Vitamin D** None.
**Vitamin E** 0.2 mg.
**Vitamin B1** 0.04 mg.
**Vitamin B2** 0.02 mg.
**Niacin** 0.1 mg.
**Vitamin B6** 0.03 mg.
**Vitamin B12** None.
**Folic acid** 3 µg.
**Pantothenic acid** 0.1 mg.
**Biotin** 0.3 µg.

**A toffee apple has three times the calories of an ordinary apple so keep them for special occasions only.**

# Toffees

**Portion** One toffee.

**Weight** 7.5 g., about ¼ oz.

**Food Facts**
**Energy** 32 kcal.
**Protein** 0.2 g.
**Total fat** 1.3 g.
**Saturated fat** Not known.
**Polyunsaturated fat** Not known.
**Carbohydrate** 5.3 g.
**Sugars** 5.3 g.
**Fibre** Not known.

**Minerals**
**Calcium** 7.1 mg.
**Iron** 0.11 mg.
**Zinc** Not known.
**Copper** 0.03 mg.
**Sodium** 24 mg.
**Potassium** 15.7 mg.
**Magnesium** 1.9 mg.
**Phosphorus** 4.8 mg.

**Vitamins**
**Vitamin A** None.
**Vitamin C** None.
**Vitamin D** None.
**Vitamin E** Not known.
**Vitamin B1** None.
**Vitamin B2** None.
**Niacin** 0.03 mg.
**Vitamin B6** None.
**Vitamin B12** None.
**Folic acid** None.
**Pantothenic acid** None.
**Biotin** None.

**Toffees contain twice as many calories as boiled sweets.**

# Tomato juice

**Portion** One wine glass.

**Weight** 140 g., about 5 oz.

**Food Facts**
Energy 22 kcal.
Protein 1 g.
Total fat None.
Saturated fat None.
Polyunsaturated fat None.
Carbohydrate 4.8 g.
Sugars 4.5 g.
Fibre Not known.

**Minerals**
Calcium 14 mg.
Iron 0.7 mg.
Zinc 0.56 mg.
Copper 0.07 mg.
Sodium 322 mg.
Potassium 364 mg.
Magnesium 14 mg.
Phosphorus 28 mg.

**Vitamins**
Vitamin A 116 µg.
Vitamin C 28 mg.
Vitamin D None.
Vitamin E 0.28 mg.
Vitamin B1 0.08 mg.
Vitamin B2 0.04 mg.
Niacin 1.12 mg.
Vitamin B6 0.15 mg.
Vitamin B12 None.
Folic acid 18.2 µg.
Pantothenic acid 0.3 mg.
Biotin 1.4 µg.

**Out of all fruit juices, tomato juice
contains the least number of
calories. Try it with lots of ice and a
slice of lemon.**

# Tomato ketchup

**Portion** One teaspoon.

**Weight** 5 g., about ⅕ oz.

**Food Facts**
Energy 4 kcal.
Protein 0.1 g.
Total fat None.
Saturated fat None.
Polyunsaturated fat None.
Carbohydrate 1.2 g.
Sugars 1.1 g.
Fibre Not known.

**Minerals**
Calcium 1.3 mg.
Iron 0.06 mg.
Zinc Not known.
Copper 0.02 mg.
Sodium 56 mg.
Potassium 29 mg.
Magnesium 0.9 mg.
Phosphorus 2.1 mg.

**Vitamins**
Vitamin A None.
Vitamin C Not known.
Vitamin D None.
Vitamin E Not known.
Vitamin B1 Not known.
Vitamin B2 Not known.
Niacin 0.01 mg.
Vitamin B6 Not known.
Vitamin B12 None.
Folic acid Not known.
Pantothenic acid Not known.
Biotin Not known.

**Most ketchups contain some sugar
and quite a lot of salt. However a
small amount will add taste to food
without adding too many calories.**

# Tomato soup ready to serve

**Portion** One small tin of cream of tomato soup.
**Weight** 300 g., about 10½ oz.

**Food Facts**
**Energy** 165 kcal.
**Protein** 2.4 g.
**Total fat** 9.9 g.
**Saturated fat** Not known.
**Polyunsaturated fat** Not known.
**Carbohydrate** 17.7 g.
**Sugars** 7.8 g.
**Fibre** Not known.

**Minerals**
**Calcium** 51 mg.
**Iron** 1.2 mg.
**Zinc** 0.6 g.
**Copper** 0.18 mg.
**Sodium** 1380 mg.
**Potassium** 570 mg.
**Magnesium** 24 mg.
**Phosphorus** 60 mg.

**Vitamins**
**Vitamin A** 105 μg.
**Vitamin C** None.
**Vitamin D** None.
**Vitamin E** Not known.
**Vitamin B1** 0.09 mg.
**Vitamin B2** 0.06 mg.
**Niacin** 1.8 mg.
**Vitamin B6** 0.18 mg.
**Vitamin B12** None.
**Folic acid** 36 μg.
**Pantothenic acid** Not known.
**Biotin** Not known.

Cream of tomato soup has more calories than plain tomato soup. Choose soups which contain less fat and calories.

# Tonic water

**Portion** One small bottle.

**Weight** 113 g., about 4 oz.

**Food Facts**
**Energy** 23 kcal.
**Protein** None.
**Total fat** None.
**Saturated fat** None.
**Polyunsaturated fat** None.
**Carbohydrate** 6.3 g.
**Sugars** 6.3 g.
**Fibre** None.

**Minerals**
**Calcium** 5.6 mg.
**Iron** None.
**Zinc** Not known.
**Copper** 0.01 mg.
**Sodium** 7.9 mg.
**Potassium** 1.1 mg.
**Magnesium** None.
**Phosphorus** None.

**Vitamins**
**Vitamin A** None.
**Vitamin C** None.
**Vitamin D** None.
**Vitamin E** None.
**Vitamin B1** None.
**Vitamin B2** None.
**Niacin** None.
**Vitamin B6** None.
**Vitamin B12** None.
**Folic acid** None.
**Pantothenic acid** None.
**Biotin** None.

This is the amount of tonic you would normally add to a pub measure of gin.

# Treacle

**Portion** One tablespoon.

**Weight** 20 g., about ¾ oz.

**Food Facts**
**Energy** 51 kcal.
**Protein** 0.2 g.
**Total fat** None.
**Saturated fat** None.
**Polyunsaturated fat** None.
**Carbohydrate** 13.4 g.
**Sugars** 13.4 g.
**Fibre** Not known.

**Minerals**
**Calcium** 100 mg.
**Iron** 1.84 mg.
**Zinc** Not known.
**Copper** 0.09 mg.
**Sodium** 19.2 mg.
**Potassium** 294 mg.
**Magnesium** 28 mg.
**Phosphorus** 6.2 mg.

**Vitamins**
**Vitamin A** None.
**Vitamin C** None.
**Vitamin D** None.
**Vitamin E** None.
**Vitamin B1** None.
**Vitamin B2** None.
**Niacin** None.
**Vitamin B6** None.
**Vitamin B12** None.
**Folic acid** None.
**Pantothenic acid** None.
**Biotin** None.

**Real black treacle contains quite a lot of minerals and gives an unusual taste to puddings.**

# Trifle

**Portion** One small bowlful.

**Weight** 150 g., about 5⅓ oz.

**Food Facts**
**Energy** 240 kcal.
**Protein** 5.2 g.
**Total fat** 9.1 g.
**Saturated fat** 4.29 g.
**Polyunsaturated fat** 0.57 g.
**Carbohydrate** 36.4 g.
**Sugars** 28 g.
**Fibre** 0.4 g.

**Minerals**
**Calcium** 123 mg.
**Iron** 1.05 mg.
**Zinc** 0.6 mg.
**Copper** 0.13 mg.
**Sodium** 75 mg.
**Potassium** 225 mg.
**Magnesium** 21 mg.
**Phosphorus** 130 mg.

**Vitamins**
**Vitamin A** 90 µg.
**Vitamin C** 1.5 mg.
**Vitamin D** 0.25 µg.
**Vitamin E** 0.45 mg.
**Vitamin B1** 0.07 mg.
**Vitamin B2** 0.21 mg.
**Niacin** 1.5 mg.
**Vitamin B6** 0.09 mg.
**Vitamin B12** None.
**Folic acid** 9 µg.
**Pantothenic acid** 0.6 mg.
**Biotin** 4.5 µg.

**Make your trifle with fruit tinned in natural juice. There is no need to add jelly. It will just increase the sugar content.**

# Twix

**Portion** One Twix bar.

**Weight** 60 g., about 2 oz.

**Food Facts**
**Energy** 299 kcal.
**Protein** 3.6 g.
**Total fat** 14.6 g.
**Saturated fat** 9.6 g.
**Polyunsaturated fat** Not known.
**Carbohydrate** 38.7 g.
**Sugars** Not known.
**Fibre** 1.1 g.

**Minerals**
**Calcium** 90 mg.
**Iron** 1.0 mg.
**Zinc** 0.02 mg.
**Copper** 0.18 mg.
**Sodium** 132 mg.
**Potassium** 174 mg.
**Magnesium** 19.2 mg.
**Phosphorus** 94 mg.

**Vitamins**
**Vitamin A** 3.18 µg.
**Vitamin C** 1.6 mg.
**Vitamin D** Not known.
**Vitamin E** 3.5 mg.
**Vitamin B1** 0.03 mg.
**Vitamin B2** 0.12 mg.
**Niacin** Not known.
**Vitamin B6** 0.03 mg.
**Vitamin B12** 0.24 µg.
**Folic acid** 3.06 µg.
**Pantothenic acid** Not known.
**Biotin** Not known.

**Make chocolate bars an occasional treat and not a regular part of your diet.**

# Vegetable soup

**Portion** One small tin of ready-to-serve vegetable soup.

**Weight** 300 g., about 10½ oz.

**Food Facts**
**Energy** 111 kcal.
**Protein** 4.5 g.
**Total fat** 2.1 g.
**Saturated fat** Not known.
**Polyunsaturated fat** Not known.
**Carbohydrate** 20.1 g.
**Sugars** 7.5 g.
**Fibre** Not known.

**Minerals**
**Calcium** 51 mg.
**Iron** 1.8 mg.
**Zinc** 0.9 mg.
**Copper** 0.18 mg.
**Sodium** 1500 mg.
**Potassium** 420 mg.
**Magnesium** 30 mg.
**Phosphorus** 81 mg.

**Vitamins**
**Vitamin A** None.
**Vitamin C** None.
**Vitamin D** None.
**Vitamin E** Not known.
**Vitamin B1** 0.09 mg.
**Vitamin B2** 0.06 mg.
**Niacin** 1.8 mg.
**Vitamin B6** 0.15 mg.
**Vitamin B12** None.
**Folic acid** 30 µg.
**Pantothenic acid** Not known.
**Biotin** Not known.

**Try making your own thick low-calorie vegetable soup. Cook a variety of vegetables in stock without added fat and then liquidise.**

# Vinegar

**Portion** One teaspoon.

**Weight** 5 g., about ⅕ oz.

**Food Facts**
**Energy** None.
**Protein** None.
**Total fat** None.
**Saturated fat** None.
**Polyunsaturated fat** None.
**Carbohydrate** None.
**Sugars** None.
**Fibre** None.

**Minerals**
**Calcium** 0.7 mg.
**Iron** 0.02 mg.
**Zinc** Not known.
**Copper** None.
**Sodium** 1 mg.
**Potassium** 4.4 mg.
**Magnesium** 1.1 mg.
**Phosphorus** 1.6 mg.

**Vitamins**
**Vitamin A** None.
**Vitamin C** None.
**Vitamin D** None.
**Vitamin E** None.
**Vitamin B1** None.
**Vitamin B2** None.
**Niacin** None.
**Vitamin B6** None.
**Vitamin B12** None.
**Folic acid** None.
**Pantothenic acid** None.
**Biotin** None.

**Vinegar adds bite not only to salads, but also to cooked dishes, such as stir-fried ones.**

# Water biscuits

**Portion** Four water biscuits.

**Weight** 20 g., about ⅔ oz.

**Food Facts**
**Energy** 88 kcal.
**Protein** 2.2 g.
**Total fat** 2.5 g.
**Saturated fat** Not known.
**Polyunsaturated fat** Not known.
**Carbohydrate** 15.2 g.
**Sugars** 0.5 g.
**Fibre** 0.6 g.

**Minerals**
**Calcium** 24 mg.
**Iron** 0.32 mg.
**Zinc** 0.12 mg.
**Copper** 0.02 mg.
**Sodium** 94 mg.
**Potassium** 28 mg.
**Magnesium** 3.8 mg.
**Phosphorus** 17.4 mg.

**Vitamins**
**Vitamin A** None.
**Vitamin C** None.
**Vitamin D** None.
**Vitamin E** Not known.
**Vitamin B1** 0.02 mg.
**Vitamin B2** 0.01 mg.
**Niacin** 0.62 mg.
**Vitamin B6** 0.01 mg.
**Vitamin B12** None.
**Folic acid** 2 μg.
**Pantothenic acid** Not known.
**Biotin** Not known.

**Water biscuits are best complemented with a lower-fat cheese in order to take advantage of their relatively low calorie value.**

# Weetabix

# White sauce, savoury

**Portion** Two Weetabix.

**Weight** 37.5 g., about 1¼ oz.

**Portion** A quarter of a pint or five tablespoons.

**Weight** 140 g., about 5 oz.

**Food Facts**
Energy 126 kcal.
Protein 3.9 g.
Total fat 0.7 g.
Saturated fat 0.13 g.
Polyunsaturated fat 0.48 g.
Carbohydrate 25.1 g.
Sugars 2.4 g.
Fibre 4.8 g.

**Food Facts**
Energy 211 kcal.
Protein 6 g.
Total fat 14.4 g.
Saturated fat 10.5 g.
Polyunsaturated fat 1.4 g.
Carbohydrate 15.4 g.
Sugars 7.1 g.
Fibre 0.4 g.

**Minerals**
Calcium 13.1 mg.
Iron 2.3 mg.
Zinc 0.75 mg.
Copper 0.2 mg.
Sodium 140 mg.
Potassium 140 mg.
Magnesium 45 mg.
Phosphorus 109 mg.

**Minerals**
Calcium 196 mg.
Iron 0.42 mg.
Zinc 0.56 mg.
Copper 0.06 mg.
Sodium 574 mg.
Potassium 224 mg.
Magnesium 22.4 mg.
Phosphorus 154 mg.

**Vitamins**
Vitamin A None.
Vitamin C None.
Vitamin D None.
Vitamin E 0.37 mg.
Vitamin B1 0.26 mg.
Vitamin B2 0.37 mg.
Niacin 3.75 mg.
Vitamin B6 0.09 mg.
Vitamin B12 None.
Folic acid 18.7 µg.
Pantothenic acid Not known.
Biotin Not known.

**Vitamins**
Vitamin A 144 µg.
Vitamin C None.
Vitamin D 0.88 µg.
Vitamin E 0.98 mg.
Vitamin B1 0.08 mg.
Vitamin B2 0.22 mg.
Niacin 1.68 mg.
Vitamin B6 0.06 mg.
Vitamin B12 None.
Folic acid 5.6 µg.
Pantothenic acid 0.4 mg.
Biotin 2.8 µg.

**Two Weetabix provide nearly one sixth of the recommended daily amount of fibre.**

**If you want to eat less fat, make your white sauce with cornflour and milk only, preferably semi-skimmed or skimmed milk.**

# White sauce, sweet

**Portion** A quarter of a pint or five tablespoons.
**Weight** 140 g., about 5 oz.

## Food Facts
**Energy** 240 kcal.
**Protein** 5.5 g.
**Total fat** 13.3 g.
**Saturated fat** 6.63 g.
**Polyunsaturated fat** 1.49 g.
**Carbohydrate** 26.6 g.
**Sugars** 18.9 g.
**Fibre** 0.4 g.

## Minerals
**Calcium** 182 mg.
**Iron** 0.28 mg.
**Zinc** 0.56 mg.
**Copper** 0.06 mg.
**Sodium** 154 mg.
**Potassium** 210 mg.
**Magnesium** 18.2 mg.
**Phosphorus** 140 mg.

## Vitamins
**Vitamin A** 130 μg.
**Vitamin C** None.
**Vitamin D** 0.81 μg.
**Vitamin E** 0.84 mg.
**Vitamin B1** 0.07 mg.
**Vitamin B2** 0.21 mg.
**Niacin** 1.54 mg.
**Vitamin B6** 0.06 mg.
**Vitamin B12** None.
**Folic acid** 5.6 μg.
**Pantothenic acid** 0.4 mg.
**Biotin** 2.8 μg.

**Sauces containing brandy or rum, will be even higher in calories than the basic white sauce.**

# White wine

**Portion** One wine glass of medium white wine.
**Weight** 140 g., about 5 oz.

## Food Facts
**Energy** 105 kcal.
**Protein** 0.1 g.
**Total fat** None.
**Saturated fat** None.
**Polyunsaturated fat** None.
**Carbohydrate** 4.8 g.
**Sugars** 4.8 g.
**Fibre** None.

## Minerals
**Calcium** 19.6 mg.
**Iron** 1.69 mg.
**Zinc** Not known.
**Copper** 0.01 mg.
**Sodium** 29.4 mg.
**Potassium** 123 mg.
**Magnesium** 12.6 mg.
**Phosphorus** 11.2 mg.

## Vitamins
**Vitamin A** None.
**Vitamin C** None.
**Vitamin D** None.
**Vitamin E** Not known.
**Vitamin B1** None.
**Vitamin B2** 0.01 mg.
**Niacin** 0.11 mg.
**Vitamin B6** 0.02 mg.
**Vitamin B12** None.
**Folic acid** 0.3 μg.
**Pantothenic acid** None.
**Biotin** Not known.

**Dilute white wine with a sparkling mineral water. It makes a cooling low alcohol summer drink.**

# White wine, sparkling

**Portion** One wine glass.

**Weight** 140 g., about 5 oz.

## Food Facts
**Energy** 106 kcal.
**Protein** 0.4 g.
**Total fat** None.
**Saturated fat** None.
**Polyunsaturated fat** None.
**Carbohydrate** 2 g.
**Sugars** 2 g.
**Fibre** None.

## Minerals
**Calcium** 4.2 mg.
**Iron** 0.7 mg.
**Zinc** Not known.
**Copper** 0.01 mg.
**Sodium** 5.6 mg.
**Potassium** 79.8 mg.
**Magnesium** 8.4 mg.
**Phosphorus** 9.8 mg.

## Vitamins
**Vitamin A** None.
**Vitamin C** None.
**Vitamin D** None.
**Vitamin E** Not known.
**Vitamin B1** None.
**Vitamin B2** 0.01 mg.
**Niacin** 0.1 mg.
**Vitamin B6** 0.02 mg.
**Vitamin B12** None.
**Folic acid** 0.1 µg.
**Pantothenic acid** None.
**Biotin** Not known.

Sparkling white wines are now available at reasonable prices. Red wine has less calories than white.

# Yeast extract (Marmite)

**Portion** Enough to spread thinly on a slice of bread.

**Weight** 5 g., about ⅕ oz.

## Food Facts
**Energy** 9 kcal.
**Protein** 2.07 g.
**Total fat** None.
**Saturated fat** None.
**Polyunsaturated fat** None.
**Carbohydrate** 0.09 g.
**Sugars** None.
**Fibre** Not known.

## Minerals
**Calcium** 4.7 mg.
**Iron** 0.02 mg.
**Zinc** 0.1 mg.
**Copper** 0.01 mg.
**Sodium** 225 mg.
**Potassium** 130 mg.
**Magnesium** 0.9 mg.
**Phosphorus** 85 mg.

## Vitamins
**Vitamin A** None.
**Vitamin C** None.
**Vitamin D** None.
**Vitamin E** Not known.
**Vitamin B1** 0.25 mg.
**Vitamin B2** 0.33 mg.
**Niacin** 3.75 mg.
**Vitamin B6** 0.06 mg.
**Vitamin B12** 0.41 mg.
**Folic acid** 62 µg.
**Pantothenic acid** Not known.
**Biotin** Not known.

Yeast extract adds taste and B vitamins to soups and stews. It is quite salty so spread it thinly on bread.

# Index

**A**

Alcohol, 7, 8
All-Bran, 15, 19, 22, 28, 29, 31, 33, 167
Almonds, 109
Anaemia, 18, 32
Anchovies, 47
Apple, eating, 109
Apple, baked, 110
Apple juice, 167
Apricot, 110
Artichokes, 111
Asparagus, 28, 111
Aubergine, 28, 112
Avocado pear, 112

**B**

Bacon, back, grilled, 47
Bacon, back fried, 48
Bacon, streaky, grilled, 48
Baked beans, 15, 113
Banana, 113
Beansprouts, 114
Beefburger, 49
Beefburger in a bun, 49
Beaf cheeseburger, 50
Beef extract, 28, 29, 33, 168
Beef, minced, 50
Beef, roast, 19, 51
Beef sausages, grilled, 94
Beef steak, 29, 30, 31, 100
Beef stew, 51
Beer, 168
Beetroot, 114
Beta carotene, 24
Biotin, 33
Biscuits, chocolate, 169
Biscuits, cream sandwich, 169
Biscuits, digestive, 170
Biscuits, plain, 170

Blackberries, 15, 115
Blackcurrants, 115
Blackcurrant drink, 171
Black pudding, 19, 52
Bones, 17, 26
Bovril see Beef extract
Bowel cancer, 15
Brazil nuts, 116
Bran, 171
Brandy, 190
Bread, granary, 172
Bread, white, 172
Bread, wholemeal, 173
Bread roll, 173
Bread and butter pudding, 174
Breast feeding, 17, 40
Broad beans, 116
Broccoli, 117
Brown sauce, 174
Brussels sprouts, 33, 117
Butter, 52

**C**

Cabbage, red, raw, 33, 118
Cabbage, white, cooked, 119
Cake, see Gateau
Calcium, 17, 22, 23, 26
Calories, 7
Camembert-type cheese, 53
Carbohydrate, 7, 12, 28
Carrots, raw, 24, 119
Carrots, boiled, 119
Cashew nuts, 22, 120
Cauliflower, 120
Celery, 121
Chapatti, 175
Cheddar cheese, 53
Cheese:
    Camembert, 53

Cheddar, 53
Cottage, 63
Edam, 64
Feta, 67
Parmesan, 86
Sauce, 17, 176
Spread, 54
Stilton, 86
Cheese and tomato pizza, 54
Cheeseburger, 50
Cheesecake, 13, 175
Cherries, 121
Chestnuts, 122
Chicken, breast, roasted, 30, 55
Chicken, leg, roasted, 56
Chicken pie, 56
Chicken roasted, 55
Chicken soup, 176
Chickpeas, 15, 19, 21, 22, 33, 122
Chicory, 123
Children, 35, 36
Chilli con carne, 15, 19, 22, 31, 57
Chillies, 123
Chinese leaves, 124
Chocolate bar, milk, 13, 177
Chocolate bar, nuts, 177
Chocolate bar, plain, 13, 22, 178
Chocolate cake, 178
Chocolate drink, 179
Chocolates, boxed, 179
Cholesterol, 12, 26
Chutney, 180
Cider, 180
Cockles, 19, 57
Cocoa, 181
Cod, grilled, 31, 58
Cod in a bag, 58
Cod in batter, 31, 59
Coffee, 182
Cola, 13, 181
Coleslaw, 124
Common cold, 26
Constipation, 15
Copper, 20
Corn oil, 59
Corned beef, 19, 60
Cornflakes, *see* Kellogg's Corn Flakes
Cornish pastie, 13, 21, 28, 60
Courgettes, 125
Cottage cheese, 63
Crab, 19, 63
Cream double, 62
Cream cheese, 62
Cream crackers, 183
Cream, single, 63
Crispbread, 183
Crumpet, 184
Cucumber, 125

Custard, 184

**D**
Danish pastry, 27, 185
Dates, dried, 126
Deficiency:
    Calcium, 17
    Copper, 20
    Folic acid, 32
    Iron, 18
    Niacin, 30
    Pantothenic acid, 33
    Protein, 9
    Vitamin A, 25
    Vitamin B2, 29
    Vitamin B3, 30
    Vitamin B6, 31
    Vitamin C, 26
    Zinc, 18, 20
Dental decay, 14
Diabetes, 8
Dietary guidelines, 34
Doughnut, 185
Duck, 28, 29, 63
Duck's egg, 64

**E**
Edam cheese, 64
Eel, 24, 65
Egg, boiled, 65
Egg, fried, 66
Egg omelette, 21, 27, 66
Egg, ducks, 64
Elderly, 9, 17, 20, 25, 26, 32
Energy, 7
Exercise, 8

**F**
Fat, 7, 11
Feta cheese, 67
Fibre, 15, 44
Figs, dried, 126
Figs, fresh, 127
Fish cakes, 67
Fish fingers, 68
Fish paste, 68
Flour, white, 186
Flour, wholemeal, 186
Folic acid, 32
Frankfurters, 72
Frozen food, 33
Fructose, 12
Fruit cake, 187
Fruit crumble, 13, 187
Fruit gums, 188
Fruit pastilles, 188
Fruit pie, 13, 189
Fruit salad, tinned, 160

Fruit yoghurt, 107

**G**
Gammon rasher, 19, 21, 28, 30, 69
Garlic, 127
Gastric cancer, 26
Gateau, 13, 189
Gherkin, 128
Gin, 190
Ginger ale, 190
Glucose, 12, 14
Goat's milk, 17, 69
Golden syrup, 191
Goose, 13, 19, 70
Gooseberries, 25, 128
Grapefruit, 25, 129
Grapes, black, 129
Grapes, white, 130
Gravy, 192

**H**
Haddock, smoked, 98
Ham, 70
Hazel nuts, 28, 130
Heart, 19, 28, 29, 32, 71
Heart disease, 8, 12, 15
Height, 10
Herring, grilled, 27, 31, 32, 71
Herring, pickled, 27, 72
High blood pressure, 13
Honey, 192
Hot dog sausages, 72

**I**
Ice cream, 193
Iced bun, 13, 193
Instant pudding, 194
Iron, 18

**J**
Jam, 194
Jelly, 195
Jelly sweets, 195

**K**
Kellogg's Corn Flakes, 28, 33, 182
Kidney, 19, 28, 29, 30, 32, 73
Kidney beans, 15, 19, 22, 28, 33, 131
Kipper, 21, 27, 31, 32, 73
Kiwi fruit, 25, 131

**L**
Lactose, 12
Lamb chop, 74
Lamb, leg, roasted, 19, 74
Lamb, shoulder, roasted, 13, 19, 75
Lamb's kidney, 19, 28, 29, 30, 32, 73
Lamb's liver, 19, 24, 28, 29, 30, 32, 33, 76

Lager, 196
Lard, 75
Lasagne, 13, 76
Leeks, 15, 132
Lemon, 25, 132
Lemon curd, 196
Lemonade, 197
Lentils, 133
Lettuce, 133
Liquor, 197
Liquorice sweets, 198
Liver, lambs, fried, 19, 24, 28, 29, 30, 32, 33, 76
Liver, pigs, braised, 19, 24, 29, 30, 31, 32, 33, 77
Lobster, 77
Low fat spread, 78
Luncheon meat, 78
Lychees, 134

**M**
Macaroni cheese, 17, 79
Mackerel, 13, 22, 27, 29, 30, 32, 79
Magnesium, 22
Malt loaf, 198
Malted milk drink, 27, 199
Mandarin oranges, 134
Mango, 13, 135
Margarine, hard and soft, 80
Margarine, polyunsaturated, 80
Marmalade, 199
Marmite *see* Yeast extract
Marrow, 135
Mars bar, 200
Marzipan, 13, 22, 28, 200
Mayonnaise, 201
Meat pie, 13, 81
Melon, canteloupe, 24, 136
Melon, honeydew, 136
Melon, water, 165
Men, recommended daily amounts, 42, 43
Milk, condensed, 81
Milk, evaporated, 82
Milk, fresh whole, 17, 29, 82
Milk, goats, 69
Milk, semi-skimmed, 17, 83
Milk, skimmed, 17, 29, 83
Milk, skimmed, powder, 17, 84
Minced beef, 50
Mince pie, 201
Mincemeat, 202
Minerals, 8, 17
Minestrone soup, 21, 202
Mints, 203
Mixed vegetables, 24, 137
Mono-unsaturated fat, 11
Mousse, 203
Muesli, 204

Mushrooms, raw, 137
Mushrooms, fried, 138
Mussels, 84
Mustard, 204
Mustard and cress, 138

**N**
Nectarine, 139
Niacin, 30
Nicotinic acid, 30

**O**
Oil, corn, 59
Oil, olive, 85
Oil, safflower seed, 91
Oil, sunflower seed, 102
Okra, 139
Olives, 140
Olive oil, 85
Omelette, 27, 66
Onion, raw, 140
Onion, fried, 141
Oral contraceptive, 31
Orange, 25, 141
Orange juice, 205
Orange squash, 205
Overweight, 8
Oxtail soup, 21, 206
Oysters, 19, 85

**P**
Pancake, 206
Pantothenic acid, 33
Parmesan cheese, 86
Parsley, 142
Parsnips, 142
Passion fruit, 143
Pasta, boiled, 207
Pastie, Cornish, 13, 21, 28, 60
Pâté, 24, 86
Peach, fresh, 143
Peaches, tinned, 13, 144
Peanuts, salted, 144
Peanut butter, 145
Pear, 145
Pear, avocado, 28, 112
Peas, frozen, 15, 33, 146
Peas, tinned, 146
Pellagra, 30
Pepper, green, 25, 147
Pepper, red, 147
Phosphorus, 23
Piccalili, 207
Pickle, 208
Pie, chicken, 56
Pie, meat, 13, 81
Pie, pork, 89
Pie, steak and kidney, 101

Pig's liver, 19, 24, 27, 29, 30, 31, 32, 33, 77
Pilchards, 17, 19, 22, 27, 29, 30, 32, 87
Pineapple, fresh, 147
Pineapple juice, 208
Pineapple, tinned, 148
Pitta bread, 209
Plaice in breadcrumbs, 87
Plaice, steamed, 28, 31, 88
Plain yoghurt, 107
Plantain, 15, 148
Plum, 149
Polyunsaturated fat, 11
Pork chop, 19, 28, 30, 31, 88
Pork, leg, roasted, 28, 89
Pork pie, 13, 89
Pork sausages, grilled, 21, 94
Pork sausages, fried, 21, 95
Porridge, 21, 209
Port, 210
Potassium, 21
Potato chips, 22, 25, 149
Potato crisps, 150
Potato salad, 150
Potato, sweet, 24, 158
Potatoes, boiled, 151
Potatoes, jacket, 151
Potatoes, roasted, 152
Prawns, 90
Pregnancy, 17, 20, 26, 32
Premature babies, 20
Premenstrual tension, 31
Protein, 9, 11
Prunes, 152
Pyridoxine, 30

**Q**
Quiche, 90

**R**
Rabbit, 31, 32, 91
Radishes, 153
Raisins, 153
Raspberries, 154
Ratatouille, 154
Ravioli in tomato sauce, 17, 210
Recommended daily amounts:
    Children aged 1 to 6 years, 35
    Children aged 7 to 12 years, 36
    Teenagers aged 13 to 18 years, 37
    Women aged 19 to 54 years, 38
    Pregnant women, 39
    Breastfeeding women, 40
    Women aged over 55 years, 41
    Men aged 19 to 64 years, 42
    Men aged over 65 years, 43
Red wine, 211
Retinol, 24
Riboflavin, 29

Rice, brown, 28, 211
Rice, white, 212
Rice Krispies, 212
Rice pudding, 213
Rhubarb, 155
Runner beans, 155

S

Safflower seed oil, 91
Salad cream, 213
Salami, 13, 92
Salmon, tinned, 27, 31, 92
Salmon, fresh, 93
Salmon, smoked, 98
Salt, 20, 45
Sardines, 27, 33, 93
Saturated fat, 11
Sausages, beef, grilled, 21, 94
Sausages, hot dog, 72
Sausages, pork, fried, 21, 95
Sausages, pork, grilled, 21, 94
Sausage roll, 95
Saveloy, 96
Scampi, 96
Scone, 17, 214
Scotch egg, 97
Scurvey, 26
Shepherds pie, 97
Sherry, 214
Shortbread, 215
Smoked haddock, 21, 98
Smoked salmon, 98
Sodium, 20
Soy sauce, 216
Soya bean curd *see* Tofu
Spaghetti bolognaise, 99
Spina bifida, 32
Spinach, 15, 17, 19, 24, 25, 33, 156
Spring greens, 156
Sponge pudding, 217
Squid, 99
Starch, 14
Strawberries, 25, 157
Steak, grilled, 19, 29, 30, 31, 100
Steak pudding, 100
Steak and kidney pie, 101
Stilton cheese, 86
Strokes, 26
Sucrose, 12
Sugar, 12, 34, 44
Sugar, demerara, 218
Sugar, Muscavado, 219
Sugar, white, 219
Sugar Puffs, 220
Sultanas, 157
Sunflower seed oil, 28, 102
Swede, 158
Sweet potato, 24, 28, 158

Sweetcorn, 15, 159
Sweets, 220
Swiss roll, 221

T

Tangerine, 159
Taramasalata, 192
Tea, 221
Teenagers, 37
Tinned fruit salad, 13, 160
Thiamin, 28
Toffee apples, 13, 222
Toffees, 222
Tofu, 17, 160
Tomato juice, 223
Tomato ketchup, 223
Tomato, raw, 161
Tomato, fried, 161
Tomato soup, 21, 224
Tomatoes, tinned, 25, 28, 162
Tomato puree, 162
Tonic water, 225
Treacle, 225
Trifle, 13, 225
Tripe, 103
Trout, 103
Tuna fish, tinned in oil, 27, 28, 30, 104
Turkey, roast, 30, 104
Turnip, 163
Twix, 226

V

Veal fillet, 19, 105
Vegans, 31
Vegetable curry, 163
Vegetable soup, 21, 226
Vegetarians, 9, 18, 31
Venison, 19, 105
Vinegar, 227
Vitamins:
    Vitamin A, 24
    Vitamin B1, 28
    Vitamin D2, 29
    Vitamin B3, 30
    Vitamin B6, 30
    Vitamin B12, 31
    Vitamin C, 25
    Vitamin D, 26
    Vitamin E, 27
Vodka, 190

W

Walnuts, 164
Water biscuits, 227
Watercress, 164
Watermelon, 165
Weetabix, 28, 29, 228
Weight, 8, 10

Weight for height chart, 10
Whelks, 106
Whitebait, 13, 106
White sauce, savoury, 228
White sauce, sweet, 229
Whisky, 190
White wine, 229
White wine, sparkling, 230
Wine, red, 211
Wine, sparkling, 230
Wine, white, 229

Women, recommended daily amounts, 38-40
Wounds, 26

**Y**
Yam, 165
Yeast extract, 29, 230
Yoghurt, fruit, 107
Yoghurt, plain, 107

**Z**
Zinc, 18

# ALLERGY?
# THINK
# ABOUT FOOD

'I am glad to be able to recommend a book which lists all additives at the back called Allergy? Think About Food.'
**Katie Boyle, TV Times**

'I received the copy of Allergy? Think About Food which to my mind is the best on the market of its kind. Would you kindly let me have two more copies which I want to pass on to friends.'
**Mrs M. R. Oxford**

'If you want to find out whether food or drink is the cause of your – your child's – allergy, Susan Lewis has written a helpful, easy-to-understand book.'
**Weekend**

## ASK YOUR BOOKSHOP FOR COPIES OR USE THE ORDER FORM BELOW

To: **Wisebuy Publications, 25 West Cottages, London NW6 1RJ**

Please send me _____ copies of ALLERGY? THINK ABOUT FOOD at £2.95 a copy plus 40p p+p or £5 airmail including p+p.

Please send me _____ copies of THE SAVERS AND INVESTOR GUIDE at £2.95 a copy plus 50p p+p or £6 airmail including p+p.

Please send me _____ copies of CRYING BABY HOW TO COPE at £3.50 a copy plus 40p p+p or £5 airmail including p+p.

Please send me _____ copies of HEALTHY EATING at £3.95 a copy plus 50p p+p or £6 airmail including p+p.

I enclose cheque/PO for £ _____ payable to Wisebuy Publications

Name _____
Block letters please

Address _____

_____

_____ Post code _____

# Other Popular Titles

**THE SAVERS AND INVESTORS GUIDE 1987–88   DAVID LEWIS**
Sixth edition 1987. 160 pages. £2.95.

David Lewis's comprehensive guide contains invaluable information to help cut your tax bill, perhaps by hundreds of pounds, as well as lots of sound detailed advice on where best to save and invest your money.
**Previously published under the title 'Money Mail Savers Guide', it has sold over a quarter of a million copies.** In clear no-nonsense language, this fact-packed book analyses 78 different types of savings and investments. **Not to be missed.**

**ALLERGY? THINK ABOUT FOOD   SUSAN LEWIS**
Second edition 1986. 224 pages. £2.95.

This book explains **how natural foods and additives can cause allergic reactions like asthma, eczema, migraine, hyper-activity, bedwetting, aches and pains and even depression.** *The Daily Telegraph said:* "One of the major problems with many additives is that they are known to cause allergies. If you do have one which you cannot trace, **it would be worth investing in a paperback called ALLERGY? THINK ABOUT FOOD.**"

**CRYING BABY HOW TO COPE   PAT GRAY**
First edition 1987. 144 pages. £3.50.

Pat Gray helped start CRY-SIS, the national support group for parents with crying babies. *The Guardian* said: **"Full of tips on the problems of yelling infants including how to help yourself survive."** Dr Miriam Stoppard in her foreword says she wished she had had the book when she had her two crying babies.

**ASK YOUR BOOKSHOP FOR COPIES OR USE THE FORM OVERLEAF**